Robert Andrew Macfie

Recent discussions on the abolition of patents for inventions in the

United Kingdom, France, Germany and the Netherlands

Robert Andrew Macfie

Recent discussions on the abolition of patents for inventions in the United Kingdom, France, Germany and the Netherlands

ISBN/EAN: 9783337271473

Printed in Europe, USA, Canada, Australia, Japan

Cover: Foto ©Suzi / pixelio.de

More available books at **www.hansebooks.com**

RECENT DISCUSSIONS

ON THE

ABOLITION OF PATENTS FOR INVENTIONS

IN THE

UNITED KINGDOM, FRANCE, GERMANY, AND THE NETHERLANDS.

𝕰𝖛𝖎𝖉𝖊𝖓𝖈𝖊, 𝕾𝖕𝖊𝖊𝖈𝖍𝖊𝖘, 𝖆𝖓𝖉 𝕻𝖆𝖕𝖊𝖗𝖘 𝖎𝖓 𝖎𝖙𝖘 𝕱𝖆𝖛𝖔𝖚𝖗

BY

Sir WILLIAM ARMSTRONG, C.B.; M. BENARD, Editor of the "*Siècle*" and "*Journal des Economistes;*" Count Von BISMARCK; M. CHEVALIER, Senator and Member of the Institute of France; M. FOCK; M. GODEFROI; Mr. MACFIE, M.P., Director, or Member, of the Liverpool, Edinburgh, and Leith Chambers of Commerce and Merchants' House of Glasgow; Sir ROUNDELL PALMER, M.P., late Attorney-General, &c.; Right Hon. LORD STANLEY, M.P., Chairman of the late Royal Commission on Patent-Law; JAMES STIRLING, Esq., Author of "Considerations on Banks and Bank-Management," "Letters from the South," &c.; and others.

WITH SUGGESTIONS AS TO INTERNATIONAL ARRANGEMENTS REGARDING INVENTIONS AND COPYRIGHT.

LONDON:

LONGMANS, GREEN, READER, AND DYER.

1869.

"La legislation des brevets d'invention peut avoir l'effet d'entraver notre commerce d'exportation, et de priver l'industrie nationale de débouchés utiles. . . Un brevet est uo privilége et un monopole. Pour que le monopole puisse être reconnu par la loi, il est indispensable qu'il repose sur un droit certain ou sur une utilité publique parfaitement établie. Le peu qui précéde suffit ce me semble a démontre que l'utilité publique n'existe pas. . . . Le brevet d'invention a-t-il pour base un droit positif? Il semble pourtant que non. . . .

"Telles sont les réflexions qui sont venues à un certain nombre d'hommes éclairés depuis quelque années et qui ont l'assentiment d'un bon nombre d'hommes des plus notables parmi les chefs d'industrie. Elles ont de l'écho dans touts les pays civilisés, et en Angleterre pour le moins autant qu'en France—(1) Elles ne tendent à rien moins qu'à renverser le systéme méme des brevets d'invention, sauf à rémunérer par une dotation spéciale tout homme ingénieux qui serait reconnu, après un certain temps d'expérience, avoir rendu à la société un service signalé par quelque découverte. C'est ainsi qu'il a été procédé en France à l'égard des inventeurs de la photographie."—From the Introduction to the "Rapports du Jury International de l'Exposition 1862, publies sous la direction de M. Michel Chevalier, President de la Section Française."

"Selon moi donc, le char du progres social doit être mu par l'industrie et dirigé par l'esprit chrétien. Il s'arrête à défaut de travail, il déraille à défaut de charité. . . . Et s'il est prouvé que c'est industrie qui nourrit l'humanité, que c'est elle qui la chauffe et la préserve contre toutes les intemperies, n'est il pas juste de dire que pousser au développement du travail, comme nous nous proposons, répandre dans l'esprit des travailleurs des idées qu'ils peuvent féconder pour arriver à une invention, a un perfectionment, a un nouveau procédé quelconque diminuant le prix de ce qui entretient la vie, que c'est là, messieurs, de la bienfaisance par excellence."—President's Opening Address of the Industrial and Scientific Society of St. Nicolas, 1866.

CONTENTS.

A 2

COPYRIGHT.

To all who are serving their generation as employers and employed, in the Arts, Manufactures, and Trades, of Leith, Musselburgh, and Portobello, and have seen and felt the evils inherent in the present State method of dealing with Inventions, these pages are inscribed,—with congratulations that in the front rank of statesmen, as well within the Cabinet as beyond it, there are earnest advocates of that emancipation of British productive industry from artificial restraints which is the needful accompaniment and the complement of free trade ;—and in hope that public attention will now at length be turned towards procuring such a solution as will satisfy at same time all just pretensions of meritorious inventors and men of science.

My own bulky contribution to the attack on the last stronghold of monopoly is to be regarded as but a rough-and-ready earthwork thrown up by a pair of willing hands in front of powerful artillery whose every shot is telling. It comprises the jottings and materials which I collected for a speech intended to be delivered on 28th May, when proposing a motion in favour of abolishing Patents for Inventions.

Notwithstanding imperfections in execution, the present compilation may acceptably supply a *deside-*

ratum and prepare the way for further discussions, and especially for the Committee which Her Majesty's Government continue to view with favour and will heartily support.

R. A. M.

June 9, 1869.

While in the hands of the printer, fresh matter has, through the kindness of honoured fellow-workers in the cause, reached me almost daily, part of which is added. The reader will find in this accession to the testimonies on behalf of freedom of industry, besides some new arguments, such a striking concurrence and oneness in the principles enunciated, and even in the illustrations made use of, as, coming from various quarters independently, may fairly be regarded as presumptive proof of their accuracy.

The Government has been so good as agree to produce, in conformity with a request from Parliament, any documents in possession of the Foreign-office which show the reasons or motives of the Prussian and Dutch Governments for proposing the abolition of Patents in Germany and the Netherlands. The adoption in the latter country of abolition pure and simple, without (so far as I can see) the slightest indication of a substitute, may well reconcile professional inventors and all who unite with them to the propositions with which I close my "speech." Now that the continental stones are dropping out of the arch which forms the System of Patents, the rest cannot long keep their place. The antiquated fabric may be expected to tumble. For public safety, the sooner Parliament and all concerned set themselves to take it down, the better.

A communication from Professor Thorold Rogers, and remarks on a recent Review, are given herewith, the former on account of its value as a vindication of economic truth and justice, the latter by way of correcting the reviewer's accidental mistakes.

The *Daily News*, in a leading article on the 27th July, having attached importance altogether undue to a small meeting called under peculiar circumstances on the 24th, which was supposed to express opinions and wishes of artisans and operatives,* I addressed letters to that influential paper, which will be found in its issues of the 29th, 30th, and 31st. Of course Sir Roundell Palmer, who did the promoter of the meeting the honour to take the chair, had not, any more than myself, the smallest connexion with its origination and arrangements.

Appended are suggestions and information regarding Copyright, which came in my way while in the press about Patent-right, and which may be useful if international negotiations are contemplated for one or other or both of these kindred subjects.

I hope imperfections of translation, which I regret, and errors of the press, for which I take blame without correcting them, will be indulgently pardoned, as well as faults entirely my own in the unaccustomed part of advocate and compiler.

July 31.

*** No rights are reserved. Mr. Macfie will be glad to be favoured, at Ashfield Hall, Neston, Chester, with a copy of any transcripts made or any printed matter illustrating the question of Patents.

---

* When members of "Inventors' Associations" ask mechanics to join a crusade against freedom of industry, the best rejoinder is to ask a statement in writing to show how it can be for the interest of the millions to perpetuate fetters for the sake of investing a few hundred individuals with a chance of obtaining personal advantage by means of the power of fettering.

My dear Sir,—. . . . The fact is, no one, I presume, wishes to say that an inventor is undeserving and should go unrewarded. All that the opponents of the Patent system do say is, that the present machinery gives the minimum advantage to the inventor, and inflicts the maximum disadvantage on the public. Besides, in ninety-nine cases out of a hundred, the patentee is only a simultaneous inventor with a number of others, who lose their labour and ingenuity because one man happens to get in first. . . . . .

It has always seemed to me that the weakness of the inventor's case lies in the fact already alluded to, that he rarely is the sole inventor. Hence the fundamental distinction between Invention and Copyright, though 1 am no fanatical admirer of the latter privilege.

Now, if a law can confer a right on one person only by inflicting a wrong on a number of other persons, it is intrinsically vicious, and cannot be defended on the ground of its intentional goodness.

Yours faithfully,

JAMES C. THOROLD ROGERS.

July 29.

REMARKS ON A RECENT ARTICLE.

The *Westminster Review* for July contains an article on Patents. Its proofs should have been corrected with more care. In my answer to question 1947 in the Royal Commission's Report, the word " patented " in the following the *Review* misprints " neglected :"—

As a matter of fact, patentees have patented things of so little value.

And in question 1954 a worse mistake is made by substituting " *some*" for "none" in the following :—

There being 400 Patents now in existence affecting your trade, none of which are made use of by you.

I have right also to complain of mistakes which do not originate with the printer. The following opinions and arguments imputed to me I disclaim :—

Had Mr. Macfie said this, we should not have been surprised. It closely resembles his contention that a book should be protected because it is something tangible, whereas an invention is something which, if not invisible, is in the nebulous condition of an idea.

What I wrote will be found below, page 241. My argument is, that the subjects of Copyright being tangible *can* be identified as the author's production, and nobody else's; and that the subjects of Patent-right being modes or plans, belong to the region of ideas which may easily occur to anybody besides the first inventor.

Again : the reviewer says of Lord Stanley :—

> The latter, while supporting Mr. Macfie on the main issue distinctly repudiated his leading arguments.

This would be strange if true, seeing I coincide in all his Lordship's arguments. How, then, can he, twelve pages further on, say again :—

> As for Lord Stanley, he did not hesitate to dissent from Mr. Macfie's arguments, while giving a qualified support to his motion.

Perhaps I should object to the following representation :—

> It has been proposed to replace Letters Patent by grants from the national purse. This is to revert to an obsolete custom. During the eighteenth century it was fairly tried, and the result should serve as a warning now. Seventy thousand pounds were distributed among plausible inventors in the course of fifty years. The advantage to the public was *nil.* The encouragement given to impostors was the only tangible result. Johanna Stephens obtained 5,000*l.* for disclosing the secret of her cure for the stone. A Mr. Blake got 2,500*l.* to assist him in perfecting his scheme for transporting fish to London by land, while a Mr. Foden was greatly overpaid with 500*l.*, " to enable him to prosecute a discovery made by him of a paste as a substitute for wheat-flour." Give a man a sum of money for his invention, and you run the risk of paying him either too much or too little. Give him a Patent, and you secure the invention for the public, while his remuneration in money is absolutely determined according to its value.

The *system* of State-rewards has *not* been tried. The reviewer's cases do not apply. The scheme that I submit could never be abused so as to sanction such follies. It may not be a generous and royal way of dealing with inventions, but it is equitable and safe ; whereas, *pace* the reviewer, the remuneration from a Patent is not at all "determined according to its value" (that of the invention).

This interesting article is remarkable for what it omits rather than what it contains. Like almost every, if not every, defence of Patents which I have seen, it ignores the grand objection to Patents—their incompatibility with free-trade. From the beginning to the end there is not in the article the slightest allusion to the hardship they inflict on British manufacturers in competing with rivals in home, and especially in foreign, markets. Reformers of the Patent system fail to realise this—that no conceivable mere *improvement*, even, though it should clear away the present encumbrance of a multiplicity of trifling Patents, can be more than an *alleviation* of the mischief now done. The remaining few would be the most important and valuable ones, and therefore the most burdensome, because those which, on account of the heavy royalties that will be legally claimed, must subject British manufacturers to the largest pecuniary exactions—exactions that they cannot, but their rivals often would, escape.

The writer of the article has a way of pooh-poohing adverse arguments, even when he mentions them.

That no two men produce the same book is true. It is almost as difficult for two men to give to the world two inventions identical in every detail, and equally well-fitted to subserve the same end. Much has been said about the case with which this may be done, but authentic proofs are lacking of this having been done on a large scale.

And

Again, then, we ask for proofs of the allegation that six men are often on the track of the self-same invention.

Why, the simultaneousness, or rapid succession, of identical inventions is notorious.

He goes in the face of the strongest evidence when he says—

It is doubtful even if these objectionable Patents do any real harm. An invention which will answer no purpose is simply useless, whether it be patented or not.

And, elsewhere,

The truth must not be blinked that, if a multiplicity of worthless Patents be an evil, if the profits of manufacturers are diminished owing to the battle they have to fight with patentees, if the bestowal of Patent-right be the source of mischief and the occasion of pecuniary loss, the like complaint may be laid at the door of Copyright, and its abolition might be demanded with as great a show of fairness.

How lightly he can regard arguments of his opponents is also seen in the following passage :—

Another of Lord Stanley's objections is that the right man hardly ever gets the reward. As he puts it, litigation being costly, and the grant of Patent-right merely amounting to permission to take legal proceedings against infringers, the poor man has no chance of asserting and defending his rights. " If a poor inventor took out a Patent, and the Patent promised to be productive, in nine cases out of ten he was obliged to sell it to some one who could command capital enough to defend it in a court of law." We submit this proves nothing more than that the poor inventor, in nine cases out of ten, deserves our pity. But then, if these nine inventors are unfortunate, that does not justify the ill-treatment of the tenth.

The source of the writer's idea, that cessation of Patents is ill-treatment, lies in the assumption which pervades the whole article, that to inventors belongs property in inventions—*i.e.*, *exclusive* right of property ; or, in other words, right to require the State to use its power to prevent other persons from doing what they do, and what every other man has a natural and inalienable right to do.

Still further: shutting his eyes to the difficulty of

mollifying the grievance of invention monopoly by means of "*compulsory licences*," which the Royal Commission declared they found no way of rendering practicable—and, I add, if practicable, would be no cure of the evils, which are radical—he writes—

If to this were added a system of compulsory licences, the amount of royalty to be determined by a tribunal, in the event of the parties failing to come to terms, nearly all the really serious and valid objections to the working of a Patent-Law would be obviated.

Yet, believing himself the friend of *the public*, in spite of all the strong arguments *against* his views and the little he himself adduces *for* them, he very complacently tells us—

Speaking on behalf of the public, we maintain that a Patent-Law is necessary in any uncivilised community, because, without its protection, industry cannot flourish, and ingenuity can have no scope for its triumphs.

The reviewer can hardly have consulted any practical man when he pronounces it—

absurd to plead that a Patent has been infringed in ignorance, when it is certain that the ignorance, if not wilful, is wholly inexcusable.

Undoubtedly, infringements often are not acts done blamelessly in ignorance ; still, I would be surprised in most cases if the infringer knew he was infringing. He is not likely to know it in making trivial improvements, for how can he know without subjecting himself to no small trouble and expense, such as ought not to be laid upon him.

There is an important point as to which the reviewer and I perhaps differ, "the extent to which Letters Patent give a monopoly in ideas." The fact is, that the whole breadth of a *principle* is patentable, provided any single mode of applying it can be specified.

The reviewer, adverting to the changes which have taken place in the Law of Patents since the days of Elizabeth, characterises them as " changes towards greater freedom of action on the part of the State, and greater liberty of choice on the part of the people." This, I confess, I do not understand, except so far as it may mean there has been less and less control exercised by the State, and more and more advantage taken of this supineness by all sorts of persons. I am quite prepared to admit that in my speech I have exhibited rather a popular than a strictly legal and logical view of the meaning and legitimate applicability of the words in the statute, "nor mischievous to the State by raising prices." All that I maintain is this,—that the spirit of the proviso is opposed to any individual Patent that keeps prices up at a level below which, if there were no grant, they might, by the natural progress of industry, be expected to fall, and to a Patent system that characteristically has that effect and is also chargeable with "hurt of trade" and "generally inconvenient."

SPEECHES AND PAPERS ON THE ABOLITION OF PATENTS.

The following petition, which Mr. Macfie had the honour to present, contains the motion which gave occasion for the speeches that form the principal part of this compilation :—

To the Honourable the Commons of the United Kingdom of Great Britain and Ireland in Parliament assembled.

THE PETITION OF THE NEWCASTLE AND GATESHEAD CHAMBER OF COMMERCE

Humbly sheweth,—

That your petitioners have had many opportunities of becoming acquainted with the working of the laws under which Patent-rights are granted to inventors in the United Kingdom.

That your petitioners are informed that notice has been given in your honourable House of a motion in the following words :—

" That in the opinion of this House the time has arrived when the interests of trade and commerce, and the progress of the arts and sciences in this country, would be promoted by the abolition of Patents for inventions."

That your petitioners, believing the proposed total abolition of Patent-Laws will be of great benefit to the country, are most desirous that the above-named resolution should be adopted by your honourable House.

Your petitioners, therefore, humbly pray that the said motion may pass your honourable House.

And your petitioners will ever pray, &c.

NOTES OF SPEECH OF MR. MACFIE, M.P.

Mr. Macfie, after apologies founded partly on the circumstance that, so far as he knew, this was the first occasion when the policy of granting Patents for Inventions had been discussed in Parliament, proceeded to say, that manufacturers could not be indifferent to improvements. It is indeed significant that they do dislike Patents, while they appreciate and honour inventors, even those inventors who claim from the State exclusive privileges, some of whom have the glory of being among the greatest benefactors of mankind.

In considering the important subject which he now brought forward, he submitted that it is not the interest of inventors, nor even the interest of manufacturers, of agriculturists, of miners, nor of shipping, that this House should consult, but those of the nation. The question to be considered is, do Patents, on the whole, promote our national welfare?

Another principle on which he proceeded is, that there can be no property in ideas. The Creator has so constituted nature that ideas can be held in common, which is not the case with things material. Letters Patent for inventions have been instituted in order to confirm to certain persons, and deprive every

B

other person of, the common, natural right to act on the ideas or knowledge there patented. These exclusive privileges, while they last, are, of course, property.

Further : It is a recognised principle, that the State is not bound to grant Patents. These are grants dictated by royal favour. In the words of Stephens' Commentaries: "The grant of a Patent-right is not *ex debito justitiæ,* but an act of royal favour." Every Patent is a voluntary transference by the State to an individual of power for fourteen years to tax at pleasure other persons for making or doing the thing patented ; aye, if he likes, to prohibit or withhold the thing altogether.

Patent-right must not be confounded with Copyright. The latter stands on perfectly different grounds, and can be advocated and upheld, as he (Mr. Macfie) himself does, in perfect consistency with disfavour for the former. There can be no rival claimant to the authorship of any particular book ; many persons may honestly and indisputably claim originality in an invention. The true similarity between these two subjects of privilege is not between the book and the invention or machine, but the book and the specification of the invention. When you buy a Murray's handbook, a book on medicine, or a commercial guide, you are at liberty to act on information you find in it, and to travel, trade, or prescribe, according to the directions you find there. But mark the contrast in what Patent-Law creates. When you buy a specification, you know it tells only of certain things that you are not at liberty to do.

Lastly : I acknowledge that it is legitimate to legislate with a view to promote or protect trade. The interference, however, which is now wanted is not a return to the old protective system of discriminative duties, but the clearing away of evil laws, and especially deliverance from the bondage and wrongs involved in Patent monopolies.

For the origin of our definite Patent legislation we go back to the famous statute of James I. of England. At that time the people of this kingdom were in a state somewhat resembling our present state. They were desirous to extend trade and introduce new arts and manufactures. Parliament was powerful and hated monopolies, under which the people had been writhing. These it reprobated in the spirit of the jurists of antiquity. While by that statute it swept away all other monopolies, it permitted, or tolerated, that the Crown should grant the exceptional privilege for " the sole working or making of any manner of new manufactures ,within this realm, to the true and first inventor and inventors of such manufactures, which others at the time of making such Letters Patent and grants shall not use, so as also they be not contrary to the law nor mischievous to the State, by raising prices of commodities at home or hurt of trade or generally inconvenient."

The House will keep steadily in view the wholly different condition of commerce and the arts at that time. When these monopolies were spared, trade was very far from being developed. The field of commerce

was still in a great measure clear and unoccupied.
The kingdom was, commercially as well as geographi-
cally, detached from the continent. The operations of
trade and the arts were slow, were conducted on a
small scale and on rude systems, and yielded large
profits. Exports to foreign parts were inconsiderable.
There were no periodicals to give information as to
anything new in the arts and sciences. Under such
circumstances, if new kinds of business were to be
established, it was not unreasonably thought safe, or
even needful, to allure by promise of exclusive
privileges. The very reverse are our present circumstances and condition.

May I be allowed now to call particular attention to
the Act. Anybody may see that it authorised exclusive
privileges as something exceptional, something almost
loathed, as " monopolies." The House may remember
how, in conformity with this view, Patents used to be
construed by the judicial bench with a leaning against
them. It was clearly not contemplated that they
were, as they are now, to be had at a comparatively
easy price, by a very simple course of procedure
organised to hand, at an office established and with
machinery ready to be set in motion for the
purpose. A rigid testing examination, or severe, perhaps somewhat adverse, scrutiny was implied. They
were granted for England only, then containing a small
population, and requiring not very much for its supply
of any new article. Moreover, the coveted privilege
was a concession of no more than leave or right to
" work " or " make " (not vend), and that within the

kingdom, which, although it is the only thing the Act allows Patents to be granted for, is not required now-a-days. The right was conferrible only on the patentee himself; whereas now-a-days, and perhaps from the first, the usage is altogether different; for the patentee is now allowed to transfer his right, by licence, to others : that is, to vend his "invention," taking the noun, not in its sense of a thing made, but of a method, or idea, or right to make or do a thing. Without this licensing, it is of consequence to remember, the monopoly would be too grossly and glaringly bad to be defensible or maintainable. There is another contrast : by the words of the statute nobody could be patentee but only the true and first inventor. Besides, the subject of a Patent clearly was to be something palpable and visible—something that admitted not of doubt as to what it was or as to its being novel—something respecting which there could be no fear whatever that it would interfere with any already existing trade. Above all, a process or operation, especially in a trade that already existed, does not appear to be contemplated by the statute. How entirely and sadly different is the present practice in this respect. Let me first quote from Brande's Dictionary the opening definition that shows how naturally, and as it seems, unconsciously, writers speak of "processes," as the great or only subject-matter :—

" The word Patent is commonly used to denote a privilege accorded to an inventor for the sole use of some process by which an object in demand may be supplied to the public; or some product already familiar to the public may be made more easily and efficiently."

So the commencement of a Paper on Patents, in the last volume of the Proceedings of the Association for the Promotion of Social Science—in the following words, " The point asserted in the following paper is, that in a grant of Letters Patent, the subject of the grant is a 'process,' and not 'product' "—shows as decisively the complete change that has taken place, and, let us not forget it, without consent of Parliament, who indeed have never been consulted. The alteration of the practice, which is nothing less than a new law—a law diametrically opposed to the spirit of the statute—is the work of the courts of judicature. Better principles might have been expected to prevail, for how just is the following reflection, taken from the most important " Treatise on the Law of Patents :"—

" Every member of the community receives many benefits from the society in which he lives, and he is therefore bound, by every means in his power, to advance its interests. And it seems to be but reasonable that he should be expected to promote the public weal by putting the community in possession of any discovery he makes which may be for the public good."

The observations I have been making are founded on the words of the statute. It is possible, and perhaps I may say probable, that outside of the statute there was an influence drawing in an opposite direction, which found expression in the Letters Patent. If these were scrutinised, it is not unlikely even the earliest would be found not to contain the strict conditions and limitations which are laid down in the Act. An incidental proof of this tendency I notice in one Patent which has met my eye, where, though the duration of the

Patent in England was confined within the permitted period of fourteen years, the duration in Ireland, which was not subject to the limitation, was in same grant made so long as between thirty and forty years. I do not find, in the excellent Chronological Index issued by Mr. Woodcroft on behalf of the Patent-office, anything at all to indicate that desire to favour trade was the motive for granting Patents even after the statute was passed. On the contrary, a money consideration seems to have been customary. The Crown stipulated for yearly payments of various amount, some of these being fixed sums, others a tenth, or three-tenths, or a quarter, or a half, of the clear benefit. In one case 4d. per bushel of salt was claimed. In another case 6d. per 100lbs. of bones was stipulated for. In another I find 5s. per ton of metal stipulated. All this is suggestive, but not less the condition, introduced occasionally, that the articles manufactured should be sold at moderate rates. The moderate rates appear to have been sometimes defined, e.g., 100 seals of a new kind were to be sold for 1d. Similar and more stringent care was taken when Copyright first became the subject of systematic legislation, to prevent the monopoly from making books dear. All such precautions have, in our modern unwisdom, disappeared. Grotius requires under monopoly a restriction on price.

One thing, I presume, may be regarded as certain, that neither in the Act nor in the Letters is there any vestige of the modern political heresy that an invention may be legislated for as in any sense property. Even the high-sounding phrase, "the rights of inventors," appears a recent introduction.

It is not forty years since the greatest number of persons allowed to participate in a Patent was five. This limitation was a lingering remain of the traditional character of Patents, as monopolies which ought not to be provided with facilities for extension but rather be confined within the narrowest bounds.

It is proper I should now prove from that and other authorities in law, what is the correct interpretation of the word "manufactures" in the statute, on whose meaning so much depends. My quotations will exhibit progressive development—a thing justly viewed with suspicion, whether its sphere be the ecclesiastical or the legal. What I now bring under notice, taken in connexion with the startling perversion of the words "first and true inventor" and the setting at nought the letter and spirit of the words "to make within this realm," matches the whimsical and ruinous sophistications we smile at in the "Tale of a Tub."

My first appeal is to Sir E. Coke's "Institutes :"—

"If the substance was in being before, and a new addition made thereunto, though that addition made the former more profitable, yet it is not a new manufacture in law."

That by a manufacture was meant something so definite as to involve or imply an art in the sense of a trade, will be seen by another quotation which I make from Serjeant Hawkins, who says—"the King may grant the sole use of an art invented or first brought into the realm." So also in "Bacon's Abridgment." The Court of King's Bench held—

"A grant of the sole use of a new invented art is good. . . . . This is tied up by the statute to the term of fourteen years ; for after that time it is presumed to be a known trade."

Mr. Hindmarch writes—

"It was long doubted whether a mode, method, or process of itself, and apart from its produce or results, could legally be made the subject of a Patent privilege."

After citing cases, he adds—

"These cases show clearly that a process of manufacturing, separate and apart, may be made the subject of a Patent privilege."

Mr. Coryton, in his volume on "The Law of Letters Patent," expresses his mind thus plainly :—

"On the assumption that a Patent confers a monopoly, it follows directly that the subject-matter of the Patent must be a material thing, capable of sale,* and cannot be either an improvement, principle, method, process, or system. In other words, the subject-matter must be, as it was originally defined, a 'new manufacture.' A thousand evils have arisen from affixing other than the literal interpretation to the terms," &c.

He quotes Justice Heath, who said—

"That which is the subject of a Patent ought to be vendible; otherwise it cannot be a new manufacture."

So Tyndal—

---

* Another illustration naively presented us, even by Mr. Hindmarch, of the characteristic logic and boldness of the Patent interest, which may surprise "inventors' friends" accustomed to rely that our system of Patents is legal and constitutional, will be found in the Appendix.

"That it is a manufacture can admit of no doubt : it is a vendible article, produced by the art and hand of man."

Mark from the words of Justice Buller, on the same occasion, the sentiment which was permitted to prevail and neutralise the statute :—

"Few men possess greater ingenuity, or have greater merit. If their (Boulton and Watt's) Patent can be sustained in point of law, no man ought to envy them the profit and advantages arising from it. Even if it cannot be supported, no man ought to envy them the profit," &c.

We come to C. J. Eyre :—

" According to the letter of the statute, the words...fall very short... but most certainly the exposition of the statute, so far as usage will expound it, has gone very much beyond the letter. 'A deliberate surrender,' comments Mr. Coryton, ' of judicial power in favour of an accumulation of popular errors.'...Later judges, following in the same course, have striven rather to regulate the inconsistencies they found, than to address themselves to the cause and thus prevent the possibility of their recurrence. Writers on this subject have on this head followed in the course indicated by the Bench."

A practical commentary, and a confirmation of Mr. Coryton's views, are furnished by the fact that the number of Patents granted in the six reigns preceding that of Geo. III. was only 540 in 85 years, or less than $6\frac{1}{2}$ a-year ; whereas now a greater number is granted daily.

The actual administration of Patents is exhibited to us by a Return which the House has been good enough to order on my motion. That return shows how the rate of multiplication has increased, especially in Scotland and Ireland.

There have been granted for—

	England.	Scotland.	Ireland.	In England for the Colonies.
In 1650—None.		...	...	...
1700	2	...	...	...
1750	7	...	...	...
1800	96	13	2	6
1825	250	62	33	87
1850	523	227	531	191
1866	2,121	2,121	2,121	none
1867	2,292	2,292	2,292	none

There were in operation in the United Kingdom at the end of last year no fewer than 11,369.

The House is aware that the Patent-office makes a classification of Patents. The classification for 1866, the latest year that could be given in the Return, shows that there are nearly 300 classes, and there were Patents granted that year affecting those classes to the number of more than thirty each on the average. Taking the manufacture and refining of sugar as a test of other classes, the Return shows that in that trade there were granted more than thirty " affecting processes or operations " (without including hundreds of others of a more general character, to which manufacturers of all sorts are subjected, as, for instance, Patents for motive power, heating, &c.). Many noteworthy matters will meet the eye of any person who examines the Return, such as the following : For medical, curative, and similar "revelations," there were granted about 80 ; for improvements tending to safety, nearly 350 ; affecting food, about 400 ; affecting steam-boilers, about 160 ; steam-engines, about 120.

But we have yet to consider the most material points in the Act. To these I now call attention. The conditions or limitations which the statute makes necessary are extremely significant. They are in these words—" Not contrary to the law nor mischievous to the State, by raising prices of commodities at home or hurt of trade or generally inconvenient." On these words Sir Edward Coke remarks—

" There must be *urgens necessitas* and *evidens utilitas*."

What might be understood by being " generally inconvenient " in the statute, and how little disposition there was to render that disqualification a dead letter, we may gather from the following extract, which shows that saving of labour was in those early days, so far from being a recommendation, an inconvenience. Hear the same authority :—

" There was a new invention found out that bonnets and caps might be thickened in a fulling mill, by which means more might be done than by the labours of fourscore men who got their living by it. It was ordained by an Act, 7 Edward VI. c. 8, that bonnets and caps should be thickened and fulled by the strength of men, and not by a fulling mill, for it was holden inconvenient to turn so many labouring men to idleness."

On which passage Mr. Farey (a gentleman eminent on Patent questions), who quotes it in an elaborate review of Patent-Law at the end of the Blue Book of 1829, the Report of the Committee on Patents for Inventions, makes the following remarks : " If this decision had been followed, it would have set aside every Patent for invention." True, and the more's the pity, perhaps ! Let us hail the admission.

Sir Edward explains, and I read, the whole passage that I have cited, not as a lawyer might who wished to ascertain whether by oversight in drawing the Act or by the malleability and elasticity of language it could be interpreted even non-naturally to suit a purpose, but as honest, blunt Englishmen would understand it, as the English gentlemen who passed the Act must have understood it and meant the Crown to understand it. I submit, Mr. Speaker, that at this moment, and by this statute, and according to the common law which this statute declares, Patents are illegal which raise prices or hurt trade. The framing of the sentence leaves no doubt whatever that the antecedent to the words "they be not contrary to the law nor mischievous to the State, by raising prices of commodities at home or hurt of trade," are these words, "Letters Patent and grants of privilege." The preceding section contains the same words. That section was introduced in order to shorten the duration of Patents granted previously, and to nullify any that raised prices or hurt trade. It is plain that the intention of Parliament and of the Sovereign was to allow no monopoly to exist whose effect would be either to interfere with the extent or efficiency of industrial occupations, or to make prices, even of the new manufacture or commodity, dearer under the restriction than they would be without it. Even so late as the last century, the consistency of monopoly with cheapening of prices was believed in. As an example, I have been told that when the Paraphrases of the Church of Scotland were issued, the monopoly was given to a particular printer, with this purpose expressly stated.

What language can be plainer than that of the statute? As that statute is still the charter of our commercial freedom and the chart by which we may discover the track we must follow in order to our return to the open and safe, and as its sound limitations are still the law of the land, I am entitled at the outset to contend that they ought to be put in force. They have been utterly neglected, and the nation suffers much from the neglect. As to this, hear my witnesses. I produce them chiefly from the following Blue-books : That issued by the Committee of this House which sat in 1829, that issued by the Committee of the House of Lords which sat in 1851, and that issued by the Royal Commission in 1865. Here remark the strange failures of expectations that characterise the proceedings of Parliament in regard to Patent-Law. The Committee of 1829 recommended that they should be allowed to continue their investigations next Session, but they appear not to have been allowed. After the inquiries of 1851 there was, as a Petition which I have perused, presented to this House, shows, an understanding that the whole subject would be inquired into; but this never has been done down to this day. A Commission was indeed appointed in 1862, but they were confined to the question of the " working" of the laws. Indications were given, both before and after it, that the question of the policy of these laws should be examined into. The Liverpool Chamber of Commerce repeatedly urged this ; *e.g.*, in March, 1862, when that body petitioned the House thus : " They therefore pray that your honourable House will appoint a Select Committee to inquire into the policy and operation of those laws." But the matter is still in abeyance, and, notwithstanding promises in a Royal Speech, legislative action is suspended.

To proceed : Mr. Lennard in this House, in April, 1829, declared his opinion—" It was not desirable to facilitate overmuch the obtaining of Patents by any reduction of expense."

So Sir Robert Peel, in the interest of the manufacturers of Lancashire, Cheshire, and Yorkshire, deprecated cheapening of Patents and their consequent multiplication. At that period another member objected even to the publishing of specifications, because

" It enabled persons to carry the invention abroad, where, of course, the Patent article was made, the foreign market shut against the real invention, and the undue benefit granted foreigners of having the free use of the invention fourteen years before the patentee's countrymen."

The House will observe that the complaint here is not that we were hurt in British markets—for these the protective system of duties closed—but that we lost our hold of foreign markets.

Sir Mark Isambard Brunel, the eminent engineer, told the Committee of 1829 :—

" I have had several Patents myself ; I think that Patents are like lottery offices, where people run with great expectations, and enter anything almost.

" And if they were very cheap, there would be still more obstacles
in the way of good ones. I think the expense of Patents should be
pretty high in this country, or else, if it is low, you will have hundreds
of Patents more yearly, and you would obstruct very much the valuable pursuits."

That Patents are, indeed, a lottery in respect to the
uncertainty whether the patentees draw a prize or a
blank, I refer to the words of Mr. Curtis before the
Royal Commission :—

" We have taken out a number of Patents, and frequently those to
which we have attached the least importance have become the most
valuable, and, on the contrary, those from which we have expected
large things we have reaped comparatively no advantage."

Mr. Coryton says in a note :—

" The opinions of the witnesses examined before the Committee of
the House of Commons in 1829 were almost unanimous to the effect
that Patents should not be too cheap, lest the country should be inun-
dated with them."

Among my private papers, I find in 1851 the
Manchester Chamber of Commerce expressing the
same fear in a letter to Mr. F. Hill, a portion of which
I now present :—

" It is considered by this Board to be a primary axiom that every
Patent granted is, during its exclusiveness, a limitation to a certain
extent of the general rights of the people, and that in those Patents
which have reference to manufacturing processes there may be a
disturbance of the general industry of the people. This Board would,
therefore, deprecate a too great facility in the obtaining of Patents. If
the cost be made cheap, every trifling improvement in every process of
manufacture would be secured by a Patent. In a few years no man
would be able to make such improvement in his machinery, or processes, as his own experience may suggest, without infringing upon
some other person's Patent. Endless litigation would follow, and the
spirit of invention in small matters would be rather checked than
encouraged."

The realisation of these fears, as well as the inconsistency of our practice with the conditions which our forefathers, more wise than the present generation, imposed, will be seen from the specimen extracts which I will now read, begging that it be remembered a very large reduction in the cost of Patents was made in 1852. The House will pardon me if it finds these extracts are not arranged with any rigid regard to order, but form a too *rudis indigestaque moles.*

The following prove that there is a natural tendency to excessive multiplication of Patents, and to the making of the same inventions, and of inventions directed to the same end, or moving on the same line, by a number of persons at or about one and the same time.

This very week you read in the papers a judgment given by the Lord Chancellor, which contains the declaration that a person in specifying an invention may be held as preventing " the loss for a year or more to the public of the fruits of the ingenuity of many minds which commonly are working together in regard to the same invention."

The *Journal of Jurisprudence* says well :—

" The rights of the inventor are also liable to interference of another kind. A rival manufacturer invents independently the same machine, or one involving the same principle. He is then, by natural law, at liberty to publish his invention without regard to the rights of the first inventor, seeing that he did not acquire his knowledge of its powers from the latter, and experience proves that, in point of fact, the same processes are frequently discovered by different individuals independently of each other. In an age of mechanical invention, an inventor cannot deprive the world of a new process by keeping it a secret. He can at most only retard the progress of discovery by a few years. . . .

We submit that the fundamental principle of any legislative contract between inventors and the public should be, that the right of using the invention should be open to all Her Majesty's subjects. Exclusive privileges, conferred for the purpose of enabling patentees to divide their profits with a few favoured manufacturing establishments, are indefensible upon any recognised principles of economy. Patents are in fact, as they are in law considered to be, trading monopolies; and the interests of the public imperatively require that, as monopolies, they should be swept away."

Mr. Webster, Q.C., a high authority, says :—

" I mean the discovery, for instance, of some chemical property, or the application of some property, of matter of recent discovery, or a certain effect, for instance, in dyeing; that becoming known as a chemical law, then persons rush to obtain Patents for different applications and different modifications of it."

See by my next quotations how great is the obstruction the multiplication of Patents creates, or, in the words of the Act, the "general inconvenience" they occasion.

Mr. James Meadows Rendel, Civil Engineer, in 1851 :—

" During the twenty-five years that I have been in practice, I have frequently felt the inconvenience of the present state of the Patent-Law, particularly with reference to the excessive number of Patents taken out for frivolous and unimportant inventions, which I think are much more embarrassing than the Patents that apply to really important inventions.

" I have found them interfere in a way that very much embarrasses an engineer in carrying out large works, without being of the slightest advantage to the inventors, excepting that in some cases a man who takes out a Patent finds a capitalist (however frivolous the invention) who will buy the Patent, as a sort of patent-monger, who holds it, not for any useful purpose, but as a means of making claims which embarrass persons who are not prepared to dispute questions of that sort. I think that in that way many Patents are granted which are but of little benefit to the real inventor, serving only to fill the coffers of parties who only keep them to inconvenience those who might have occasion to use the particular invention in some adjunct way which was never contemplated by the inventor.

" After you have designed something that is really useful in engineering works, you are told that some part of that design interferes with some Patent granted for an entirely different purpose, and which might in itself be frivolous, but important in the new combination ; and one has such a horror of the Patent-Laws, that one evades it by designing something else, perhaps as good in itself, but giving one infinite trouble, without any advantage to the holder of the Patent. I have frequently found this to be the case."

Mr. W. S. Hale, candle manufacturer, said in 1851, in answer to the question—

" At present they are obstructions to you ?—Decidedly.

" You say that, practically, you have found the existence of Patents in themselves useless—a great obstruction to the introduction of inventions which would otherwise have been of value ?—Certainly.

" The great objection which I conceive many parties have to introduce real improvements arises from useless Patents. I am in treaty now for one or two which in themselves are useless, yet they contain the germ of something, and it is worth my while, if I can get them for a small sum, to purchase them ; but directly you make application for a Patent of that description, it becomes very valuable all at once ; the party conceives you are desirous of possessing yourself of it, and that you will be inclined to give anything for the use of it."

In like manner Sir William Armstrong answered this question, put in 1864—

" Is it within your knowledge that considerable inconvenience does exist in those branches of business with which you are most conversant from the multiplicity of Patents ?—Most certainly, and great obstruction."

So also Mr. James Spence, of Liverpool, a well-known correspondent of the *Times* during the American war, said—

" It is difficult for a manufacturer to move in any direction without treading on the toes of some sort of a patentee."

Likewise Mr. Montagne E. Smith, Q.C., M.P., said :—

"In several cases in which I have myself been counsel, very great inconvenience has arisen from the multiplicity of Patents which an inventor has had to wade through to see that he has not been anticipated."

How truly did Sir W. Armstrong observe to the Commission—

"You cannot grant a monopoly without excluding other persons who are working upon the same subject."

Again :—

"Here the State grants to an individual a monopoly, and therefore the public are at his mercy."

Mr. J. S. Russell, who himself has taken out a good many Patents, speaks more specifically :—

"There are a great many Patents of that kind taken out for boilers of steam-engines, and boilers of steam-engines admit of a very enormous variety of shape and proportion without damaging their efficiency . . . . The consequence is, that I have not defended any of my own. I have never made of mine more than a mere registry of priority of invention. I have not made mine a source of money, but I have suffered in this way from Patents : I have gone on, in the course of my business, doing my ordinary work, and I have found other people taking out Patents for what I was doing without calling it an invention, and then prosecuting me under the Patent they had taken out for my own inventions, and it appears that there is nothing to prohibit them from doing that."

This I can from experience endorse. He is then asked—

"If you were able to prove that you had been carrying on an invention, whatever it might be, at the time when the person claiming to hold a Patent for it took out his Patent, would not that relieve you from all difficulty in the matter?—It would only give me the pleasure of defending a law-suit."

Mr. Curtis, engineer, Manchester, said :—

" Many parties in trade have made alterations without being aware of their being patented, and when they have used them for a length of time, they have found that the patentee has come upon them and made a claim for Patent-right."

Mr. Platt, of Oldham, whom you are happy to see as a member, said :—

" I think that there is scarcely a week, certainly not a month, that passes but what we have a notice of some kind or other of things that we have never heard of in any way, and do not know of in the least, that we are infringing upon them, and the difficulty is to get at any knowledge. We may be now infringing, and may have been infringing for years, and a person may have been watching us all the time, and when he thinks that we have made a sufficient number he may come down upon us, and there is no record. A very large number of Patents are now taken out for what is termed a combination of known things, and known things for the same purpose, and the descriptions of those Patents are generally so bad that it is impossible to tell the parts that are actually patented; in matters of that kind it has become a very serious question as to conducting a large business."

In 1851, Sir William Cubitt spoke of an inventor of filters :—

" After he began to supply his customers, he received notice from a house in Liverpool that he would be prosecuted; he received intimation of legal proceedings against him for interfering with his, the Liverpool man's, Patent. I have some of those filters. The manufacturer of these things, who had no Patent, came to me to consult me upon the subject. I at once saw how the case stood, having regard to the specification of the Liverpool patentee, that he (the latter) had taken out a Patent for that which another man had before done, so exactly that the words of the specification and the drawings fitted the first man's invention, which was without a Patent, therefore his Patent would have been null and void. I advised my friend to write to the patentee to inform him of the fact that he had taken up a case which he could not support, and that he himself was infringing upon the invention of the first man, who had no Patent; that brought the Liverpool man to me, I having been referred to as having one of these filters in use. I explained to him that I had had the patent filter of the other man for two or three years. Then what was to be done ? I advised my friend, who was in fact one of the Ransomes, of

Ipswich, to tell the Liverpool patentee if he did not come to some arrangement of a business-like nature, he himself would have to become the prosecutor, and to sue out the ' *scire facias* " to make him prove his Patent-right, which is an expensive legal proceeding, and very troublesome to a patentee. I believe they have since made some business arrangement ; but that shows how Patents may be, and are frequently, taken out for things which have been previously invented."

As to the bad effects of Patents, I quote again from Mr. Scott Russell :—

" The unlimited power given by a monopoly to an inventor has this practical effect at present, that when an invention has been made the subject of a Patent, everybody shrinks from it, everybody runs away from it, everybody avoids it as an unlimited evil, because the person who has the monopoly can subject you to a most expensive prosecution, and can charge you a most inconvenient sum for what you have done, and can punish you in every way for having touched his invention."

Mr. Grove says it is natural that people should yield to the holder of the Patent, for, if

" He has a letter from a patentee saying, ' You are infringing my Patent ;' I do not believe that the tradesman would go to the expense of litigation with the patentee, and for this reason, it is the patentee's interest to give a very large sum of money to support his Patent. His Patent, although for a very trivial thing, may, taking the vast extent of sale, be a very lucrative affair, and therefore it is worth his while to lay out a large sum of money to support his Patent. It is not worth the while of the opponent, because he has only a little stock which affects him ; the patentee has his whole interest consolidated in the Patent. All those who might oppose the Patent are a scattered body, namely, the public generally, not one of whom has any strong interest in opposing the Patent ; and I believe that that has been very much worked by patentees, particularly in a small and comparatively frivolous and perhaps an all but useless invention. The public is a scattered body, not one of whom has sufficient interest to meet with equal force the patentee."

Mr. Platt, M.P., presents the following case, to show how unprincipled people use the power which the law gives them, and how, even with a good case, if they but knew it to be so, people in business are led to succumb to extortion :—

" The fourteen years of the Patent had expired, and five years, so that it was nineteen years from the date of the Patent before the action that I now speak of was commenced. It was commenced by the parties, and I may say that the person who was the original patentee was a person of no money whatever ; but he persuaded some party, I believe some lawyer, to advance some money in order to take up this case. I know that many machine-makers, rather than contest the case, absolutely paid the money—the different sums of money that were demanded of them. I came up this afternoon with a gentleman in a train from Manchester, who mentioned this case to me, and who stated that one of his own clients offered as large a sum as £2,000 in one case, to settle the matter. I found that the system was to attack the smaller men, and by that means to extract money in different ways, and there have been a number of instances in which parties have paid in that way. Although not attacked in this instance myself, a neighbour of mine was ; I looked over his evidence, and I told him that I thought I could amend it very much, and I told him further that I would be a party to the expense. I said, let me take the case in hand, which I did. Now, nineteen years is a very long time for a machine, and this machine was of a very valuable kind ; hundreds upon thousands had been made during the nineteen years, and if this person could have established his claim to a Patent-right, he would have made a very large sum of money, so large as to be almost incalculable. It so happened that I recollected, when it was brought to my memory, that we had made a number of those machines long before the date of that Patent, and the difficulty then was to prove that such a machine had been made, for in nineteen years, speaking of cotton machinery, such machines would probably all have been broken up, scarcely any were to be found in the country ; but it so happened that in one instance a very large firm of manufacturers in Preston, of the name of Horrocks, Miller, and Co., had two or three of these machines still left. I got Mr. Miller to come up to London, and we brought one of these machines with us. It was taken into court, and in a moment their own witness admitted that this was precisely the same thing that the other parties had been paying royalty to this man for, and the case was at once abandoned by Mr. Webster, who was then conducting it."

Sir W. Armstrong told the Commission :—

"Another great evil of the Patent system is this, that an invalid
Patent really answers the purpose of protection almost as well as a
valid one.   I believe that there is not one Patent in ten which would
bear scrutiny, and the mere name of a Patent often answers all the
purpose.   Nobody will face the litigation necessary to get rid of it.

" In very many cases people prefer to pay black mail rather than
undergo the expense of a law-suit ?—In almost all cases ; I know that in
my own experience, if I find that a man has a Patent which I am satisfied is not a valid one, I would rather go out of the way to avoid any
conflict with him."

So also Mr. Curtis :—

" I have in one or two cases given £200 to a party for the use of
an invention in which I have told him at once that what we used
was not an infringement in any shape or form ; but rather than run
the chance of going to a tribunal where I was fighting with a man
of straw, I have consented (thinking it was prudent to do so) to
pay £200."

Mr. Woodcroft, in keeping with all this, testified—

" I know of existing Patents which are but old inventions, as old as
the hills."

The following extract from the Transactions of the
National Association for the Promotion of Social
Science presents another illustration of the mischief
the Patent system works :—

"The Patent in question having been purchased for a trifle by Mr.
Foxwell, its merits were subjected to close scrutiny, and the specification being found to be defective in some respects, but possessing the
quality of elasticity from the vagueness of its phraseology, it was
resolved to improve it under the Disclaimer and Amendment Act.
After undergoing a compound operation analogous to pruning and
grafting, it was found to embrace almost every kind of shuttle sewing
machine.   In other words, it was hoped by the possession of this
invaluable Patent to control nine-tenths of the sewing machine
trade of Great Britain.   Fired with this idea, Mr. Foxwell commenced legal proceedings against a well-known sewing machine manufacturer for compensation for an alleged infringement of his amended
Patent, and at the third trial succeeded in driving his opponent into

a compromise, whereby the sum of £4,250 was paid in liquidation of all demands. Encouraged by this success, he, through his solicitor, apprised the trade of his intention to levy royalties on the users of all needle and shuttle machines other than those manufactured by his licences, and, failing to bring many to his terms, he filed bills in Chancery against 134 defaulters."

Mr. Abel, of Chancery-lane, in a recent pamphlet, writes thus, to show how, in self-defence, Patents require to be taken :—

" In many cases an inventor takes out Patents for immaterial improvements that he is continually making in his processes or machinery, merely for the purpose of indisputably publishing those improvements, in order thereby to prevent the chance of his being debarred from the use of the same, through a Patent being obtained for them by somebody else."

The following statement is authenticated by Mr. Grove :—

" I had at one time great doubts about it, but things have arrived at a dead lock. The Courts now really cannot try these cases. We have at these very sittings three Patent cases made remanets because they cannot be tried ; they interfere too much with other business. We have at this moment going on a Patent trial which is now in its fourth day. We have had within, I think, a week another trial of a Patent, which lasted seven, and a third which lasted five days. During the time that these Patent cases have been going on there have been heavy Patent arbitrations going on, two of which I can speak to myself ; one, I think, lasted seventeen days, and the other, which involved a very simple issue, lasted six or seven days. Those arbitrations went on contemporaneously, and the cases were obliged to be tried by arbitration because the Courts could not try them ; it would have occupied too much public time. While these cases have been going on several Patent cases have been also ready for argument in banco, and one has been postponed.

On this part of the subject I again cite Mr. Platt:—

" There being an adjournment, for example, for a fortnight or three weeks, is there constantly a fresh burst of evidence to meet the difficulty raised at the last meeting?—Yes, it is so ; and that prolongs the case very much; in fact, the case that I have in my mind now I have no doubt will cost the parties a sum of £4,000 or £5,000. I cannot see how it is possible for the verdict to be against them, for it has been a frivolous and vexatious proceeding from the beginning, and with the idea of extorting money."

And Mr. Scott Russell :—

" In your experience have you not seen a great number of dishonest litigants, plaintiffs who bring actions in the way of persecution, and defendants who desire to destroy a Patent, and where one or other of the parties for the most part acts in bad faith, trying to injure his adversary in any way that he can ?—I should say that the greater number of Patent cases are cases of oppression.

" Have you known cases of oppression where the patentee has been the oppressor ?—Yes, frequently.

" Have you known cases of patentees with a good Patent, and in which there has been what may be called a dishonest attempt to destroy it ?—Yes, I have known both on a very large scale ; for example, there was the great hot blast case. I was engaged in that from the beginning in the capacity of arbitrator ; and in that great hot blast case the whole litigation arose from the ironmasters, who were making enormous sums of money, wishing to get rid of a very small Patent rate per ton, which had accumulated to an enormous sum in consequence of the success of the Patent. The expenses in the hot blast Patent case amounted, I should think, to more than £100,000."

In the celebrated capsule case, the expenses have been somewhere about half of that enormous sum. In another case, about three-quarters of it. How true, then, is the following, from *Chambers' Cyclopædia :*—

" When a Patent has been granted, if it is of such a nature as to lead to competition, infringements are almost matter of course ; and the only mode of discovering and checking the infringement is so ineffective that inventors generally pass their lives in constant litigation, fighting a succession of imitators, who often have nothing to lose by defeat, and therefore entail all the greater burden on the legitimate manufacturer. It has been said that not more than three per cent. are remunerative. A Royal Commission has lately been engaged in inquiries as to the best mode of remunerating inventors and improving the law with reference to infringement; but it is doubtful how far the subject is capable of being put on a better footing, so many difficulties being inherent in it."

And how many of these pernicious Patents do honourable members think have been repealed? Allow me, as to this, to quote Mr. Grove—

" . . . . . Very few Patents have been repealed, and, generally speaking, the patentee has been victorious."

And the Commissioners' Report:—

" Number of Patents repealed by *scire facias* from 1617 to October, 1852 19
" Number of Patents repealed by *scire facias* from October, 1852, to December, 1861... ... ... None."

A natural question suggests itself, Who is to get a Patent, since in many cases there is a plurality of almost simultaneous inventors? Listen to the words of Mr. Webster, Q.C., author of well-known books on Patent-Law :—

" I have frequently had brought before me five or six Patents for the same thing within two or three years, or perhaps even within a year. I remember a remarkable case of a Patent for an improvement in railway wheels, where there were as many, I think, as six Patents almost within six months."

Sir W. Armstrong shows that sometimes the chief benefit of inventions goes to the wrong parties :—

" A person obtaining a Patent for a crude invention prevents other persons from entering upon the same ground unless at their own peril, and I have known cases where, in the ignorance of the existence of a Patent, improvements have been made, and practical value given to an invention which has been previously patented, and then that patentee has come forward and said, ' That is my invention, and you must pay me for using it.' Other people have given additional value to his Patent, that is to say, they have made improvements which he can appropriate to his Patent, and in that way it gives it an additional value. The mere conception of primary ideas in inventions is not a matter involving much labour, and it is not a thing, as a rule, I think, demanding a large reward ; it is rather the subsequent labour which the man bestows in perfecting the invention—a thing which the Patent-Laws at present scarcely recognise.

"But you are unable to do so, because you cannot interfere with the Patent over it. Do you find practically that that clogs the progress of invention? — I will take one of my own inventions. I will take an hydraulic crane, for example, which I will suppose that I do not patent, and I will suppose that another person invents an improved valve and applies it to hydraulic cranes, and that he patents that improvement upon hydraulic cranes ; clearly the result of that is, that if it gives an improved character to the whole machine he will obtain the monopoly of the machine, because he has a Patent for the improvement, and that carries with it the machine itself."

Mr. Webster shows how it is that men of science, the real discoverers, miss reward :—

" The number of inventions brought out by purely scientific people I believe to be very few, and for this reason : purely scientific people want practical knowledge to enable them to carry out their own ideas ; the mass of inventions, I have no doubt, are made by workmen, or persons of skill and science engaged in some actual manufacture."

Mr. I. K. Brunel tells—

"Cooke and Wheatstone derived, I believe, a large sum of money from the electric telegraph ; and I believe you will find fifty people who will say that they invented it also. I suppose it would be difficult to trace the original inventor of anything."

Sir W. Armstrong speaks regarding that frequent case—

" An idea which is present to the minds of very many persons at the same time. Without any reference to his competency to develop that idea, and to give it practical value, he is allowed to have a monopoly of it, and thereby to exclude all other persons."

He points out that—

" As soon as a demand arises for any machine, or implement, or process, the means of satisfying that demand present themselves to very many persons at the same time, and it is very unfair, and very impolitic

I think, that the person who gets first in the race to the Patent-office should have the means of preventing all others from competing with him in the development of that particular means of process."

Mr. Grove, Q.C., eminent in science as in law, hints at a remedy :—

" I am speaking of classes of inventions which, if they may be called inventions at all, would inevitably follow the usual course of trade and the fair scope which every man should have for modifying or improving his commodity. I would not shut out the public from those things. I would exclude from Letters Patent those changes which would naturally follow in the ordinary uses of the machines. I would not prohibit a tradesman from exercising the same ordinary skill in using his machine as we should all be expected to exercise in anything which we happened to make or from changing its form."

Another question as naturally thrusts itself forward, How far have we benefited by having more Patents ? Although the Act of 1852 has greatly multiplied the number, Mr. Woodcroft, the intelligent head of the Patent-office, gives the following answer :—

" There has been no considerable increase of bonâ fide Patents compared with the old law ?—No."

Very suggestive are the following observations of Mr. Grove, as showing which are the kinds of invention, so-called, that pay best, and how absurd, if people would reflect, they must consider our present mode of rewarding and stimulating invention :—

" A Patent may be an extremely valuable invention ; for instance, the manufacture of aluminium is of the utmost importance, but it was of very little trade value for a long time. When aluminium was first made what I may call a practical manufacture, it was of no value to any tradesman at all ; it would take probably ten or twenty years before such a thing could have any approach to practical value. On the other hand, the most frivolous Patent—the turn of a lady's hat, the cutting of a shirt-frill, or a new boot-heel—may be of very considerable value, from the number of bootmakers all over the

country who would have to order it, every one of whom would pay
an extremely trifling licence duty, and therefore the Patent would be
a very good Patent to the patentee. In my judgment those are not
good subjects for Patents, and there the opponent would have no
interest equivalent to that of the patentee to meet him.

"Although I know that the Law Courts have come step by step to
include a greater number of inventions, yet I should not call an
improvement in a shirt-frill, that is to say, a peculiar method of
cutting the little puckered linen which is sewn and used for shirt-
frills, or a particular shape of the brim of a lady's hat (I am speaking
of existing Patents), a proper subject for a Patent."

The following is from the evidence of Sir Francis
Crossley, Bart., M.P. :—

"A Patent was taken out for simply putting india-rubber at the
end of a glove, so as to make it tight round the wrist ; that might have
been considered a frivolous Patent, but I believe that it was thought
to be a very good one in the trade, and it was new and useful."

So Mr. Richards Roberts, of Manchester—

"In the case of an improved button, the Patent pays very well."

Of another class of illegitimate Patents, Mr. Newton,
the eminent Patent Agent, says :—

"Patents for obvious applications.—I may take for instance the use
of alpaca for covering umbrellas. There is no invention in it."

In 1851 Mr. Carpmael was as distinct and condemnatory :—

"A multitude of things for which Patents are granted have no
invention in them ; in nineteen cases out of twenty, if there were cheap
Patents, they would be for things which already exist, and people
would only use Patents for the purpose of advertisement and publication.

"If you grant a Patent, and give to a man the means of advertisement, for a small sum of money, he will not investigate it in the
slightest degree in the world; he does not inquire, and does not wish
to inquire, but he goes and spends his money, and then he advertises,
because the Patent appears to give him a standing different from his
competitors in the same way of business."

In 1829 Mr. Farey, Patent Agent, went further :—

"I have urged the utter worthlessness of their Patents, but they did complete the specification; they have sometimes acknowledged, and said perhaps they might nevertheless sell the Patent to some one who did not know that fact."

Mark now how Patents hinder progress in manufacture. Hear Mr. Brunel :—

" Take the Electric Telegraph Company. I believe we should have had that telegraph much improved, and that it would be working much cheaper, and that we should have had it all over the country, but for the misfortune they laboured under, of having Patents which they were obliged to protect; and they were obliged to buy up everybody's inventions, good or bad, that interfered technically with theirs. I firmly believe that they have been obliged to refrain from adopting many good improvements which they might have introduced themselves, but did not, because they were afraid that it might shake their Patent; and I believe that the stoppage put to inventions by this state of things is far greater than would result from secrecy."

The same is certified by Sir W. Armstrong :—

" I am quite satisfied that a very great number of inventions which have remained inoperative for years and years, many of which I could easily name, would have been brought to perfection very much sooner if it had been open to all the intellects of the country to grapple with the difficulties of them.

" May we take it that under the present system, if a man has obtained a Patent with little or no inquiry, although that Patent would not stand investigation if opposed, yet if the patentee is content to impose a moderate tax upon those who want to use his invention, they will pay that sum without its being worth anybody's while to contest it?— Yes.

" Do you believe that the cases of that kind are very numerous?— Very numerous, and the cases are still more numerous in which the existence of a monopoly simply has the effect of deterring other persons from following up that particular line of improvement."

Another effect is the restraining of publication. Hear Mr. Richard Roberts' thrilling representations :—

"I have a list of something like 100 inventions that I should have patented thirty or forty years ago, but for the cost.

"I could mention one by which many lives would have been saved if I had had a Patent for it.

"I very rarely make models, but I had one made for this.   It was made many years ago.   I invented it in 1830, and I mean to say that, if it had been put into practice, things would not have happened which have happened, and which have caused the loss of many lives, as connected with railways."

I adduce this evidence to prove that inventions actually made are kept back just now.   I don't require to go far for a party who has two or three small inventions (not connected with his own line of business) ; but—such is our "system"—no ready means to publish, and so has for years kept them back.   But a more remarkable instance is present to my mind.   Since about twenty years the same party, having been then consulted by an *employé* of a house near Birmingham, is the reticent possessor of an inventor's secret.   That inventor's name he does not know.   His invention is ingenious, and may be practicable.   It affects an article of universal consumption, and, so far as I know, has never been patented or thought of by anybody else than he who confided the secret, nor introduced to use by him, although, in my opinion, sufficiently promising to be worthy of attention.

One of the ways in which Patents hurt trade is shown by Mr. Platt :—

"Are there not some large manufacturers who like to keep the monopoly of a Patent in their own hands, who obtain money and go on manufacturing without granting licences to others ?—Yes."

Sir W. Armstrong testifies to this power to refuse licences :—

" Is it not the case that such possessor could refuse you a licence, and so prevent you from making the improvements altogether?—Certainly he could."

Lord Chelmsford confirms the legality of this procedure :—

" If he chooses to work the Patent himself exclusively, it is only doing what the law permits him to do."

Where there is not downright refusal, Sir W. Armstrong shows that patentees ask too much :—

" I have known patentees very exorbitant in their demands for licences—far beyond the merits of their inventions.

" In that case the power of fixing an exorbitant price, really preventing the use of the article altogether, operates very disadvantageously to the public ?—No doubt of it."

So Mr. Newton :—

" The claims of patentees are very frequently, and I may say generally, excessive, and beyond the real value of their inventions ; but there may be cases in which new conditions of things arise, and the invention, if invention it may be called, becomes a matter almost of necessity, and the public must have it. The case which has been put, I think, is a very strong one, in which a public company or a large capitalist buys up all the existing Patents, and thereby acquires a power which may be exceedingly oppressive.

" . . . . I have seen much folly in the refusal of licences. I introduced the sewing machine into this country. I sold it for a small sum, and I offered some years afterwards to the owner of the Patent as much licence-money as 10l. per machine, and that was refused.

" A poor man invented and patented the making of ' cock-spurs ' (supports for dishes and plates while submitted to furnace heat) by means of dies, and established a small business upon the manufacture. Some years later a gentleman improved upon the invention so far as to make the cock-spurs 500 at a time instead of singly. The earlier Patent being brought to his notice, he desired to make terms with the original inventor, and offered him a liberal sum, together with the sole right to sell the new manufacture in his own locality (the potteries). He could not, however, be brought to accept these, or indeed any terms ; but, contrary to advice, commenced an action for

D

the infringement, and was cast by reason of an unimportant claim in his specification being untenable."

As a preventive of this abuse, and almost as a *sine quâ non* in the Patent system, " compulsory licences " have been proposed (see the proceedings of the Social Science Association, 1858, 1860, '61, '62, '63, '64), but the Royal Commission has reported against them as impracticable.

No wonder, then, that it is said the system hurts inventors themselves, even those inventors who are patentees :—

" Nothing could work greater injustice *qua* the inventors themselves than the present Patent-Law does.   Many most meritorious inventors under the present Patent-Law are utterly ruined, enrich others, and never pocket a farthing themselves ; therefore the present law is as unjust as a law can be in its practical working."

Listen to the elder Brunel :—

" Almost invariably when the Patents come before the public, the beneficial interest in them is not held, to any great extent, by the original inventor, but that it has changed hands many times before it comes out before the public.   I should say that, in the majority of cases, the original inventor gets little or nothing.   In most cases the original inventor has a very small beneficial interest left-in it, and in most cases I doubt whether, even in Patents that are saleable, he is much the gainer on the whole, taking into account his previous loss of time and money."

Sir W. Armstrong points out how, and how much, poor inventors suffer :—

" I have every week letters from inventors, and I dare say you have the same ; I have scores of them.   Poor men very often come to me imagining that they have made some great discovery.   It is generally all moonshine, or, if it looks feasible, it is impossible to pronounce upon its value until it has passed through that stage of preliminary investigation which involves all the labour, and all the difficulty, and all the trouble.   Many a poor man is ruined by fancying he has made a discovery which, by means of a Patent, will bring him a fortune. He loses all relish for his usual pursuits, and sacrifices his earnings to a phantom."

Mr. Spence agrees :—

" I do not believe that any system of law could be devised which would enable a poor inventor in this country to fight his own battle. He can only fight it by interesting some capitalist, more or less wealthy, in the probable promise of his invention; the result is, as all know, that some ninety-eight out of every hundred Patents end in loss to the parties and are worthless to the public."

Mr. Grove leads to the same conclusion from another point :—

" If the patentee himself was a wealthy man and a large manufacturer, having 20, 30, or 40 Patents in his possession, he would struggle to the utmost to maintain his Patent; he would retain the ablest advocates and the ablest scientific witnesses; and there would be no chance of repealing the Patent unless the person opposing it had something like an equality of purse to go into the field. You never could get the battle fought if one side was wealthy, without the opposite party having something like equal powers to oppose him."

Mr. Brunel thus states his conclusion :—

" I believe them to be productive of almost unmixed evil with respect to every party connected with them, whether those for the benefit of whom they are apparently made, or the public."

I proceed to call attention to the effect of Patents as seen and felt in Government establishments. Before doing so I quote experience in a private shipbuilding-yard.

Mr. Hall, the eminent builder of the Aberdeen clippers, says :—

" As the sailor with his pockets full is a prey to the crimps, so is a ship-contractor a prey to Patent-mongers—patent windlasses, patent reefing apparatus, patent blocks, patent rudders, patent chain-lifters, patent capstans, patent steering gear, patent boat-lowering apparatus, patent paints, and numberless others, all attempting to hook on to the poor contractor. This would be no grievance, were we not aware that most of them are patent humbugs."

Like many others, he thinks it very doubtful whether the inventor

" Would not be as well without a law which still allows the strong to prey on the weak."

The following is from the evidence of the Duke of Somerset :—

"I appear to bring under the notice of this Commission the great inconvenience to the Admiralty of the present state of the law. The inconvenience consists in the apparent facility with which persons can obtain Patents covering a very large number of different inventions under one Patent. For instance, there is a Patent which one gentleman obtained some years ago in building ships for a combination of wood and iron. Now, it is almost impossible to build ships in these days without a combination of wood and iron. Therefore a Patent of that kind, where it is wide-spread, as it is in this case, brings us continually under difficulties with this patentee. Whenever we apply wood and iron, he is watching to see whether or not his Patent is invaded, and he complains and says that different improvements which we have made without any notion of his Patent have been infringements of his Patent rights. . . . We do not know what Patents are now lying dormant ; we never move without knocking against several. I think that we are stopped at every turn. . . . In the case of the screw-propellers the Admiralty, in 1851, purchased five different Patents, hoping that they should have peace by that means, but they had all sorts of claims afterwards ; they were told that they had infringed different Patents, and they have had to pay for other Patents since.

" Persons run and take out a Patent for what they think is going to be done in that way. There are a great many in the case of iron ships. I think that when the Warrior was built there were five or six persons who all said that their Patents were infringed, though I believe that, when the Warrior was designed, none of their Patents were known to the designer, and they had never been used. . . . They showed me different forms of shot which had been made in the Arsenal a great many years ago, but all of which had since then been patented by different persons, who claimed these forms of shot under their Patents.

" Then there are cases of disputed claims by rival inventors, which are embarrassing to a department ; we do not know who has a claim to a Patent, and sometimes when we buy a Patent of one person we are told that we have done a great injustice to another. I remember that when we paid for the Griffith patent screw, which was cutting off a small portion of the screw, I had repeated letters from Sir Howard Douglas, telling me that it was a great injustice to him ; that he had invented all this, and that his fame was diminished, and that his rights were taken from him by the Admiralty, who had most unjustly and unfairly paid Mr. Griffith.   Those cases are continually arising, and of course they are very inconvenient for a department : they not only take up a great deal of time, but they very often prevent some very desirable process being gone on with."

Admiral Robinson said—

" There have been twelve upon the construction of ships since 1861.

Mr. Bush	Construction of ships.
Mr. J. Clare	Construction of ships.
Mr. P. Drake........................	Construction of ships.
Mr. A. Lamb	Construction of ships.
Mr. W. Rae	Keels, stern posts, &c.
Mr. Thomas and Col. De Bathe	Mr. G. Clarke's target.
Mr. Truss	{ Animal fibre. { Armour plates.
Mr. Beslay	Preservation of iron.
Capt. Wheatley	Position of guns in ships.
M. De Lapparent..................	Carbonising timber.
Commander Warren...............	Bow rudder.
Mr. Feathers........................	Construction of ships.
Messrs. Woodcroft, Smith, Ericsson, Lowe, Blaxland, and Mr. Currie.	Purchase of Patents for screw propellers.
Capt. Carpenter	Screw propeller.
Capt. Trewhitt	Disconnecting apparatus.
Mr. Griffith	Screw propeller.
Mr. J. O. Taylor	Screw propeller.
W. Ireland	Cupola.
Messrs. Laird and Cowper	Trimming coals in ships.
———	Distilling apparatus in 'Defence.'

" In those cases the patentees claimed compensation for infringement?—Yes; and it was necessary for the Admiralty to have recourse to their solicitor, and to enter into a very long correspondence.

"It is very possible that you may infringe upon these Patents without knowing it?—Constantly. The inconvenience which the Duke of Somerset has mentioned resulting from Patents applied to shipbuilding is so very great that it is scarcely possible to build a ship, being a combination of wood and iron (and you always have some of each in a ship), without treading upon somebody's Patent; and I am entirely of opinion that the Patents are drawn up for that especial purpose, without any idea of their being practically applied for the benefit of the public, but only that the patentee may lie in wait for a colourable evasion of his Patent taking place."

Now I present the evidence of General Lefroy, deputed by the War-office :—

"The expectations of patentees are very extravagant, generally speaking, and prior to trial it is very difficult to determine at all what is the value of an invention. As an example, a gentleman some time ago made a great improvement in cooking apparatus, and he assessed his own reward at a large portion of the whole saving in fuel which might be effected by the application of this improvement to an enormous extent upon the whole military consumption of the Crown, which would have come to many thousands of pounds. Such an improvement should not be assessed by the value to the Crown, but by what it cost the originator in intellectual labour or previous experiment, and its importance in a large sense."

Let me next cite Mr. Clode, Solicitor to the War-office :—

"If he has not the power either of keeping those improvements perfectly secret, or of securing them to himself by Patent, then the War-office authorities are placed in the position of having in all probability to pay private individuals for inventions or improvements actually made by their own officers."

Next Mr. Abel, F.R.S., Head Chemist to the War Department :—

"In your experimental inquiries, when you have happened to fall upon any discovery, you have not been much annoyed by claimants saying that they have had precedence of you?—Not at all, and it is to that that I referred in my first answer. We do not meet practically with those embarrassments during experiments, but we may meet with them in applying the details of improvements. For instance, I am at present engaged upon the working out of the application of gun cotton, the whole details of which application were communicated as a great secret to this Government by the Austrian Government. . . . While every care was taken by this Government to keep them secret, a Patent was taken out in this country for the whole improved process of the manufacture."

Mr. Clode again :—

" Some time after I commenced these experiments, while they remained a perfect secret, and while every care was taken by this Government to keep them secret, a Patent was taken out in this country for the whole improved process of the manufacture. . . . One of them who is present is experimenting upon gun cotton, but it is with him a matter of extreme embarrassment to know how to deal with the subject ; if he discloses by way of specification all that he knows, he sends the invention or discovery he has made away to the winds—the very night that it is put upon the file it goes to Paris, Dresden, Berlin, and elsewhere. If he does not do that, he is afraid that some man will find out precisely what he has in view, and put a Patent on the file, and tax the Government in that way. So that we are upon the horns of a dilemma."

If I were now to stop, and say not a word more, I might trust to the candour of the House for an admission that the case against Patents is proved, on the ground that the conditions of the Statute of Monopolies have been systematically violated, these violations being of the very texture and vitals of the institution.

But I proceed. If the House permit, I will now advert to the new phases the question has assumed since the inauguration of free trade, understanding by that term *le libre echange*, and not *la liberte du travail*.

The pernicious effect of home Patents on trade with our Indian empire, is stated thus by Mr. Rendel, in 1851 :—

"As engineer to the East India Railway, we had a little inconvenience the other day; we wanted to manufacture articles patented
in this country, and we would have had to pay Patent-rights; it was a
question whether we had not better buy the iron in India, and avoid
the Patent-rights. Those cases, I think, are constantly occurring.
The Patent-Laws not being applicable to India, people will not unfrequently order things to be manufactured in India to avoid the licence
dues in this country; and the consequence was that I made an
arrangement with the patentees at about one-half of the ordinary
charge for the Patent in this country."

In 1851 it was proposed, and in 1852 an Act was
passed, to limit British Patents to the United Kingdom, with exclusion of the Colonies. This change
was desired by an influential and intelligent portion
of the West India Association. Their conduct contra-
dicted, and their experience proves the fallacy of, the
allegation so confidently made and repeated in spite
of its futility, by some interested or else ignorant
parties, that inventions thrive most where Patents
exist—*i.c.*, where trade is trammelled with prohibitions
or burdened with royalties. The home sugar refiners
exclaimed against an exemption which, being partial,
operated against their trade. The following is an
extract from one of the petitions presented by that
body :—

"That, so far as regards home manufacturers and producers, such
a change of the immemorial usages of the kingdom is virtually a
bestowal on parties carrying on the same businesses in the colonies of
a right to use patented inventions fourteen years sooner than they.

"That if, at any time, the British Parliament might have put home
manufacturers on such an unfavourable footing, surely this cannot
be supposed under free-trade and equalised duties, when they must
task their utmost energies, and adopt every improvement in mechanism
and processes, in order to maintain their ground.

"That the use of future Patents, at the rates that have been freely
paid by sugar refiners for Patents granted before now would subject

each sugar house, of average size, to a payment of about £3,000 a year.

"That to exempt their competitors in the colonies from such a tax (for tax it is, payable by order of, though not to, the State) is really to give them a bounty of that very large amount.

"That, in so far as patent fees may be considered a premium for stimulating improvements, an equal share of the benefit is enjoyed by the colonists, who, therefore, should bear a due share of the burden."

Soon after that time, protection having ceased, the unfairness of burdening British manufacturers came more vividly into sight. How can they compete with Prussia and Switzerland? Here is evidence regarding those countries. From a Prussian witness :—

"I am a member of the Board of Trade and Commerce, and at the same time a member of the Patent Commission.

"Will you be good enough to state what is the system adopted in Prussia with regard to protection to inventions?—We have the principle in our country to give as much liberty as possible to every branch of industry and art, and, considering every sort of Patent as an hindrance to their free development, we are not very liberal in granting them. We merely grant a Patent for a discovery of a completely novel invention, or real improvement in existing inventions."

From an important Swiss witness :—

"There is no want of persons to import them into Switzerland, although those persons thus importing them obtain no monopoly?— When a Patent is taken out in France or England, the process is published; therefore it becomes the property of the public in Switzerland; the Swiss have access to the French or English Patents.

"In that way the Swiss have the benefit of the invention without the charge of the licence?—Yes.

"And so far they have an advantage?—Certainly.

"When inventions in the watchmaking trade are made in France, are they immediately introduced into Switzerland?—I should think so, if they are useful."

How, I ask, can British manufacturers compete with

Prussia, which prudently grants less than 100 Patents in a-year ; or with Saxony, which grants only about 134 ; or the Netherlands, which grant only about 42 ? Rather, I may ask, how can they compete with other countries in general, even those that grant Patents freely, seeing that it is not incumbent on the British patentee to take a Patent in any other country whatsoever ; seeing also that, unlike some countries which grant Patents, we in most cases do not terminate the currency of those we grant at the time when the Patents taken elsewhere expire ? Honourable members will understand how serious is the disadvantage under which our manufacturers, and with them, of course, the labourers and artisans who co-operate in manufactures, are placed if they are precluded from using inventions which their continental rivals may use. When licences are given by patentees, the disadvantage is lessened, but not very greatly. The House will agree when it hears how enormous are the royalties sometimes exacted. For a set of inventions in the iron trade, which is not the subject of Patents in Prussia, a single firm is said to be paying at the rate of £16,000 every quarter. Let me quote from a leading article in the *Engineer :*—

" Owing to the invalidation of his Austrian Patents, Mr. Bessemer derives no pecuniary benefit from the working of his inventions in that country. This is also the state of things in Prussia, whose really iniquitously-managed Patent Commission have refused to give Mr. Bessemer any Patent at all. The great Prussian steel works there manufacture Bessemer steel unweighted by any royalty. We regret this, not merely for Mr. Bessemer's sake, but also on public grounds. Our steel makers are thus heavily handicapped in the industrial race with royalties of from one to even three pounds per ton."

See a confirmation of this in the following piece of a private letter :—

" The very heavy royalty payable under Bessemer's Patent does, to a very great extent, prevent English manufacturers competing on the Continent for steel rails; but, from the accidental circumstance of continental manufacturers being obliged to buy a considerable portion of their raw material from this country, we have not been exposed to competition in England, as the cost of carriage backwards and forwards about equalled the benefit which the Germans enjoyed of paying no royalty."

The sugar-refiners, in a printed document before me, put the case, convincingly no doubt to all who will consider how small is the percentage margin of profit in great businesses :—

" If, for any invention, French producers of refined sugar should have only royalties of one per cent. *ad valorem*, while the British should have to pay royalties of five per cent., it is obvious the Patent-Law may in effect impose. on the latter a most onerous differential duty."

In that trade I myself, shortly before my retiring from commerce, paid £3,000 for a year's right to use a new process, which proved unworkable, and had to pay a *solatium* of £1,000 for leave to discontinue it.

The agricultural interest should not remain indifferent. Mark what was told the Commission by Mr. Reeve, Registrar to the Privy Council. In Mr. Bovill's Patent there was charged a royalty of 6d. a quarter on all the corn ground in Great Britain by millers who thought it desirable to adopt his plan. Obviously the royalty in that case had the effect of a protective duty leviable for individual benefit, and enabling foreigners to undersell in the British markets.

And what title to this power had Mr. Bovill? He was not the inventor. Another case is exhibited in the following extract from a private letter with which I am favoured, from a highly respectable quarter :—

" Patents have become so numerous and so various, that it is not safe to use any piece of machinery, or make any variation without first making a careful search to ascertain whether it is not protected by a Patent. The Patent-Law has also been the cause of much litigation, there being very few Patents of any real worth but have had to go through the ordeal of the Law Courts, and there can be little doubt that injustice has frequently been done both to patentees and to the public. A case of considerable hardship connected with our own trade occurred regarding the application of the exhaust to grinding purposes. It was clearly proved at the trial that the machine for which the patentee claimed protection had been in public use in Denmark, where it had been seen by a Glasgow miller, who erected a similar machine on his premises in Glasgow, but hastily threw it aside without putting it to a proper test prior to the date of the Patent, but it was held that no profitable use having been made of the machine by the Glasgow miller, the Patent was good and perfectly protected. In our opinion a Patent obtained in such circumstances should never be allowed to stand, and if some means could be devised for ascertaining the circumstances beforehand, it should never be granted. The trade suffered very considerably in consequence of this Patent being sustained, and the consequence was, that although the patentee was not the original inventor, he pocketed a very large sum of money.

" A more recent instance has occurred, however, of a large sum being pocketed by parties not the inventors of the article patented. We can, however, only give you the figures as popularly reported, without vouching for their accuracy, and in relating the story we shall endeavour to reply to your queries *seriatim*. 1st, The patented article is a machine for dressing millstones by means of a black diamond, or piece of 'bort,' instead of by the hand with picks. It was originally patented in France by the party said to be the inventor, and shortly afterwards was patented by him in this country. 2nd and 3rd, A Leith commission agent (a German) and an Edinburgh miller saw the machine in the Paris Exhibition of 1867, and induced the patentee to bring it over to Scotland for trial, and ultimately they, in con-

junction with a third party, purchased the patentee's right for
the whole kingdom for £4,000. 4th, These parties immediately
put the machine in the market, and it was at once seized hold of
by speculators, who readily gave most extraordinary sums for it.
One party is said to have paid £40,000 for the right for a dozen
counties in England; another £15,000 for three counties; and another
£20,000 for some counties in Ireland: the whole sum realised by the
original purchasers amounting, it is said, to upwards of £150,000.
5th, The consequence is, that such enormous sums having been paid by
the speculators, the trade can only get the use of the machine by
paying a most exorbitant price, and hitherto it has remained all but a
dead letter. We cannot give you in round numbers the amount
expected to be realised by the speculators, but the price originally
charged by them would have yielded four or five times the amount
they paid if the whole trade had become purchasers. This machine
has not yet been the subject of litigation, but there is every probability that it soon will be."

But I can reproduce a case where the effect was far,
far worse, communicated to me in a private letter:—

"The patentee of the Howard series of improvements in sugar-refining
granted licences to houses in Liverpool and Hull, with a condition in
each case that he would not grant a licence to any party carrying on
business within seventy miles of either town. A sugar refiner of long
standing, established in Sheffield, applied for a licence, and was refused
for the reason above stated, Sheffield being just within the prescribed
distance. The consequence was, he had to carry on his manufacture
for nearly fourteen years on the old system; and during this period
sustained great losses by working, which he, as well as parties cognisant
with the facts, attributed to the disadvantage he was compelled to carry
on under. His fortune disappeared, and he became insolvent.—I am, &c.
"Sheffield, December 17, 1863."

This distressing result will, I trust, drive home the
conviction that, great as is the evil of multiplying
Patents, it would be but a mitigation not worthy of being
looked to as a cure, to get the number lessened.

If in an earlier part of this address I have shown
that the condition not to produce "general inconvenience" has been preposterously set at nought, surely

these passages prove no less conclusively that there has been equal disregard of the condition not to "hurt trade." I will satisfy myself, and I hope the House, with one extract only to prove what I apprehend is the rule rather than the exception, that Patents offend against the other condition, not to "raise prices." It is from a paper read by Mr. Lowry Whittle before the Statistical Society of Dublin :—

"I was informed lately of a case in the North of England where a successful patentee produced a machine at the cost of £200 for working in the linen trade. On this machine his royalty is £1,000."

I may give one instance from my own experience, where the pretensions of the applicant for a Patent were equal to about a farthing a pound on all the sugar that the process perfected. The House may understand the hardship this would inflict on the population when told that it was for the use of a single process only, or rather of a machine invented by another, an engineer firm, who had overlooked, and not included in their Patent, its applicability to sugar. My experience in that case was very instructive. Pardon my introducing a few particulars. I have no reason to think the idea of applying the machine to the refining of sugar was original; on the contrary, it had been already made practical on the Continent. Nor was the idea patented by my friend alone; on the contrary, to several persons it had occurred, by some (I forget how many) it had been patented. One of my partners and I had a good deal of travelling in England and Scotland, when we discovered the first patentee of the application at length. We traced the indubitable priority home to a good neighbour, whose office was within a bow-shot of a sugar-house of which I myself was managing partner. He told me, when I called about his Patent, that he had not attended to it for years. I regret to be able to add that he was afterwards led, by representations which I will not characterise, to part with his privilege—it was really a very valuable one—for a most inadequate consideration, to a person who had applied for a parasitical Patent for something, the value of which could not be substantiated. Perhaps the worst of all is, that the really most meritorious person, the patentee of the machine, got comparatively little advantage from its new but natural application. A coalition was formed whose terms violated one of the conditions to which I have called attention, by charging an exorbitant price for the machines, and, what is the greatest mischief of Patents as now administered, by further charging high royalties proportioned to the quantity of work they did.

Now will the House consider why it subjects the nation to all this inconvenience, loss, and expense? It is not because without it we would miss many important inventions. The groundlessness of such a fear has already been indicated with sufficient plainness.

The House can hardly doubt, from its individual acquaintance with what goes on in the world, and from the extracts I have troubled it with, that whatever argument in favour of maintaining a Patent system may be founded on the claims of inventors, the material interests of the nation would suffer little from the cessation of Patents as a stimulus. Unquestionably, if the system induces some inventions to be made and published, it deters others. What we gain is a matter of doubt. That much inconvenience is inflicted by it, and much' disadvantage and very heavy burdens, is no matter of doubt. It is a case in which we have to balance the positive disadvantages against the supposed advantages. To enable the House to weigh these, by seeing how few inventions we would lose by total abolition, a few more quotations may be permitted.

Very significantly Mr. Richard Roberts answers :—

"Would the absence of Patents for inventions, in your judgment, have any effect in producing secret trades ; or have you had any opportunity of judging whether non-patented inventions are used much in secret trade ?—I do not think there is much secret trade, but I know this, that no trade can be kept secret long ; a quart of ale will do wonders in that way."

Let me adduce Mr. Woodcroft :—

"Do you think there is any natural tendency or propensity in inventors to keep to themselves their inventions, or have they a natural tendency to make them known ?—The natural tendency of an inventive mind is to make the invention known."

I now adduce the late able Mr. Fairrie :—

"You believe that the same energy of mind would be displayed, and the same anxiety to make new discoveries felt, whether there were this hope of protection or not ?—I think so ; in the case of manufacturers certainly. I think the great bulk of improvements proceed from the manufacturers themselves, and not from mere inventors."

Hear Colonel Reid, so well entitled to speak :—

"Supposing the law were so modified as to make the acquisition of a Patent easy and simple, and to provide for the publication at the earliest possible period, do not you think there would be more inducement to the disclosure of the secret under such a system than if all privileges of the kind were abolished ?—I am inclined to think that the advance in improvement in all our arts would be greater by leaving them entirely unshackled."

Sir W. Cubitt was asked—

"Have you ever been an inventor yourself?—Yes, of many things; but a patented inventor of but one.

"You have taken out a Patent?—I took out a Patent in the year 1807.

"Has your attention been at all directed to the advantages or disadvantages of the present system?—Yes, it has been drawn to the subject very frequently indeed; but the more it was drawn to it, and the more I saw of it, the less I approved of it; but with that disapproval I could not satisfy myself how to devise anything much better; whether to make alterations, or whether to do away with Patents altogether would be best, I can hardly determine.

"Will you state, generally, your objections to the present system? —The objections to the present system are the very advanced state of scientific and practical knowledge, which renders it difficult to secure anything. The principles of mechanism being very well known and very well understood, inventions involving exactly the same principle and to effect the same object may be practically and apparently so different, that Patents may be taken out for what is only a difference in form, intended to produce the same effect, without there being any difference in principle."

So Sir W. Armstrong :—

"My firm conviction is, that if there was no artificial reward for invention you would have just as much as at present."

Mr. Grove perhaps goes at least part of the way :—

"The Patent is to encourage invention; if, therefore, you would get the same inventions as we now get without Letters Patent, I would have no Letters Patent at all. I believe that, with respect to the minor class of inventions, you would get them."

Mr. Platt also has his doubts :—

"Is not almost every Patent which is now granted a Patent for an improvement?—A great many Patents are granted for things which are no improvement at all.

"I would simply limit the Patent-Law to that extent. I think there are so many Patents granted that it is a great question with me, I confess, if Patents for these combinations are to be granted, whether it

E

would not be better to abolish the Patent-Laws altogether, as it becomes such a nuisance in conducting a large business."

How emphatic was Mr. I. Kingdon Brunel :—

"Do you think that there would be an equal inducement for a man to turn his attention to improvements if there were no Patent-Laws, as compared with the present state of things, which lead him to the expectation and hope that he will obtain some exclusive advantage from the discovery of some new improvement ?

"I feel certain of it; I have felt it very strongly, and it always struck me as surprising that it was not seen by everybody else; but we have so long been in the habit of considering that the granting of an exclusive privilege to a man who invents a thing is just and fair, that I do not think the public have ever considered whether it was, after all, advantageous to him. My feeling is, that it is very injurious to him.

"My impression is, that in every class of inventions you would practically in the end have a more rapid supply and increase of inventions than you have now; I believe that men of science, and all those who do it for pleasure as well as for profit, would produce more, they would be less interfered with by existing Patents, and they would really produce more; I believe that the working class, the smaller class of inventors, would introduce very much more. With respect to that class of inventions, which I believe to be very few in number, though they are talked of very much, which really involve long-continued expenses, I believe they would probably be brought about in a different manner. I wish, however, to have it understood that I limit my observations to the present state of things. I do not wish to express any opinion as to what might have been formerly the effects of Patents, or whether they did originally encourage inventions or not. I believe that in the first place they are very prejudicial, on the whole, to a large class supposed to exist of inventors, and principally from these circumstances : the present state of things is this, that in all branches, whether in manufactures or arts of any sort, we are in such an advanced state, and every process in every production consists of such a combination of the results of the improvements which have been effected within the last twenty or thirty years, that a good invention now is rarely a new idea."

So likewise Mr. James Spence :—

"The evils of the present system are serious. There is a charm in the name of a Patent which entices large numbers of men to neglect their own affairs in pursuit of some phantom. Where intellectual power exists of an inventive character, it will develop itself without any spur; it is, indeed, irrepressible in its nature. To such minds the stimulus of a Patent is superfluous.

" Besides the progress of the arts, another change has occurred whic affects this question. Formerly improvements made slow progress, and unless an inventor were protected for many years he had little chance of recompense. Now the power of advertising is so great and intelligence is so diffused, that any really useful invention can be brought immediately into operation and profit. Were Patents abolished, any one with an invention of value could find a manufacturer to take it up. It is true it would be open to the rest of the world as soon as found out, but the manufacturer would obtain the first start of all others, in itself a profit. Under the present system the legal protection breaks down in practice. The moment a specification is published, competing manufacturers strain their wits to contrive how to reach the same result through other means or modifications; in other words, how to infringe. Against this the patentee has no remedy, except proceedings at law of the most costly nature.

" No change can be proposed in Patent-Law that will not be open to objections based on individual cases of hardship; but, on a comprehensive view of the subject in all its bearings, I hold that it would benefit the country to abolish the system *in toto*. Manufacturers would be relieved from present perplexity, delusions would no longer be kept up by excitement, an enormous waste of money would be stayed; and whilst the mass of worthless Patents would disappear, any of real value would be taken up on its merits and produce sufficient remuneration to the inventor."

The Report of the Commission, founded on the evidence of which I have shown the general character, contains the following just observations :—

" The majority of witnesses, however, decidedly affirm the existence of practical inconvenience from the multiplicity of Patents. It is clear that Patents are granted for matters which can hardly be considered as coming within the definition, in the Statute of Monopolies, of 'a new manufacture.' It is in evidence that the existence of these monopolies embarrasses the trade of a considerable class of persons, artisans, small tradesmen, and others, who cannot afford to face the expense of litigation, however weak the case against them may seem to be ; and a still stronger case is made out as to the existence of what may be called obstructive Patents, and as to the inconvenience caused thereby to manufacturers directly, and through them to the public.

" Other instances will be found in the evidence of particular manufactures and branches of invention which are so blocked up by Patents, that not only are inventors deterred from taking them up with a view to improvement, but the manufacturer, in carrying on his regular course of trade, is hampered by owners of worthless Patents, whom it is generally more convenient to buy off than to resist. The evil also results in another practice, having the same obstructive tendency— namely, that of combination amongst a number of persons of the same trade to buy up all the Patents relating to it, and to pay the expense of attacking subsequent improvers out of a common fund. From a comparison of evidence, it cannot be doubted that this practice prevails to a considerable extent. We must also conclude that when the obstruction is not to be got rid of without the expense and annoyance of litigation, in a large majority of cases the manufacturer submits to an exaction, rather than incur the alternative.

" We desire to call special attention to the evidence given by the First Lord of the Admiralty, and by various witnesses on behalf of the War Department, showing the embarrassment which has been caused to the naval and military services by the multitude of Patents taken out for inventions in use in those departments.

" It has long been the practice, founded on judicial decision, to consider that the use or publication of an invention abroad did not deprive that invention of the character of ' a new manufacture within this realm.' It appears to us, and is generally admitted in the evidence, that the present facilities of communication subsisting between all parts of the world have done away with the only valid reason for such a construction of the words of the Statute of Monopolies. The object of allowing such Patents might fairly be, in an age of slow international communication, to encourage enterprising persons to go in search of, and to introduce to this country, useful processes employed abroad, but not otherwise likely to be adopted here, for the want of which we should long have been behind other nations. It does not, however, seem worth while to continue the same facilities now, when foreign inventions are most frequently patented in this country and in their native land simultaneously ; especially, as we are well informed, that one result of the practice is to encourage unscrupulous persons to steal the inventions of foreigners and to run a race with the legitimate owner to get them patented here."

The extracts which I have culled sufficiently prove that, in the opinion of men selected because they were competent to speak with authority on account of their character, ability, and experience, our Patent system is "generally inconvenient" and is "hurtful to trade." Being so, it is inconsistent with the conditions on faith of which, while other monopolies were prohibited by the Act, it was spared. But I rest my case on absolute evils, without regard to that inconsistency. I am sure nobody can go over the evidence as a whole, or even those scraps of evidence which I have presented—I am well aware in a very promiscuous and ineffective manner—without becoming convinced that the trade and manufactures of this country are seriously obstructed, fettered, retarded, harassed, and burdened, sometimes demoralised, often wronged, or even robbed, by the multitude and vexatious character of Patents, and by the claims and conduct of patentees ;—that these Patents, though very numerous, in general possess little merit, yet often produce large revenues, the result of exactions from persons who use them, to the assignees, rather than to the original grantees,—that the uncertainty of receiving a good return (in place of which experience shows there is, in most cases, disappointment or even positive loss), and the utter incongruity existing between the earnings, where there are any, and the merits of inventions, render the system of Patents an exceedingly

unsatisfactory way of stimulating invention or rewarding inventors ;—and that there is wide-spread dissatisfaction with things as they are, yet despair of amendment, among the most intelligent of those portions
of the community for whose benefit the system is
plausibly represented to exist.

The evidence goes to show that the poor man and
the working man suffer in two ways. Such cannot
bring their inventions into play for want of capital,
and they could not, even if it were in that respect
different, make head against rich infringers who are
able by the costliness of law proceedings to set them at
defiance. I might allege, also, that while the expenses
of patenting are clearly too heavy to suit the circumstances of the poor, there is little or no favour shown
by any influential witnesses to propositions for reducing them, because of the tendency that a suitable
reduction would have to still further multiply Patents.
Surely this indicates sufficiently that there is something radically wrong in the principle on which we
proceed.

Allow me, while adverting to the case of the
poor, to express my belief that the Patent system
has an effect on wages which demands the serious
consideration of the friends of working men. I believe
it helps to keep wages low. The abolition would work
in this manner : whenever, in any establishment, an
improvement is introduced, the fact of its use becomes,
of course, speedily known throughout the establishment and in other establishments. The *employés* who
in their ordinary occupations must come to know

what the improvement is and how to work according
to it—for this is a matter of necessity, especially now
that operations are conducted on a large scale, with
the indispensable aid of men intelligent and independent—very soon find they are in request. To
prevent their leaving, they are offered an advance,
which itself in its turn may be outbid. The rise which
indisputably would result in the case of individuals
will, in my opinion, tend towards a general rise. If I
am correct in my anticipations, operatives and artisans
are much injured by Patent-Laws. But independently
of this hypothetical advantage, a good system of dealing
with inventors will be beneficial directly to operatives,
by removing from trade the present hindrances.

Having seen how little store there is set on Patents
by eminent engineers, by manufacturers, and by the
public services, let me appeal to eminent statesmen.
Among these I name foremost the apostle of free-trade.
Mr. Cobden told me, many years ago, that he was
opposed to Patents ; and at a later period, Oct., 1862,
he wrote :—

" I have a growing doubt of the value and justice of the system,
whether as regards the interests of the public or the inventors."

Lord Granville, then Vice-President of the Board of
Trade, the Chairman of the Committee on the Patent
Bills, told the House of Lords, on July 1, 1851—

" The last witness was the Master of the Rolls, who, notwithstanding
the experience he had had as one of the law officers of the Crown in
administering the Patent-Laws, and although he took charge of the
first Bill which the Government proposed on the subject, was
decidedly of opinion that Patent-Laws were bad in principle,

and were of no advantage either to the public or inventors.
. . . . All the evidence that had been brought before the
Committee, both of the gentlemen who were opposed to the
system of Patents and those who were most strongly in favour of
it, had only tended to confirm his previous opinion that the whole
system is unadvisable for the public, disadvantageous to inventors,
and wrong in principle. The result of the experience acquired by the
present Vice-Chancellor and Lord Chief Justice of the Queen's Bench
had raised great doubts in their minds as to whether a law of Patents
was advantageous. The Chief Justice of the Common Pleas likewise
had written him a letter, which he authorised him to make what
public use of he pleased, declaring his concurrence in his opinion that
a law of Patents was neither advantageous to the public nor useful
to inventors. . . . The only persons, he believed, who derived any
advantage from the Patent-Laws were members of the legal profession.
Except perhaps warranty of horses, there was no subject which
offered so many opportunities for sharp practice as the law of Patents.
As regards scientific men, too, the practice of summoning them as
witnesses on trials respecting Patents had an injurious, if not a demoralising, effect. . . . They sometimes allowed themselves to be
betrayed into giving a more favourable opinion of the merits of an
invention than was strictly accurate."

Lord Harrowby judiciously said, in reference to the
proposition then for the first time made to exempt the
Colonies from the incidence of British Patents—

" The colonial refiner would be enabled to avail himself of every new
invention in the manufacture of sugar, to the prejudice of the home
refiner, who would have to pay for the Patent-right."

Lord Campbell—

" Having been some years a law officer of the Crown, had some
experience as regarded the question at issue, and he begged to say
that he entirely approved of the view of his noble friend, Earl
Granville."

Sir James Graham, on Aug. 5 of the same year, observed—

" There was also evidently great division of opinion among Her
Majesty's Ministers upon this subject. The Vice-President of the

Board of Trade, in the House of Lords, when introducing this Bill, expressed a decided opinion adverse to the principle of Patents altogether. The noble Secretary for the Colonies (Earl Grey) agreed with the Vice-President of the Board of Trade, and now it was found that the advisers of the Crown had put an end altogether to Patents in the colonies. Was it right, then, to continue a system in England which had been condemned in principle by the advisers of the Crown? And were they to legislate upon a question which the divisions in Her Majesty's Council rendered still more doubtful?"

Mr. Cardwell, sensibly and patriotically,

"Would remind the House of the case of the sugar-refiners of Liverpool, who complained of this part of the Bill."

I need not quote Mr. Ricardo, whose lamented death prevented him from urging the present subject as he intended. Allow only the following observations of

Mr. Roche, who on the same occasion—

"Entirely agreed that the Patent-Laws should be abolished altogether. They might depend on it that nine-tenths of the Patent inventions, under any law that could be passed, would be nothing less than so many stumbling-blocks in the way of improvement."

Here is an extract from the proceedings of the British Association at Glasgow :—

"Mr. Archibald Smith was convinced that a majority of scientific men and the public were in favour of a repeal of the Patent-Law, and he believed its days were numbered. He held it was the interest of the public, and not the patentees, that should be consulted in the matter. This was a growing opinion amongst lawyers and young men of his acquaintance."

I revert to the injurious influence of Patents in incapacitating manufacturers to compete with their foreign rivals, and am able to submit Continental testimony that such is the inevitable effect. The following lengthy quotation will suffice from M. Legrand, Auditor of the Council of State of France :—

"There is in this institution not only an obstacle to the development of home trade, but also a shackle on foreign commerce.

"The doors which we open by our Treaties of Commerce may by means of Patents be closed.

"Let an invention be freely worked in Belgium; if in France it be patented, Belgian produce cannot enter there. Let the contrary be the case; we cannot export to Belgium the production which is free with us, but patented at Brussels.

"Let us suppose, for example, that a new colour is patented alone in France, and that the patentee only permits the manufacture of the colour on payment of a high royalty: this colour will become dear, to the profit of the patentee alone, and the detriment of all; its exportation, or the exportation of articles dyed with this colour, into a country where the manufacture is free, will become impossible, because in that country they will begin to fabricate it, and its price will be diminished to the extent of the royalty exacted for it by the patentee.

"The French producer will necessarily be placed in such a situation that he will be unable to sustain any foreign competition.

"It is of consequence, so far as it depends on legislators, to place those countries on the same footing who unite in the peaceful, beneficent struggle of competition.

"But with the sound notions which prevail amongst persons of intelligence, it is evident that the uniform solution to which every one would adhere cannot be one which would recognise Patents.

"The making all discoveries free is the system which alone would have the chance of being adopted by all nations.

"It would certainly put an end to more injustice than it would originate."

I had the pleasure of being present at a numerously-attended meeting of the Economists of Germany held at Dresden in 1863, which almost unanimously adopted a resolution against all Patents; quite in harmony, I may say, with formal resolutions of commercial and industrial associations in that country and France.

The House must long ago have been prepared for the following conclusions, which close the Royal Commission's Report on the Law relating to Letters Patent for Inventions:—

" That in all Patents hereafter to be granted a proviso shall be inserted to the effect that the Crown shall have the power to use any invention therein patented without previous licence or consent of the patentee, subject to payment of a sum to be fixed by the Treasury.

" While, in the judgment of the Commissioners, the changes above suggested will do something to mitigate the inconveniences now generally complained of by the public as incident to the working of the Patent-Law, it is their opinion that these inconveniences cannot be wholly removed. They are, in their belief, inherent in the nature of a Patent-Law, and must be considered as the price which the public consents to pay for the existence of such a law."

This is signed by Lord Stanley, Lord Overstone, Sir W. Erle, Lord Hatherley, Lord Cairns, H. Waddington, W. R. Grove, W. E. Forster, Wm. Fairbairn.

The public understood this to mean that the Commission were by no means satisfied that there should be any longer any Patent-Law at all. The *Journal of Jurisprudence* gives it this interpretation.

But I can adduce a higher and more authoritative exposition with regard to the views of at least the noble Lord the Chairman of the Commission. When the question was put as to legislation in conformity with the Report, Lord Stanley told this House on June 10, 1865 :—

" The House ought first to have an opportunity fairly and deliberately of deciding upon that larger question which had not been submitted to the Patent-Law Commission—viz., whether it was expedient that Patents for invention should continue to be a part of the law."

We all know there is in general society, and even among politicians and men in business, an acquiescence almost amounting to approval of Patents in the abstract. Its existence I attribute to unacquaintance with actualities. I acknowledge that when the more able advocates of the system state their reasons, these look conclusive enough, and would be so if there were but one side of the case. What we, their opponents, claim is that our objections be met. This, I apprehend, cannot be done without, at least, leaving so much inevitable evil confessed as must turn the scale. Some of these arguments that we hear are futile and far-fetched enough to deserve to be repeated. Admitting obstructiveness, a Chancery-lane writer pleads thus :—

> "This very prohibition causes others to exert themselves to invent different means by which the same or a better result may be obtained than by the invention which they are prevented from using, except by payment, and the result is competition, in the highest degree beneficial to trade, and an unceasing advancement and striving."

Really no better is the reasoning of an official witness, who told the Commission :—

> "Three-fourths of the Patents, Inventions of Englishmen.—Three-fourths of the applications for Patents, or thereabouts, are for the inventions of Englishmen; the remaining one-fourth are for the inventions of foreigners, for the most part Frenchmen and Americans. The country in which inventions are of the highest value will draw inventions to it from all others, and so long as any one country protects inventions by Patent, so long must all countries protect. Were England to abolish protection of inventions, inventors would carry their inventions to other countries. Switzerland does not protect, and consequently the Swiss take their inventions to other countries."

Why? What harm though the British inventor should go abroad to patent or even to work his invention? He must specify it in the country he goes to ; and cannot, will not, our artisans at once avail themselves, and revel in the free use, of what he there records? Call our nation's not rewarding him a piece of doubtful policy, or want of generosity ; but banish the notion that our trade will suffer. It will gain.

But there are defenders of very different calibre : Mr. MacCulloch,* Sir David Brewster, Mr. John Stuart Mill. It is meet I should inform the House what are their arguments. I find them succinctly stated and well put in Mr. Mill's " Political Economy." I will read the whole of that gentleman's observations, inter-lacing, for brevity's sake, very short and unargumentative dissents, if not replies :—

" The condemnation of monopolies ought not to extend to Patents, by which the originator—"

Does Mr. Mill know that many an invention is patented by some person who is not the originator, but only the first promulgator in Britain; still more often, who is not the only originator ?

" of an improved process—"

I have already shown that the law, rightly read, can hardly be said to sanction the patenting of a "process."

" is allowed to enjoy, for a limited period, the exclusive privilege of using his own improvement."

Which means, the privilege of debarring all other people—some of whom may, after him, or at the same time as he, or even before him, have invented it—from doing what he is, and they also should be, allowed to do.

" This is not making the commodity dear for his benefit, but merely postponing—"

For his benefit, and still more frequently and surely for the benefit of a multitude of other individuals, who have less claim, or no claim at all.

* What would Adam Smith think of his commentator ?

"a part of the increased cheapness, which the public owe to the inventor—"

But not to him only, for he invents often along with others, and always in consequence of knowledge which he derives from the common store, and which he ought, as its participant, to let others share, if doing so does himself no harm.

"in order to compensate and reward him for the service."

The real service, if it be "service," is the communicating his knowledge.

"That he ought to be both compensated and rewarded for it, will not be denied;"

But it does not follow, surely, even in Mr. Mill's logic, that he should be invested with monopoly powers, which "raise prices" and "hurt trade," and cause "general inconvenience."

"and also, that if all were at once allowed to avail themselves of his ingenuity, without having shared the labours or the expenses which he had to incur in bringing his idea into a practical shape—"

But which, very likely, were trifling, and if heavy, were incurred for his own sake, and may have produced benefits to himself that sufficiently compensated all.

"either such expenses and labours would be undergone by nobody—"

Which is a wild assumption.

"except very opulent and very public-spirited persons."

The former are numerous; the latter ought to be; and the service is one the nation may well expect of them. Why should not there be innumerable Lord Rosses, Sir Joseph Crossleys, Sir David Baxters, and Sir William Browns, promoting beneficent commerce by their generosity; and why should not manufacturers systematically combine as an association to procure through science and experiment every possible improvement?

"Or the State must put a value on the service rendered by an inventor, and make him a pecuniary reward."

And why should we not prefer this alternative?

"This has been done in some instances, and may be done without inconvenience in cases of very conspicuous public benefit."

Well: that is a great deal; but why not in cases that are not conspicuous?

"But in general an exclusive privilege of temporary duration is preferable—"

Now, mark the only reasons adduced:—

"because it leaves nothing to any one's discretion—"

That is, I suppose, Mr. Mill, to avoid trusting anybody—the danger from doing which is imaginary, or at least avoidable—would let the nation remain subject to proved frightful inconvenience and loss.

"and the greater the usefulness, the greater the reward—"

Which, Mr. Mill rightly thinks, is what ought to be, but it is not and cannot be what happens under Patents; for, on the contrary, rewards depend mainly on the extent of use and the facility of levying royalties.

"and because it is paid by the very persons to whom the service is rendered, the consumers of the commodity."

Here Mr. Mill appears to regard, and it is right he should, manufacturers as mere intermediates. Well: can they shift the burden which they, in the first instance exclusively bear, from their own shoulders to those of the consumer? Perhaps they could have done so before the inauguration of Free Trade ; but since that time, the thing is impossible, and so will it ever be until the day arrive when either Patents shall apply to all countries, and in all countries exactly the same royalties shall be charged for their use, or else they are abolished.

"So decisive, indeed, are these considerations, that if the system of Patents were abandoned for that of rewards by the State, the best shape which these could assume would be that of a small temporary tax imposed for the inventor's benefit—"

Would he in general get it ? And, let me ask, how collected—how distributed ?

" on all persons making use of the invention."

A thing impossible, however, even for conspicuous inventions ; and to which there is the further fatal objection that there must be none but such recognised, which might be unfairness, as it certainly would be partiality. If, as indicated, a tax on all users and consumers, will not grants from the Exchequer be in the main fair enough as to incidence ?

" To this, however, or to any other system which would vest in the State—"

Why the State ? Why not let inventors decide ?

" the power of deciding whether an inventor should derive any pecuniary advantage for the public benefit which he confers, the objections are evidently [!] stronger and more fundamental than the strongest which can possibly be urged against Patents. It is generally admitted that the present Patent-Laws need much improvement."

It is not admitted that they can be made satisfactory, do what we will ; and I contend that no extent of mere improvement can overcome the objectionableness of the restraints and burdens inseparable from the system.

"But in this case, as well as in the closely analogous one of Copyright, it would be a gross immorality in the law to set everybody free"—

Why, everybody is naturally free, and would continue free if the law did not step in and cruelly take their freedom away, doing which is the real immorality.

" to use a person's work "—

A fallacy—to use, it may be, his thoughts, which, as soon as they are communicated, are no longer his only —and not at all to use his " work " in any proper sense.

" without his consent, and without giving him an equivalent."

As if consent were needed to use one's knowledge, and as if there could or should be any equivalent.

" I have seen with real alarm several recent attempts, in quarters carrying some authority, to impugn the principle of Patents altogether; attempts which, if practically successful, would enthrone free stealing under the prostituted name of free trade, and make the men of brains, still more than at present, the needy retainers and dependents of the men of money-bags."

As to "free stealing," hear what the greatest political economist of France thinks—

" C'est dans une mesure la meme question que le free trade."

As to the "money-bags," Mr. Mill plainly is not aware that the dependence he deprecates is the invariable, almost the inevitable, consequence of a Patent system.

I am extremely sorry to differ on a question of political economy from Mr. Mill. But with all due respect I submit that he has not, when writing the passage which has now been given *in extenso*, realised what a Patent is in practice. It is the price at which

F

the State buys a specification. The purchase is a compulsory one, with this peculiarity, that whereas the inventor may or may not offer to sell—for he is left at perfect liberty, as in a free country he ought to be, whether to patent and reveal (sell) or not—yet if he do offer, it is the State, the maker of the law, which, through the Sovereign, voluntarily puts itself under compulsion to accept the offer, and—with a defiant violation which the frequency of the deed in my view makes flagrant of sound principle—pays not out of public revenues or any funds over which it has legitimate control, but out of the means of private individuals, reached and extracted either in the form of exceptional profits on goods the monopolist makes, or by his levying of a tax called royalties on any of his fellow-subjects whom he may of grace, if they comply with his demands, associate with himself as sharers of the monopoly.

Such opponents' impulses are excellent, but their plan is incompatible with actual pre-existent interests. They omit to take into full account the conditions of the everyday world which the statesman has to do with, and might not unprofitably call to mind a story or parable of juvenile days wherein certain wise men were represented as, after due counsel, placing a favourite bird within high and close hedges in order to gratify their tastes and enjoy melodious notes all the year round. The conditions of winged existence had not been taken into account; theory and sentiment could not be reduced to practice. Favouritism, constraint, and isolation, being contrary to nature, failed. The nightingale loved, needed, sought, and found freedom. To recall another book of youthful days. Think of Robinson Crusoe, and the many new inventions his peculiar position required and elicited. Let me suppose the neighbouring islanders saw for the first time in his hands a cocoa-nut turned into a cup, in his hut potatoes roasting in the fire, in his garden guano used as manure. What would they have thought of Christianity and civilization, if he, anticipating the pretensions of modern inventors, had alleged, on the ground of first use, exclusive property in these manufactures, processes, and applications, and had debarred the imitation for fourteen years? The unsophisticated savages would have said, "We understand and allow your claims to possess what you yourself make, but we do not understand, and we dare not allow, your claim to possess what we make ourselves. You are welcome to learn what we shall learn, and to do whatever you see us do. We cannot sell for money the odours that rise from the fruits that sustain our life; should we forbid to pick up and plant their seeds that we throw away? Should we grudge the runnings over from the brimming cup of knowledge which heaven puts into the hand, and the froth at the top which the wind blows away?" Heathens are pleased to even work at what is good for all according to opportunity. The fact is, the right of inventors is too shadowy to have any recognisable existence where there is not a submissive society to vend to or trample on, and a complaisant state to compel their submission.

If he were a member this night present with us, I would appeal to Mr. Mill as a philosopher. Seeing that the world is so framed that whereas acquisitions of material property or things cannot be possessed in common without the share or enjoyment of each person being lessened or lost, it is universally possible that any number of persons, however many, can possess and use, without any diminution of individual enjoyment, knowledge or ideas in common, do not wisdom and humanity justly interpret this as an indication that to interfere is to oppose the order of nature ?

Let me appeal to him as a moralist. Seeing that to so interfere with the communication and enjoyment of knowledge or ideas by limiting the power and right to apply inventions to use is to withhold that whereby one man, without loss to himself, may benefit his fellows, do not ethics favour the philanthropic course which accords with the course that Nature indicates ?

I appeal to Mr. Mill as a political economist. Seeing that the order of nature and the promptings of philanthropy are favourable to the communication of inventions and their free use, is it the part of a State to provide for the gratification of the selfish principle in man by legislation framed to endorse, and facilitate, and almost to necessitate it ?

I appeal to Mr. Mill as a statesman, and ask, Is it consistent with enlightened policy to place manufacturers in such a position, that they are constantly tempted to conceal improvements they are using, from fear to discover that they are infringing ? Does he know so little of mankind, that he expects them, the poorest as well as the richest, to employ (and this would be requisite) suitable agents to search whether any improvement they mean to adopt is already the subject of a Patent that renders its adoption illegal, and also to institute inquiries as to who, and where, in the wide world, is the holder of the Patent or Patents, whom in that case he must first negotiate with and sue for a licence? Does Mr. Mill think a manufacturer's time is so free from absorbing occupations that he can attend to the daily transactions of the Patent-office, so as to inquire whether such and such a mysterious application is an unintended, it may be, but in result an effectual, ousting him from use of a process that he is about to introduce or has already in operation? Yet these are the superhuman efforts and gifts which compliance with, and subjection to, any Patent system presupposes and requires.

Is it nothing in the eyes of this legislator, whose absence from this House is so generally regretted, that by means of the Patent-Laws there are thrown loose on men in trade thousands of individuals whose interests run counter to those of society, men trusted with letters of marque to prey, not on foreign commerce, but on British? Is it a small matter, that, having surrendered the principle of discriminating duties leviable by the State for national purposes, we continue to expose those from whom this protection is withdrawn to an ever-increasing burden of taxes, in favour of individuals, levied without State control or any regard to equality? Does Mr. Mill conceive it is short of recklessness to continue to stimulate invention by rewards which often turn out ruinous to those whom they are meant to favour, and which bear not the smallest proportion to the cleverness, the beneficial

results, the cost of elaborating, the merits or the wants of
the inventor, and scarcely to the originality and legiti-
macy of the claim of whoever is the applicant? Is he
aware that the advantage reaped by inventors, sometimes
very large, is obtained at so frightful a cost that, as
some persons believe, for every pound which actually
reaches him the country loses to the extent of one
hundred pounds? Surely we are asked to obtain our
stimulus by a folly (only his was voluntary, and not
habitual) like that of the fabulous sailor who, for the sake
of a tumbler of rum, swallowed the bucketful of salt
water amid which the dangerous stimulant had by accident fallen. I honour the candour of Mr. Mill, and I
hope yet to have his concurrence in my views. He
cannot have reflected on and realised actual facts. One
illustration more, and this of another difficulty which I
commend to his attention and that of any honourable
gentlemen who have been carried away along with him,
I give by narrating an incident in my late canvass.

A deputation of the trades of Scotland did the can-
didates the honour of submitting to us a very judicious
list of questions. One of these concerned the Patent-
Law. They asked, would I support a motion for
reducing the cost of Patents? I answered I would,
because I think the cost too high for the working
man; but I added that I would rather see Patents
swept away. One of the deputation properly animad-
verted on the hardship this might inflict, and he
instanced the case of his brother, who had invented an
improved apparatus for use on board ship. I rejoined
that I accepted the case as sufficient to confirm the con-

viction that Patents are on the whole not good, but bad, for working men or any men. My reasoning was substantially this: In order to reap his reward, the inventor is required or expected to visit every ship or shipowner at the port, and endeavour to get the apparatus understood, believed in, and adopted; and not at Leith only—at every Scotch port, every English port, and every Irish port. But not to let British shipowners suffer by the inequality of paying, while rivals use without paying, and at the same time to promote his own interests, the inventor must take out Patents in France, Belgium, Holland, and all maritime countries and their colonies. After he obtains these many Patents he has to sell his apparatus at all the ports of those countries. The first thing obvious is, that to do a tithe of that work the inventor must relinquish his own business, which is the solid beef in the mouth of the dog in the fable, for the delusive shadow in the water. But never mind that in the meantime: after the business is relinquished, there remains the insuperable difficulty of conducting a business so much beyond the power of man as that I have sketched. He might of course attempt to overcome that by appointing agents to manufacture abroad or act abroad for him; but where is the capital to hazard on so great an enterprise? If he were as rich as a Rothschild, has he the gift of tongues to enable him to correspond in all languages? And if he had, how can all this work, requiring simultaneity, be done at once? The end, of course, must be, at the very best—the Patents, if, indeed, actually taken, are sold for a trifle, and the persons who secure them, which they only do if valuable, in their turn sell, for a trifle too ; so that the lucky inventor gets but little out of the tens of thousands or hundreds of thousands of pounds which the public are made to bear the burden of. *Ex uno disce omnes.*

I am unwilling to leave this part of my theme without adverting to a point which deserves some attention—I mean the tendency the Patent system has to lower the tone of men of science. In a quotation from Lord Granville it is seen to be more than insinuated that the sacred claims of truth are in danger of being compromised by the evidence men of science are asked and tempted to give in courts of law. But the evil of Patents begins in the laboratory and the closet; for there is felt the impulse to conceal anything new and likely to be useful, in order to patent ; so that a conflict is generated between, on the one hand, the theory of the academic chair which supposes in the very name "university" universalism, community of knowledge, and on the other, law-created personal interests, whose nature it is to stifle the man of science's inherent desire to spread knowledge and exchange thoughts in order to benefit mankind.

But Mr. Mill presents an alternative. I, for one, have no objection to see it considered. I have long advocated State rewards ; they cannot be condemned on principle ; they are sanctioned by another philosopher. When I say that I had the honour long ago to receive the following from M. Chevalier, I am sure of this House's attention.

Extract of a Letter from M. Michel Chevalier to Mr. Macfie.

" The Patent system, as constituted in all countries where it is established, is a monopoly that outrages liberty and industry. It has consequences that are disastrous, seeing there are cases where it may stop trade for exportation and even for home consumption, because it places manufacturers who work in a country where Patents are established at a great disadvantage in competing with others who live in States, such as Switzerland, where Patents are interdicted by law. Practice, experience, which is the supreme authority in the world, shows daily, in France particularly, that the system is a scourge to industry. What might be substituted is a system of recompenses, either national or European, as you have proposed, to be awarded when practical use has pronounced on the merit of each invention, and when the originality shall admit of being established. All the friends of industrial and social progress ought to unite their efforts to liberate industry from the shackles that have been bequeathed from the past. That of Patents is one of those which there will be most urgency to get rid of."

The Continental Association for Promoting the Progress of Social Sciences favours such rewards. Allow me to quote from a Report of M. Tilliere, Avocât of Brussels, which was adopted by that body :—

" It is proper to introduce, in respect to industrial inventions, the principle of *expropriation* [or acquisition for behoof of the public], with a view to general benefit, in order to reconcile the interests of industry and the requirements of free trade (*libre échange*) with the interests of the inventor.

" It is desirable, for the satisfaction of the same interests, to establish between the different countries by means of stipulations with reference to Patents in International Treaties, uniformity of system, and, pursuant thereto, to provide a depôt where, without the necessity to patent in every particular country, specifications might be lodged that shall be recognised and published in all."

The House will observe that in connexion with the principle of State rewards, or, what is nearly allied to it, of expropriation, the Association commended another principle, that of international arrangements as to inventions. On the occasion when the report I quote from was adopted, another eminent French economist, Professor Wolowski, spoke as follows :—

"The free competition which ought to exist between peoples requires that Patents should be everywhere ruled by uniform laws. Intellectual property must everywhere have limits within which there shall be exchange, in order that its products may everywhere circulate under the same conditions. International legislation with regard to Patents is an object to be earnestly pursued. It responds to the demands of free-trade, satisfies the needs of liberty of manufacture, and provides a compensation for a shortened term of Patent-right by extension of area."

But I come nearer home, and am happy to be able to quote concurrence in the idea of national rewards on the part of one of our great staple manufacturers, the sugar refiners. The refiners of Scotland many years ago petitioned Parliament in the following terms :—

"That, in the opinion of the petitioners, it is highly desirable that your honourable House should devise some means whereby discoverers of valuable inventions (to whom alone Patents should be granted) might be rewarded by the State, and trade be relieved from the restrictive operation and expense of Patents altogether."

Tending in favour of rewards rather than Patents is the following evidence, given before the Royal Commission by Sir William Armstrong :—

"How would you give these rewards in the absence of a Patent-Law ?—I am not prepared to say that. If the country would expend in direct rewards a tithe of what is paid for Patent licences and expenses, there would be ample provision for the purpose. As a matter of opinion, I believe that if you let the whole thing alone, the position which a man attains, the introduction and the *prestige*, and the natural advantages which result from a successful invention and from the reputation which he gains as a clever and able man, will almost always bring with them a sufficient reward."

A successful inventor writes me :—

"I should be very glad to see a good round sum set apart by Government for the purpose of being awarded to real inventors by competent and impartial authority. Then the poor inventor might have some chance."

It is not out of place to inform the House that so far back as the earliest years of the Patent system a precedent can be adduced. In 1625, Sir F. Crane received a grant of £2,000 a-year for introducing a tapestry manufacture. There are several other precedents for similar grants of public money.

Of course, to reward is not to purchase. We do not buy any man's invention or secret. But if he thinks proper, as a good subject, to reveal that secret, we mean he shall have a substantial mark of favour. Something like this was, no doubt, the original intention of Patents ; only the favour took the form of monopoly for introducing and working a manufacture, whereas we prefer to pay, as soon as the value and benefits of the invention made can be guessed at, such a sum of money as will be neither, on the one hand, from its magnitude made oppressive to the people, nor, on the other, from insignificance or paltry conditions unworthy of a noble mind, whatever the rank, to accept. What is given will be proportioned to merit or service, and will be, in the fullest sense, a *honorarium*, a complimentary gift, a mark of national approbation and gratitude. We all know, though few of us think of it as a striking proof how Patents have declined in public esteem, that among us to be a patentee is by no means usually reckoned an honourable distinction. It is the same in France.

" The title of patentee is falling into greater disrepute every day from the abuse which is made of it."

This prejudice we must remove, and we can do it. I believe in the possibility and advisableness of presenting, as a substitute for Patents, a system of rewards which will reconcile the honour and interests of men of science and those of practical men, the interests of the master and those of his workmen, the interests of the many and those of the few. Such a system, while entirely emancipating commerce and industry, must, as its condition, deal out its rewards more equitably than the Patent system does, and with more regard to the just claims of inventors. It must distribute these without the tedious delays now suffered from. Its rewards must, in contradistinction to present experience, be sure, easily attainable, and suitable for poor as well as rich. I respectfully submit the following scheme as one that at least may form a basis for some system that will obtain general acceptance.

New System of Rewarding Inventors and Promoting the Publication of Inventions.

1. The Patent-office to be turned into an office for recording inventions.

2. (Forms for specifications to be furnished gratuitously.)

All specifications to contain a certificate that the inventions promise to be useful, and are believed to be new, from three persons familiar with the trade chiefly concerned; one of whom, if the inventor is an *employé*, to be his employer.

3. These specifications to be registered.

4. Any time after an invention has been tried and proved practically useful, a fact to be duly certified, the inventor to be allowed to claim that the invention shall be reported on.

5. A Chief Commissioner for Inventions shall appoint one or more examiners for this purpose, whose duty it shall be (after, if needful, first visiting the scene of operations, and conferring with practical manufacturers) to recommend, if they think it worthy, classification for a reward, prize, or certificate of merit.

6. Once a year the head of the Invention-office, with the help of an Adjudicatory Committee, who shall form an Invention Commission, shall classify the several inventions that have been in the previous twelve months certified as having been for the first time brought into beneficial use.

7. In this classification the first rank shall entitle to a

reward of . . .	£10,000.
2nd.	5,000.
3rd	1,000.
4th	500.
5th	100.
6th	50.

7th, Gold Medal, or value in money.
8th, Silver Medal   ,,
9th, Bronze Medal   ,,   ,,
10th, Certificate of Merit.

8. Parliament shall annually place at the disposal of the Invention Commission £200,000, from which shall be defrayed the expenses of the staff, and fees to " re-

porters," as well as of the several publications showing the progress of Invention that shall (as now, but on an improved system) be issued; the balance to be distributed in rewards and prizes, with an understanding, however, that the amount must be reduced if the total awards of the Commission shall exceed the money at its disposal.

9. In appointing Commissioners Government shall consult the various trading interests of the nation in order to select the most acceptable persons. Inventors collectively might have a veto or the initiative.

10. The prizes may be divided between the originator of the idea of any invention and the successful introducer into practical use.

11. Where there are rival claimants, the expense of deciding priority in respect of time and merit to be borne by themselves.

12. The Commission to be at liberty to correspond with foreign nations, and act in concert with any that shall establish instead of Patents a system of rewards.

13. In cases in which pre-eminent merit, especially if there has been a course of costly experiments antecedent, appears to entitle to a reward greater than the largest in the schedule, Government may propose to Parliament special augmentations. I do not presume to recommend Royal decorations and titles, though such honours would be much valued.

A writer on Patents has judiciously said—

"It would seem very desirable that a system of registration for all improvements or ideas which an inventor may think of minor importance should be instituted, whereby any one could, at a moderate cost to defray expenses, deposit at the Patent-office, a description of any new idea, improvement, or invention."

My scheme is calculated to answer this good end.

Here I may fitly call attention to an interesting and instructive analysis which Mr. Woodcroft submitted to the Commission.   He showed—

RESULTS of the EXAMINATION of the first hundred inventions, for which applications for Patents were made in each of the years 1855, 1858, and 1862 (abridged).

1855.

"Of the first hundred inventions for which applications for Patents were made in the year 1855, none are apparently of considerable value.

" Four of the hundred inventions appear to be of some, but not of great value, and Patents were granted for all of them.

" The remaining ninety-six of the hundred inventions seem to be of little or no value; and Patents were granted for sixty-six of them."

1858.

" Of the first hundred inventions for which applications for Patents were made in the year 1858, none are apparently of considerable value.

" Three of the hundred inventions appear to be of some, but not of much value.

" The remaining ninety-seven of the hundred inventions seem to be of little or no value; and Patents were granted for sixty-two of them."

1862.

" Of the first hundred inventions for which applications for Patents were made in the year 1862, one is apparently of considerable value.

" Of the same hundred inventions one appeared to be of some, but not of great value.

" The remaining ninety-eight of the hundred inventions seem to be of little or no value.   Patents were granted for fifty-nine of them."

I conceive, on the basis of this evidence, that the estimate I am now about to give represents, relatively, but I will not venture to say absolutely, a fair view of probable claims.   It also affords some guide for anticipating what, coming from the Exchequer, would be a reasonable total vote for rewards. Such a sum, or even a larger, Parliament should willingly grant. It can be proved to be true national economy. The nation, as individuals, is paying vastly more now. For that burden Parliament, by not removing Patents, is alone responsible.

1 at	...	...	...	...	...	£10,000
3 at 5,000		...	...	...	...	15,000
12 at 1,000		...	...	...	...	12,000
84 at 500	...	...	...	...	...	42,000
250 at 100	...	...	...	...	...	25,000
400 at 50	...	...	...	...	...	20,000
Medals and Certificates of Honour and Merit...			...	...	...	1,000
750						£125,000

I am aware that inventors have hitherto drawn such large sums in some cases (in many or most cases claiming more than they got), that they may at first hardly be pleased with my proposal. But they should remember that the sums set down are those derivable from one country alone—one of the between forty or fifty countries which give Patents now. The revenues from these other countries, therefore, are to be added. They will also consider that it is optional whether or not they apply for rewards. Let them work in secret, if they will and can. But if they resolutely contend for Patents, let them know the time for abolishing these is at hand ; and abolition may come, if they resist it, without even this substitute.

I have endeavoured to show what I believe to be

true — that Parliament, when it, by the Act 21, Jas., 3, tolerated monopolies for inventions, did not sanction any system at all like that into which Patents have developed, or degenerated ; that, in defiance of the Act, Patents are granted so as to create the evils which Parliament expressly sought to shield the nation from ; that recent legislation has aggravated the great evils that pre-existed ; that a Commission has satisfied itself that no radical or sufficient remedy can be applied ; that the arguments of the defenders of Patent monopolies are untenable ; that the most eminent statesmen, lawyers, engineers, manufacturers, and philosophers plead for abolition ; that the State is at liberty, and has the power, to devise, if it wills, a better method of dealing with inventions, but that such a method must be one that leaves manufacturers free, and able to compete with continental rivals by at once adopting, without any burden of royalties, every most recent improvement.

To conclude : this great and vital question cannot longer be deferred. It must be taken up, and that early, by what is expected to be a working Parliament— a Parliament, too, which for the first time can claim to represent labour and operative industry. Parliament has legislated in order to the preservation of salmon, and required the removal of obstacles on the coasts and in the rivers. Here are far worse obstacles, affecting not a luxury, but all our necessaries of existence, and every means of earning a livelihood.

Again : are we not asked to remove light-dues at the sea and tolls on the land ? But what are these

unimportant, sparse, and withal equitable taxes, compared with the close-recurring stoppage and the inde
finite and heavy demands for questionable "service"
which Patents constitute ? Yet, again : By arrangement with France we recently abolished the time-
sanctioned petty exemptions of free-men ; but here we
are continuing to levy more burdensome private taxes,
with exemptions in favour of foreigners! It is they,
indeed, whom the provisions of the Patent-Law
strangely serve. Foreign countries are not so liberal
to British subjects as we are to theirs ;—why should
they ? The number of Patents we grant in a year to
foreigners has increased within a short period tenfold
— to about 880, or about twelve times the whole
number that Prussia grants to her own subjects and
all the world besides. Well may Sir William
Armstrong remark in his evidence :—

"Unless you wish to benefit the foreigner, unless that be the sole
object, as a matter of policy, I do not see what the motive to apply
the Patent system is."

The same witness said also :—

"Is it the fact that Patents are taken out in this country for processes which are in operation abroad, but which have not been previously introduced into this country ?—Certainly. A process in actual
operation abroad, which has not been published in this country, can
be made the subject of a Patent.   .
"Is it practically the case that processes which are carried on
abroad are brought into this country by parties who patent them here ?
—Yes.
"A great number every week ?—Yes, constantly."

Any one who has followed me in the statements I
have presented will see that, while we have been

retrograding and making our system of monopoly wider and worse, the Continent, to which a Patent system was first introduced just three-quarters of a century ago, is ahead of us in respect of the prudence with which exclusive privileges are granted and administered. There, as a rule tolerably general, Patents of importation are treated less liberally than those granted to inventors. The early and almost continuous working of the Patent within the kingdom is required; it lapses when expiry abroad exposes to foreign competition; expropriation is provided for; there is more scrutiny; medical appliances and food are excluded, &c.

But this is merely one, and a comparatively unimportant, fault of the system. There are many faults, as we have seen, much more serious, and which the Commission deem irremovable. I must, therefore, protest against injury done by the Patent system to our manufacturers and artisans, and through them to the nation.

These interests, the interests of us all, cannot with impunity be subjected longer to the hardships that I have endeavoured to expose. Times are changed. British and Irish manufacturing pre-eminence is passing away, not indeed by its actual retrogression, but by a simultaneous and relatively more rapid progression of rivals on the Continent, who, in not a few cases, are competing successfully, even in our home markets, in those articles of commerce and manufacture in which but lately we, perhaps conceitedly, supposed we had outstripped, without a chance of being overtaken, all conceivable rivals. The motion, of which notice has been given, is :—

"That, in the opinion of this House, the time has arrived when the interests of trade and commerce, and the progress of the arts and sciences, in this country would be promoted by the abolition of Patents for inventions."

Unless, indeed, Government and the House prefer in the first instance fresh inquiries through a Committee or Royal Commission, in behalf of which course it is fair to allege the circumstance that artisans and operatives were not represented among the witnesses in former investigations, I submit that this motion ought to be at once adopted. Such action on our part will command, and, in a sense, inaugurate a principle which the nations of the world, who copied our present system, will not be slow to appreciate and embrace. Restoration of that effete system to its earlier moderate dimensions—rectification, however thorough, of the wrongs it involves towards inventors, will not suffice, and need not be attempted. The time has come, not for palliatives nor remedies, but for removal out of the way.

SPEECH OF SIR R. PALMER, K.B., M.P.

Sir Roundell Palmer, in seconding the motion, said he had long felt convinced that this subject was one of great and growing importance, which it would be necessary at an early period to bring before the attention of the House. He rejoiced that it had been undertaken by a practical man like the honourable member for Leith, who could speak upon it, not under the influence of any of the partial views which possibly those who looked at it from a lawyer's point of view might be thought by some to entertain, whether they were in favour of or against Patents. He was glad to find that practical men like his honourable friend had arrived at conclusions which, in their broad principles, were substantially the same as those to which many members of the legal profession, who had had a good deal of opportunity of observing that matter, had in common with himself, come. He was bound to state that he thought the time had arrived rather for opening than for concluding the discussion of that subject ; and, therefore, he hoped he should not be thought to do anything inconsistent with the duty he had undertaken in seconding his honourable friend's motion, when he said at once that, for his own part, he was inclined to go to the root of the matter and abolish Patents altogether, and not attempt to substitute even such a system—although it might probably be preferable in many respects to the present system—of rewards, as his honourable friend had mentioned. Of course those who derived benefit—whether they were the public or were private individuals—from the discoveries that might be made if Patents ceased to exist, might always take into consideration the value they received, and pay for that benefit, as he believed the Government now did, although it was not bound by Patents, with respect to improvements which were useful to the public service. But that, he conceived, would be a very different thing from an organised system of rewards at all analogous to the present system of Patents. He might mention, in passing, a third plan, which had found very able and authoritative advocates, and which he should also greatly prefer to the present system, although he thought total abolition would be better than that likewise. He referred to the plan of putting an end to the notion that every person who invented anything had a right to a Patent, and recurring to what, he imagined, was originally the principle intended—namely, the giving of Patents as a matter of grace and favour in well-selected and discriminated cases, in the exercise of a discretion by an authority entrusted with that discretion. But, as he had already said, he confessed that he himself was not for half measures in that matter. He thought they had a right, as the motion proposed, to say that at the period of progress in the history of the arts and of trade in this country at

which they had arrived, they could do much better
without these props. He called them props because
he thought they were meant to be so, but he believed
that at present they were nothing but obstructions
and hindrances to trade and the arts. Let him, in the
first place, notice the principle on which the Patent-
Law was generally supported. Some persons imagined
that there was a sort of either moral or natural right
in inventors to some such protection as was given by
Patents, and the principle was sometimes expressed in
this way—that a man had a right to the fruit of his
brain. Now, he held that invention and discovery
were essentially unlike Copyright. Copyright applied
to a creation : a man wrote a book ; he thus brought
into existence something which had no existence in
the nature of things before. The rest of the world
were not in the race with him to write that particular
book. But in the case of inventions and discoveries,
the facts with which they were concerned lay in
Nature itself, and all mankind who were engaged in
pursuits which gave them an interest in the investigation for practical purposes of the laws of Nature, had
an equal right of access to the knowledge of those
laws and might be equally in the track for obtaining
it. All who were engaged in particular arts and
manufactures were actually upon the track which led
to the discovery of the useful application of those
laws ; and the knowledge of them was the common
stock and property of all mankind who were equally
in pursuit of it. He could not allow that the man
who was first in the race of discovery could claim for

fourteen years, or any other term, an exclusive property in a portion of the common stock of knowledge which was accessible to all who used the proper means of discovering it. It could not be said that on any considerations except those of public advantage and expediency the man who made the first discovery of a law of nature, or the right mode of applying it had an exclusive right to apply that discovery for a certain period. It was said, however, that Patents were useful to the public, either as stimulating invention, or as insuring the publication of useful discoveries; and he did not venture to say that the time might not have been when they answered both of those purposes. Bounties and premiums might be adapted to a rude state of the arts, and an early stage in the progress of commerce, but when a nation had reached so high a degree of progress in all ingenious arts and discoveries and in trade and commerce as we had, he thought that in this department, as well as in others, the system of bounties and premiums was much more likely to be mischievous than useful. But of course one could not demonstrate that point by resting merely on an abstract proposition, and therefore he would ask the House to look at two or three things which it seemed to him would put the matter in a strong practical light. Patents might be divided into those which might be popularly called meritorious, and those which were not meritorious. The former class were certainly not one in a hundred of the total number of Patents, and the latter class were very numerous in every year. How, then, did the system work as regarded meritorious Patents? He supposed it would be admitted that among the most meritorious discoveries of recent times were the steam engine, the electric telegraph, and the screw propeller for ships. These cases furnished excellent illustrations of the way in which the Patent system worked. Take the electric telegraph. According to the evidence on the subject it was not possible, even for those who best understood the matter, to say who was entitled to the merit of that invention, so gradual and imperceptible was the natural growth and progress of knowledge and discovery in reference to it. But about 400 or 500 Patents had been taken out as marking different steps in the investigation of that subject. As to the screw propeller, he had seen a book which represented the collected Patents of one company as being 90 or 100; and he understood that the case was very much the same in regard to the steam engine. They were not dealing, in the case of the most meritorious inventions, with a true discovery by a single inventor, but with an important branch of practical knowledge at which many men were working at the same time, and in regard to which each step attained indicated the next step that was to follow, and many persons together were on the road. Well, but if they were on the road, the public would get the benefit of the discovery, and the question was whether, by enabling each person on the road to stop up the road at his particular point, they were not really retarding the progress of discovery, and throwing difficulties in the way of even the most valuable inventions. There was no one better acquainted with that subject than a friend of his—a gentleman very eminent both in science and in law. He meant Mr. Grove ; and those members of the legal profession who had to encounter Mr. Grove in a Patent case knew they had a very difficult task indeed before them. Now, here were the words of Mr. Grove in reference to that subject :—

" Always when a discovery has been made when the public has reaped the fruits of it, there is no case, and never was a case, either in the history of pure science or in the history of practical discovery, where it is not alleged, ' If you look at such a book and such another book, you will find that so and so has been done, and you will find that it has been anticipated.' That is partly true and partly false. There are in all such cases approximate anticipations. The difference is, that one man gets at the points, hits the real thing which will do it, and the reason why it will ; whereas other people, although they may have got the thing, have not aquired an accurate knowledge which will enable them with certainty to produce it."

That showed the House that the race was often so close that even the man who had hit the thing might be shut out by somebody else who did it a trifle better. Nothing could be more true than that. Would the House allow him to quote the example of a very important Patent, which he thought would make the matter clear, and indicate how much they might lose by a system of that description. For a very long time the distillation of oils from shale and coal had been a matter of the common knowledge—aye, and of the common practice, of mankind. Early in the present, or towards the end of the last century, it was practised by means precisely similar in all points to those which the present patentees used in this country. But it was not known commercially that there was such a thing as paraffin, nor was it known commercially how to distil it. The oil was, indeed, obtained in a rough way, and without that nicety of discrimination which afterwards resulted from scientific knowledge of the article itself. All chemists knew that in order to distil these oils it was necessary to keep the temperature as low as possible. This was the state of knowledge when a great German chemist discovered that by operating on wood, tar, and other substances, he could produce paraffin· in small quantities. He also said it could be got from coals in precisely the same way as was subsequently done by patentees in this country. But still the German chemist's experiments were of a scientific and not of a commercial character He neither produced it commercially nor did he hit upon the material from which it could be commercially produced. The same oil could be produced from shale. Only the other day there was discovered in Scotland a new kind of mineral, as to which the scientific world were at variance whether it was coal or shale. Patents had been already taken out for distilling oil from shale, and, therefore, if the newly-discovered substance were shale, oil could not be obtained from it without an infringement of those Patents. But a Patent was taken out by a gentleman who stated that his object was to use bituminous coals for the purpose of distilling paraffin. In point of fact, he hit upon a mineral which was *in ambiguo*, whether it was coal or shale, but which the authorities ultimately pronounced to be coal. From this substance the oil could be produced in large quantities. This gentleman took out his

Patent, notwithstanding all the previous knowledge on the subject, and notwithstanding the fact to which the learned judge who decided the case in one of its branches referred in the following terms :—

"There is ample evidence that the attention of practical chemists was previously to the date of Young's Patent laboriously directed to discover the proper material and the proper means of producing these articles in sufficiently large quantities for common purposes."

The public literally had in their hands all the necessary elements of knowledge belonging to the subject, and yet the first person who found that this particular coal was more bituminous than others excluded the rest of the world from that manufacture for fourteen years, and of course amassed a large fortune. Substantially, the test in the courts of law was whether a man had made money and brought the manufacture into use. If so, the courts assumed that all previous knowledge was inadequate and useless, and the man who was successful in the manufacture was regarded as the discoverer. Was it not quite clear, however, that the public were so far on the road to this discovery that it would have assuredly been found out and enjoyed by the public at large if the path had not been obstructed by the Patent ? He would now mention another case. In the days of our youth mills were much infested with flour flying about in them. All the millers, both in this country and abroad, wanted to get rid of this nuisance, and they were possessed of the scientific principle and the mechanical means by which this desirable object would be accomplished. They tried experiments with fans which created a draught to draw the air from the millstones, and everything depended on the adjustment of a plan to draw just sufficient air and no more. People were actually on the road, and were doing the thing in an imperfect way, but in such a way that if they had continued after the granting of the Patent it would have made them infringers of it. But the man who proposed to do just enough, and no more, was held to be entitled to a Patent, whereupon all the millers in England combined to go into litigation in order to defend themselves. Law-suits of the most enormous and oppressive magnitude resulted simply from the circumstance that a man had been allowed to step in and prevent the millers from carrying on their business in the best way. That they would have found it out was certain. That was certainly the impression on his mind. He thought it was almost certain that the discovery being in the direction of their necessity, and depending on the application of a known principle and of known mechanical means, was a discovery which could not in the course of nature have been long delayed. Having said thus much about those Patents which were meritorious, he would make a few remarks on those which were not. A great number of Patents were simply frivolous, and related to practical nothings, but still nothings affecting trades, and standing like lions in the path to frighten tradespeople, and to expose them to risk, litigation, and annoyance, if they manufactured those articles which they ought to be at liberty to manufacture. Then there were other Patents of a less frivolous nature. They related to some little combination of a kind which really was so plainly in

the open path, that everybody ought to be at liberty
to use it.   These, however, furnished the staple of the
great majority of Patents, which, though they did no
practical good, operated to a great extent in hindering
subsequent inventors in effecting further improvements,
because these Patents covered almost the whole ground
of everything that could be possibly done.   An inventor, unless he paid a tax to the owners of prior
useless Patents, was exposed to litigation, and even if
he were willing to pay the tax, the owners of the prior
useless Patent might refuse to grant him a licence.
Thus for the space of fourteen years these useless
Patents might not only do no good to the public, but
might actually stop the road to all further improvement during that long period.   On this subject evidence
had been given by three persons of eminence—Mr.
Scott Russell, Sir William Armstrong, and Mr. Platt.
These gentlemen agreed in saying that the useless
Patents to which he had just referred were a practical
nuisance, and, if so, it was obvious from their number
that they must be a very great nuisance.   Mr. Scott
Russell said :—

"There are a great many Patents of this kind (practically useless,
but not appearing so on the face of them) taken out for boilers of
steam-engines, and boilers of steam-engines admit of very enormous
variety of shape and proportions, without damaging their efficiency.
The consequence is, that it is hardly possible at this moment for a
man having to scheme a boiler for a new situation or new circumstances to avoid putting his foot in so doing into a trap which somebody has previously set for boilers. . . . Nearly the whole of the
Patents for the boilers of steam-engines at this moment are of no
practical value to inventors or to the public ; but they are continually
getting every man who makes a boiler into a scrape with some

patentee, because almost every conceivable form of boiler having been previously patented, and bit of a boiler, one cannot make any sort of boiler without infringing some man's patent."

He said precisely the same thing of screws. Then Mr. Platt, a well-known machine-maker, said :—

" I think that there is scarcely a week, certainly not a month, that passes but what we have a notice of some kind or other of things that we have never heard of in any way, and do not know of in the least, that we are infringing upon them; and the difficulty is to get at any knowledge. We may be now infringing, and may have been infringing for years, and a person may have been watching us all the time, and when he thinks that we have made a sufficient number, he may come down upon us, and there is no record. If a thing is entirely new, there is a record by getting a description; but what I mean by a description is this—A very large number of Patents are now taken out for what is termed a combination of known things for the same purpose, and the descriptions of those Patents are generally so bad that it is impossible to tell the parts that are actually patented. It is only when you come into court, or after making some compromise rather than go to that expense, that you ascertain that fact, and very likely they themselves in many cases do not know the parts that they have actually claimed. It appears to me that, as to that question of combination, the granting of Patents for things to do precisely the same work in the same machine, with the addition, perhaps, of a chain or a couple of bolts, or the form of the lever changed, a straight lever made into a compound one; in matters of that kind it has become a very serious question as to conducting a large business."

These were examples which it would be very easy indeed to multiply, and if the objections he had urged against the meritorious Patents were well founded, what could be said in favour of the large proportion of Patents which were thus simply obstructing the trade and commerce of the country? Could any one doubt that in this advanced era of knowledge the public would gain, on the whole, by the abolition of the Patent-Laws? Before he left that part of the subject he wished to mention one very pregnant fact. There was in this country a powerful consumer—he meant the Government—which, with respect to fire-arms, cannon, ships, and things of that sort, would be placed in a very singular position indeed if it were subject to the Patent-Laws. During the time he had the honour of being a law officer of the Crown, an extensive war was, as the House was aware, unfortunately raging, and a large number of Patents had come under his consideration in connexion with so-called improvements in ordnance and ships. It would be seen from the evidence to which his honourable friend had referred that the authorities at the War-office and the Admiralty had patentees swarming like hornets about their ears, and that the public service seemed, in consequence, likely to be obstructed to a very inconvenient extent. The question was then tried whether the Crown was bound by Patents at all, and a decision was obtained to the effect that it was not. But while the Crown was free it should be remembered that the people at large were subject to the law as it stood, and if in the case of the Government the claims of patentees were found to be monstrously inconvenient, it might not be difficult to believe that they operated in the same way in the case of the rest of the world also. He should not enter into the minor details of the improvements which had been recommended by the Commission, but there was another point to which he wished briefly to advert before he sat down ; he alluded to the question of the protection of the public against invalid and bad Patents. The whole argument in favour of Patents proceeded on the supposition that the public were likely to be really benefited by some discovery which was worth the price of all the inconvenience and obstruction to which they were exposed under the present system. But if they said that they gained nothing by the Patent, and that they only wanted to be set free, what was the position in which they stood in reference to the cardinal point of protection against bad Patents ? Was there really any protection in that respect in the duties which were discharged by the law officers of the Crown ? It was impossible for the law officers of the Crown, acting on the mere statement of the patentee, to know with certainty whether a so-called discovery was new or not. They could only examine into the question whether an alleged invention, as described on the face of it, was or was not satisfactory, but they could in no way protect the public against having an old thing put forward as a new, or a useless as a useful invention. Indeed, the attempt by means of any sort of preliminary investigation to establish the utility or inutility of a Patent must, in his opinion, necessarily fail so long as the granting of Patents was a matter of right and not of discretion. And what was the result when a Patent came to be disputed in a court of law ? Everybody was aware that such litigation had acquired a reputation infamous beyond every other. In the Paraffin Oil Company's case, which had been referred to, the time occupied before Vice-Chancellor Stuart was not less than thirty whole days. Why was so large an amount of time consumed in those cases ? Because it

H

was necessary to enter into the whole history of the discovery in all its numerous stages, and to beat up witnesses all over the country, so that a voluminous mass of scientific evidence had to be produced. That was the reason why the expense in those cases was so enormous, while the public were in every point of view placed at an immense disadvantage, for the presumption was in favour of the patentee, who, if he happened to have succeeded in an action against another person, was entitled to have the fact put in evidence in the case, and might subject his opponent to extra costs. But that was not all. In a case, he believed, of a Patent for the purifying of gas by the use of metallic oxide of iron, it came out that there were two kinds of oxide, the hydrous and the anhydrous, and that the one would effect the object while the other would not ; but, because the terms were general, although everybody who tried the experiment might arrive at the result desired, the Patent was held to be bad, and another person who took out a Patent for the hydrate had his Patent made good. Lord Westbury, who was as well acquainted with the subject as anybody who had in recent times occupied the woolsack, said in 1862, in speaking on that point :—

" To vitiate a Patent by prior publication, whether in a prior specification or in a published book, &c., the antecedent statement must be such that a person of ordinary knowledge of the subject would at once perceive, understand, and be able practically to apply the discovery without the necessity of making further experiments. If anything remains to be ascertained which is necessary for the useful application of the discovery, that affords sufficient room for another valid Patent."

It would be seen, he thought, from what he had

stated, that the public were placed at a great disadvantage in the contest. In dealing with Patent cases in a court of law there was generally a vast array of witnesses to be examined, consisting of mechanics, chemists, and scientific men of all sorts on one side and the other. Then there were the jury, who knew nothing of the subject, and the judge, who might be placed in a worse position, because he might imagine he understood all about it when he did not. He did not, of course, mean to say that the judge did not sometimes understand it, but it might very easily happen that an ingenious professional witness might so argue the case under the form of giving evidence as to lead the judge to think that he really knew all about it when such was not in reality the fact. Then the bias being in favour of the patentee, the result of such trials almost invariably was, that if the matter happened to be of any practical importance, the public were defeated, after having endeavoured to protect themselves at an enormous expense. He would not enter into minute details, but probably he had said enough to show that a great practical evil arose out of Patent-Laws, and that for this evil there was little or no corresponding benefit. He did not think that we should lose really valuable discoveries if the Patent-Laws were abolished. There might be some rare instances in which particular circumstances might give to particular inventors motives for suppressing and facilities for suppressing discoveries which were not patented. But, assuming that to be possible in some cases, it operated even now, for it was well known that Patents were bought up for the purpose of being suppressed, and it was understood also that inventors were the persons who derived the least advantage from their inventions. His conclusion, therefore, upon the whole matter was that the time had at last arrived—even if it had not arrived some time ago—at which the public interest would be promoted by the entire abolition of the present system of monopoly.

[This speech and the succeeding one have been obligingly revised for the press by the speakers.]

SPEECH OF THE RIGHT HON. LORD STANLEY, M.P.

Lord STANLEY said that, agreeing substantially in the arguments of the honourable and learned gentleman who had just sat down, he should not have troubled the House if it had not been for the circumstance that he was chairman of the Royal Commission which sat upon the question of the administration of the Patent-Law some years ago, and he thought, therefore, that it might be expedient he should state what was the result which that inquiry produced upon his mind. There was no doubt that, quite apart from the principle of the law, the details of the law, as at present adminis-tered, were not satisfactory ; and, if the law were to con-tinue in any form, he believed that in the report of that Commission various suggestions would be found by which the most prominent objections to its present working might be removed, and fair trial might be given to the principle itself. But it was impossible to carry on an inquiry of that kind, even limited as it was —it was impossible, at least, for him, and he believed he was not the only one in that position—without finding a doubt raised in one's mind whether any Patent-Law could be framed in such a manner as not, upon the whole, upon the balance of good and evil, to do more harm than good. That conclusion, he was bound to say, was

totally opposed to his earliest impressions upon the
subject. He resisted it for some time, but the more he
had to look into this matter—the more he had to consider how great were the practical abuses and inconveniences of the existing system, and how difficult it
would be to remedy them—the more clearly it appeared
to him that the evil was really irremediable, being
inherent in the principle itself. On this subject of
Patents there had been a certain amount of prejudice,
particularly in the minds of literary men, who appeared
to think that Copyright was only a modification of the
same principle, and that if Patents were abolished Copyright would follow. The analogy seemed a plausible
one, but he thought that, on being looked into, it would
not hold water. The difference was simply this : He
did not rest it on any abstract ground as to the distinction between invention and discovery, but on the
obvious fact that no two men ever did or ever would
write, independently of one another, exactly the same
book ; each book, be it good or bad, would stand alone ;
whereas it might happen, and often did happen, that
two or three men, quite independently of one another,
would hit upon the same invention. That alone established a distinction between the two cases. He was
not disposed to place the objection which he entertained
to the system of Patents upon the ground of any abstract
impropriety in giving a man a property in ideas. To a
certain extent you did in the case of Copyright recognise
a certain qualified and temporary property in ideas ; and
if it could be shown that a man's ideas had been of a
nature to add greatly to the wealth of the country, he

did not think that any abstract considerations of the kind mentioned by the honourable member (Mr. Macfie) would induce anybody to grudge to such a man any reward to which he might fairly be entitled, provided that that reward could be given in a manner free from objection on other grounds. The objections which he felt to the principle of Patents were threefold. In the first place, you could hardly ever secure the reward going to the right man. In the next place, you could not establish any proportion between the public service rendered and the value of the reward received, nominally, for that service. And, thirdly, you could not by any arrangement that he had been able to discover, prevent very great inconvenience and injury being inflicted upon third parties. With regard to the first point—the difficulty of securing that the reward should go to the right man—it must be remembered that a Patent did not, as some people supposed, bring to the holder of it an immediate pecuniary recompense. All that it did was to give him a right to prevent any one else from using his invention without paying for it, and if that Patent were infringed he was entitled to take legal proceedings. But everybody knew that law was costly, and that Patent suits were the most costly of all. It was notorious that Patents were continually infringed by persons who well knew they were infringing them, but relied upon the inability of the inventor to incur the expense of defending his property. If a poor inventor took out a Patent, and the Patent promised to be productive, in nine cases out of ten he was obliged to sell it to some one who could command capital enough to defend it in a court of law. If the Patent remained in his own hands, it was quite sure to be infringed, and then he would probably be crushed by the law expenses. He did not know whether it would be possible to obtain accurate information upon this point, but he really did not think he should be exaggerating if he said that in nine cases out of ten—probably in 99 out of 100—the reward was obtained, not by inventors or their representatives, but by persons who had bought the Patent on speculation and at a very low rate. He said at a low rate, because there was a great deal of uncertainty about such property, and until a Patent was tested by actual working you could hardly say whether it was valuable or not. What was the practical effect of this? Why, that a few great firms in any branch of business, buying up at a low rate any new Patent applicable to their business, and prepared to fight for it, could so hamper other competitors as to secure a practical monopoly. The reward, therefore, did not, as a rule, go to the men who, on the ground of the public service rendered by them, were intended to receive it. As to the second point—that the reward might be great and the public service very small—that had been dwelt upon by the honourable and learned gentleman opposite, and little need be added to what had been said by him. The merit and novelty of the invention might in many cases be almost nothing, and, yet however obvious it might be, however much it might lie, so to speak, in the high road of discovery, if it applied to any article of general use, the pecuniary reward derived from it might be absolutely out of proportion to the novelty or value of the invention. It would be easy to give instances, but he apprehended that the fact was familiar to every one who had studied this question. Then, with regard to the injury to third parties, it commonly happened that half-a-dozen men who were competing in the same line of business were upon the track of the same discovery. Each of these half-a-dozen men would probably have hit upon the invention which was wanted, independently and without communication with the other. But the first who hit upon it, and who took out a Patent for it, was thereby entitled to exclude the general public and competitors from the use of that which, if he had never existed, they would probably have hit upon within a few weeks. A and B reached the same point, one a week or a fortnight before the other, and A became entitled, by the mere accident of such priority, to exclude B from a process which, a little later on, B would have hit upon for himself. Another case was that where the successful working of a process depended not upon one, but upon several successive inventions. The first two or three, not leading to any immediate practical result, might not have been thought worth patenting. The last link in the chain gave to the whole their commercial value, and it was the person who took out the Patent for the last invention who got the benefit of the whole, yet it might not be the most important invention in the series. He would say nothing of the inconvenience and prejudice to manufacturers in general. That was obvious enough, and the question was whether there was any counterbalancing advantage. These were the considerations which led him to the conclusion that it was impossible to defend our system of Patent-Law as it stood. At the same time, he did not at all disguise from the House that there were certain inconveniences and difficulties in the way of abolishing Patents altogether. You had to guard, in the first place, against the danger of encouraging inventors to keep their discoveries entirely to themselves. In some branches of business, no doubt, that would be possible, and the obvious effect might be to shut out the public, for a much longer period than would be the case if Patents were allowed, from the use of some valuable invention. Then it had been suggested by the honourable member who raised this debate that there might be a system of State rewards for the encouragement of really meritorious inventions. Without putting an absolute negative on that plan, he must observe that it was one which could only be established at great cost, and it would be a very difficult thing to apportion among inventors the rewards to which they might think themselves entitled. The distribution of the rewards would give rise to endless complaints, and would occasion, however unjustly, suspicions of jobbing and partiality. With regard to the suggestion thrown out by the honourable and learned gentleman, of the possibility of granting Patents, not as a right, but as matters of discretion only in certain limited and important cases, the Select Committee considered that point, and he was bound to say that the difficulty of carrying it out appeared to his mind almost insuperable. There would be found great difficulty in drawing the line, and it would not be an easy matter for any one to exercise so large a discretionary power as to decide to what inventions Patents should or not be granted. He did not know what tribunal would be fit to exercise so great an authority, and he was sure that none would be able to exercise it in a manner to give satisfaction to the public. The most fit persons to decide in such a case would be the first to see the difficulty of deciding on any intelligible principle, and would on that ground decline to undertake the duty. Under these circumstances it appeared that they were landed in a position of great embarrassment. He was convinced that the Patent-Laws did more harm than good, and if called on to say aye or no as to their continuance, he should certainly give his vote against them; but, as this was a matter which required particularly careful handling, he should be content to leave the question in the hands of the Government, and he thought it was well worth consideration whether they could not, starting on the ground that the abolition of the Patent-Laws, wholly or partially, was desirable, institute some inquiry with the view of discovering, if possible, the best substitute for them in certain cases.

PATENT RIGHT.

Paper by Mr. J. Stirling, Presented to the Glasgow Chamber of Commerce, and published by permission.

First : Patent-right cannot be defended on the ground of justice.

The object of a Patent-Law is to establish a "property in ideas :" but this involves the double fallacy that thought can and should be appropriated. The end of all law is to ensure the universal freedom of human action. Hence the law of property secures to every man the product of his own labour. It gives to each an exclusive right to the material embodiment of his productive energy, to be possessed or alienated by him at will. But in so doing it leaves unrestricted the productive energy of every other man. The freedom of one (as represented by his property) is thus consistent with the freedom of all.

But thought cannot be appropriated. In thought there is no material product to be made the object of a proprietary right. There is no "thing" to be possessed or alienated. The law can only, therefore, give the exclusive use of an idea to one person by injuriously limiting the intellectual activity of all others. A Patent-right, therefore, is less a "property in ideas" than a monopoly of thought.

Again, a true right of property is universal in its application ; it extends to the products of all industry,

however humble. But it is instinctively felt, that a proprietary right applied to every individual idea would be
essentially absurd. Patent-Law, therefore, is essentially
partial in its application. It picks out certain favourite
ideas, and confers on them an anomalous and oppressive
privilege. There seems no good reason why the ideas
of inventors should be especially favoured. An invention is a means to a special end, and should be
recompensed by him who has the end in view. If
any ideas deserve a public recompense, it is those
general ideas whose application is of universal utility.
But Patent-Law ignores the discoverer of general ideas,
and while conferring rewards, at the expense of the
community, on empty schemers and puffing tradesmen,
it passes over the services of a Newton or an Adam
Smith. The law of Copyright, indeed, gives to the
philosopher a right of property in his published and
material works, but it leaves (most justly) his ideas to
be used and elaborated by whoso can and will.

Again, Patent-Law is founded on a conventional,
not a natural, right. It is not, like the ordinary law of
property, based on an universal intuition of the human
conscience, but it is one of those laws by which unwise
legislators have striven so long and so vainly to give
an artificial stimulus to human industry. Hence the
arbitrary nature of its enactments. The ordinary right
of property is unlimited in its duration — passing
from generation to generation. But common sense
revolts, instinctively, against a perpetual monopoly of
thought. A Patent-Law, therefore, can never be more
than a weak compromise with principle—the legislator

undertaking to secure to the patentee his ideal property during the biblical term of seven or fourteen years. Now, if the inventor have a right at all, he has a right to more than this. To cut down a real and acknowledged right of property to seven, or even fourteen, years were a grievous wrong. Patent-right goes too far, or not far enough. Either a Patent is no right at all, or it is a right for all time. If ill-founded, it is a robbery of the public ; if well-founded, of the patentee.

Mere priority affords no good ground for the exclusive right to an invention. The free exercise of thought is the common right of all. Wherefore if A excogitate a principle to-day, and B, by independent thought, excogitate the same principle to-morrow, both have an equal right to benefit by the discovery ; and A has no natural right to debar B from the legitimate fruit of his intellectual effort. It may be even that A had no real priority of thought, but was only more knowing, more greedy, or was simply nearer to a patent office, and, though latest in arriving at the idea, was the first to secure a legal monopoly of its use. To found a right on such a race for priority is evidently irrational. The simultaneousness of discoveries and inventions by different minds, is a well-established fact in the history of science. Certain facts and reasonings, all tending in a given direction, are before the world. These act simultaneously on various minds, and produce in each the same development of thought. Now, with what justice do we pick out one of these many thinkers and give him a monopoly of the common thought ? Nor is the injustice confined to the original idea, of which we grant a monopoly. By tying up one idea, we stop the whole course of thought in a given direction, and thus interfere generally, and to an indefinite extent, with the intellectual activity of other men.

The inventor benefits by the ideas of the community, and has, therefore, no right to a special privilege for his idea. The universal thought of mankind is a common good; all benefit by it freely, and all are bound freely to contribute to it. Every thinker owes an incalculable debt to society. The inventor has the benefit of all foregone human thought, of all existing civilization. He has the unbought advantage of all laws, all language, all philosophy. He has the free use of all the methods and appliances, spiritual and material, which have been painfully elaborated by the thinkers and workers of all time. Why, then, should he alone have an exclusive privilege, in respect of the infinitesimal addition which he may make to the work of ages?

Secondly: Patent-right cannot be justified on the lower ground of expediency. The object of a Patent-Law, in the supposed interest of the community, is to stimulate invention. But invention needs no artificial stimulus. Nature has amply provided all needful and wholesome encouragement, in the additional profit afforded by improved methods of production. In the natural course of business, every producer is spurred on by his material interests to invent for himself or to encourage the inventions of others. The whole history of industrial progress is an unceasing striving after improvement, with a view to profit. The few thousand patented inventions are as nothing compared with the innumerable improvements produced daily and hourly in the ordinary course of business, with the vulgar view of gain. The best stimulus to invention, therefore, will be found in the natural competition of producers; but Patent-Law destroys this competition by an unjust monopoly, and thus tends indirectly to weaken the natural impulse to improvement.

Invention may be even over-stimulated. In all her arrangements, Nature provides for a due equilibrium of powers and tendencies. Thus the various faculties and temperaments of man—the sanguine and the cautious, the speculative and the practical—are nicely balanced. The result, when things are left to themselves, is a happy combination of ingenuity and caution, and, as a consequence, a continuous but prudent course of improvement. But if, by conventional rewards, we give a factitious impulse to the inventive faculty, we destroy the natural equilibrium of capacities, and foster a scheming, fanciful turn of mind, at the expense of thoroughness and a patient working out of sound ideas. This result has actually occurred in the United States, where the factitious value attached to invention has tended to produce an almost total sacrifice of solid workmanship to a flimsy ingenuity.

Patent-Law does not even attain its proposed end of quickening the progress of real improvement; on the contrary, it is found in practice seriously to hinder it, the monopoly granted to one inventor necessarily obstructing the progress of every other. Hence, an eminent inventor has lately said : "The advance of practical science is now grievously obstructed by those very laws which were intended to encourage its progress." That Patents seriously obstruct the natural development of ideas, is best seen by the sudden advance which usually follows the expiry of important Patent-rights. The natural course of improvement, dammed back by artificial obstruction during the continuance of the Patent, is set free on its conclusion, and a new impulse is given to the development of ideas and their practical application.

But the public is not the only sufferer by Patent-right. Without doubt the heaviest evil falls on the patentee. The inventor is led to give an excessive development to his talent, and is seduced into reliance on a law that can give him no substantial protection. The difficulty of defining original inventions is a practical bar to a satisfactory Patent-Law. The whole history of Patents is a long-continued story of litigation and disappointment ; and the more admirable the invention, the greater is the certainty of difficulty and loss. It must be a worthless invention that the patentee is left to enjoy in peace. Whenever a Patent · is worth pirating, the inventor may depend on being involved in a maze of litigation that disturbs his peace and ruins his fortunes. And the more the Patent privilege is extended, the worse the evil becomes ; the intricacy and the multiplicity of details baffling every attempt to define the rights of competing inventors.

At this moment the heaviest complaints against

Patents come from our great inventors. They repudiate the proffered privilege as " injurious to inventors," and complain of being " borne down by an excess of protection." As is natural, they who are most occupied with the advancement of invention, feel most acutely the grievous obstructiveness of the Patent-Law. Not enough that they have to battle with natural difficulties; at every step they meet obstructions which a well-meaning but perverse law places in their way. Nor do these obstructive privileges confer any real advantage on the empty schemers whose monopoly they establish : they merely give them the vexatious power of hindering the progress of better men. The mere " pen-and-ink inventor " has neither the energy, nor the perseverance, nor the practical ability to mature his crude "idea;" but to this man the law awards the dog-in-the-manger privilege of effectually obstructing the natural progress of practical improvement.

These practical evils the advocates of Patent-Law do not deny ; but they attribute them to the defective execution of the law, not to its vicious principle. Hence a never-ending cry, as in the case of all bad laws, for more legislation, for more stringent regulation, for stricter investigation, and more thorough registration of Patents. But no tinkering at details can avail. The whole system is radically unsound ; and the only effectual remedy is to lay the axe to the root.

A sentimental plea in favour of Patent-right has been set up by some, on the ground that the inventor

—the man of thought, as he is called—must be saved from the toils of the capitalist, ever ready to prey on his superior intellect. This silly sentimentalism could only originate in an utter ignorance of the relations which naturally subsist between capital and talent. The capitalist is the natural ally of the inventor, whom it is his interest to employ and encourage. It is a chief part of the business of every producer to search out every one who can help him to improved methods of production ; and the remuneration which, in one shape or another, it is the interest of the capitalist to offer to the really clever inventor, will always form a surer and more substantial reward than the delusive privilege of a legal monopoly. As to the complaints we hear of neglected talent, we may safely conclude that they arise more from the exaggerated pretensions of conceited schemers, than from any obtuseness to their own interests on the part of practical men of business, who refuse to profit by their inventions.

On the whole, Patent-Law seems a blunder, founded on the antiquated notion of giving State encouragement to certain favoured modes of human activity. It is no part of the duty of the State to stimulate or reward invention ; the true function of Government is to protect, not to direct, the exercise of human energy. By securing perfect freedom to each individual, we shall best provide for the progress of the community ; nor can any law be conceived more detrimental to the common weal than one which lays restrictions on perfect freedom of thought.

ARE INVENTIONS PROPERTY?

BY M. T. N. BENARD,

EDITOR OF THE "JOURNAL DES ECONOMISTES," JULY, 1868.

(Translated and Reprinted by his obliging consent.)

In the number of the *Journal des Economistes* for last December there appeared a very conscientious paper on " Property in Inventions," by our learned colleague, M. le Hardy de Beaulieu. We would have preferred that some master of the science had published an answer to this article, which it seems to us is based on a wrong principle, and that he had given to the readers of this journal the opposite view of those ideas so ably set forth by the honourable Professor of Political Economy at the Belgian "Musée de l'Industrie."

We believe that this question has acquired sufficient importance and reality to merit being fully argued and cleared up ; and, no other having taken up the pen in answer, we shall endeavour to set forth the principle which alone appears to us true and admittable.

We throw out these ideas for discussion, hoping that the subject will be taken up by one of our masters in the science, and that this great debate will be carried out in a manner suitable to the imperishable doctrines of justice and equity, which form the basis of political economy.

I.

" The man who first made a hut," says M. le
Hardy de Beaulieu, " a piece of furniture, a cloak, or
some necessary of life, would no doubt have thereby
excited the envy of his neighbours, and.he would frequently have been deprived of these objects by violence
or by strategy, before it would be generally allowed
that they ought to belong to him who made them, and
that it was at once the duty and the interest of the
community to guarantee him their possession against
every attack."

We acknowledge that the man who first constructed
a hut was perfectly right in making good his claim
against those who would have deprived him of it, and
that he was justified in vindicating his claim by force.
He had employed his time and strength in building
this hut ; it was undoubtedly his, and his neighbours
acted up to their natural right and in their own interests
in helping him to oppose the intruder.   But there
ended both the right of the individual and that of the
community.

If this first man, not content with claiming his hut,
had pretended that the idea of building it belonged
exclusively to him, and that consequently no other
human being had a right to build a similar one, the
neighbours would have revolted against so monstrous
a pretension, and would never have allowed so mischievous an extension of the right which he had in the
produce of his labour.

Nevertheless, this man had exercised imagination
and combination ; he had invented the shape, the

size, and the arrangement of the whole structure; he
was the first to conceive—probably after many
efforts of mind and thought, after long study,
after observations made on the nests of birds and
the hut of the beaver—that pile of branches, of
dead wood, of leaves and of stones, of which its
shelter is formed. He was an inventor of the first
class. How is it, then, that the sentiment of justice
which prompted him to claim his property did not
prompt him at the same time to claim exclusive
possession in the idea, the result of a long train of
reflection? How is it that the same sentiment of
justice which induced his neighbours, the community,
to lend him armed force to preserve for him the possession of his hut, did not go so far as to grant him a
property in his idea? No one dreamed of asking him
for the permission to imitate what he had made; no
one thought he was committing a crime, or doing him
a wrong, in making a copy of his hut.

Property can be a right only when its principles tend
to the general good and are useful in advancing the
interests of the human race. And if, in our day, imitation of an invention is not generally considered as
guilty an act as robbery of tangible property, it is
because every one understands the difference between
an idea and a thing made or done.

The inventor of a particular weapon, or certain
furnishings, or tools, had all possible rights in the
constructing and possession of these weapons, furnishings, or tools; but these rights could not be
extended to the hindering of his neighbours from

making tools, furnishings, or weapons, in every way similar. If the community had admitted an exclusive right in these inventions, it would have died in its germ, civilization would have been a dead letter, and man would have been unable to fulfil his destiny.

Thus far, then, there was not, nor could be in principle, any question of exclusive right of invention. This right was only thought of when all notions of social right had been obscured by laws which, like that of Henry II., declared that the right of labour belonged to the Crown, and when there had grown up the idea of licensing labour and granting exclusive privileges for its exercise. The institution of the pretended property in inventions was a retaliation against the suppression of the abusive right of masterships and corporations.

II.

Doubtless invention, as M. le Hardy de Beaulieu remarks, consists in the discovery of a new scientific principle; but we cannot admit, with the learned Professor, that the new application of a principle already known, that the discovery of a natural agent hitherto unknown, or of new properties or other modes of action of natural agents, or of materials previously discovered, are inventions.

It is probable that coal was known long before any one thought of putting it in a stove to be used as fuel. It is certain that stone was known long before any one thought of employing it in the construction of walls.

To pretend that the discovery of the combustible quality of coal, or of the use to which stone might be put, gave a right to the discoverer to exact from his neighbours the payment of a royalty before employing this fuel, or this material for construction, is also to grant that he who, centuries before, had thought of burning wood to warm himself, or of seeking the shelter of a cave, ought also to be recompensed for the trouble he had in discovering, appropriating, and working out either this source of heat or this means of shelter.

Invention, we acknowledge, consists in the discovery of a new scientific principle; it can often place, as M. le Hardy de Beaulieu says, new gratuitous forces at the disposal of the community; but does it follow that the inventor has an exclusive right in the property of this discovery? We think not. The inventor of the compass, whoever he was, has rendered an immense service to the community; but could his invention be claimed as private property? Does it not, on the contrary, enter with perfect justice into the public domain?

Napier, the discoverer of logarithms, has rendered the most signal service to calculators and navigators; but can his invention, the knowledge of which may, either orally or by the printing-press, be extended indefinitely—which any one may use privately, in the quiet of the study—be put upon the same footing as landed property, which a single man may cultivate— as house property, which may belong to one or several, and which cannot be seized upon without its being observed, and to the great scandal of all? Evidently not.

And if the law has never tried to appropriate inventions of this class, it is because there must be something tangible, limited, and final, giving the power to regulate its employment or possession.

It is not correct to say, besides, that the inventor does not deprive the community of any portion of the common property which it possessed before the invention. Before the invention the thing discovered existed in embryo—in nature. This germ was multiple; it existed as frequently as there were men; and the inventor pretends, by the property in it which he claims, to deny it to all others and to hinder its germination.

The right of the inventor is limited to that of working out his idea; it is identical with that of a man who has discovered and cleared a field; but it is not, like his, exclusive. He who invents and he who clears can possess their property as long as they like and as they like; but there is this difference between the field and the invention: the first can be cultivated only by one without doing an injury to the proprietor, while the invention may be used by several without hindering, diminishing, or suppressing the working of it by the inventor.

I have cleared a field, and cultivate it; if one of my neighbours desires also to cultivate the same field, he hinders me from exercising my right—he interferes with my working—he dispossesses me.

I have discovered the combustible nature of coal:

in what way does my neighbour, who cooks his food on a coal fire, hinder me from exercising my right, or interfere with the working of my faculties ? of what does he dispossess me ?

III.

We have not, as we think, to take into consideration more or less the difficulties of inventors ; we have not to inquire if every invention requires a more than ordinary degree of intelligence, special knowledge, great perseverance, &c.   There is a multitude of occupations in life which require all these qualities, but no one has ever pretended that on account of these qualities, probable sources of success for them, they had a right to any favours, immunities, or privileges.

The inventor of a useful discovery has quite as much, or more, chance of making a fortune as the manufacturer who confines himself to the beaten tracks, and only employs the known methods ; this last has had quite as much risk of being ruined as any searcher after discovery.   We believe that they are on an equality as to position ; for if the inventor may be ruined in not finding what he seeks, the manufacturer may see all his looms or his machines rendered useless, all his outlets closed, by the introduction of a cheaper means of production.   Why make a golden bridge for him who enters the arena with arms more subtle and more finely tempered than those of his adversary ?

Notice that the manufacturer also renders a service to the community—no doubt in seeking his own profit ; but is it not so with the inventor? Why then demand a reward for the one which is not asked for the other ?

The manufacturer who, in using the old looms, manages his factory so as to reduce his prices by 10 or 20 per cent., and who in consequence can furnish stockings (supposing him to be a stocking manufacturer) to a number of those who were not rich enough to buy them at the old prices, undoubtedly does a service to the community equal to that which it would receive from the invention of a machine which would make the stockings 10 or 20 per cent. cheaper.

The farmer who by superior ploughing, more skilful manuring, or more careful weeding, increases the yield from two to three quarters per acre—does not he also render a signal service to the community ?

The sailor, who finds the means of shortening voyages by utilising certain currents or winds, in modifying the spread of his sails, &c.—does not he increase the gratuitous natural forces placed at the disposal of the community ?

Why, then, if there is question of rewarding this class of services, should they not ask for privileges, favours, and exclusive rights ? Why not go so far as forbid any one to arrange his factory on the plan of the manufacturers of whom we have been speaking ? Why not forbid any farmer to weed, plough, or manure, like his neighbour ; or any sailor to follow the track of the first, without paying to those who gave the example a previous and perpetual royalty ?

IV.

" The property of an invention having required for its creation the same labour as that of the soil, and this work offering less chance of success and results of probable less duration, it is as legitimate at least as landed property," says M. le Hardy de Beaulieu ; "and there is no argument against it which may not be applied with equal force to the individual and permanent occupation of the soil."

The soil, to render all the productions that the community has a right to expect from it, ought to become and remain a personal individual property. Invention, on the other hand, cannot give all the results that society can draw from it, unless it be public property.

Herein lies the immense and irreconcilable difference between property in land and that of invention. Besides, land cannot become unfertile, unproductive, or lose all its value as property, except by some convulsion of nature which would deeply unsettle it. An invention, on the contrary, may become quite valueless in ten years, one year, a fortnight even, after being discovered, and that by the superiority of a subsequent invention.

What becomes, then, of the property of this invention ? What is its worth ? Has the inventor a right to damages ?

If you construct near my field a factory from which escape noxious vapours, hurtful to vegetation, and if I can show that you have deteriorated or destroyed my crops, you, according to the laws of every civilised nation, owe me damages ; would you claim damages of the inventor, whose discovery had rendered that of one of his predecessors partially or completely unproductive ? If property in invention is equal to property in the soil, damages are incontestably due. We do not think that a single advocate for this class of property has, however, dared to carry his logic thus far.

The proprietor of a field may leave it uncultivated, the proprietor of a house may leave it shut up as long as he likes ; no law obliges to put in a tenant, or to open it for lodgers. The laws of all countries contain, with slight modifications, the following clause, quoted from Art. 32 of the Law of 1844 :—" Will be deprived of all his rights . . . . . . the patentee who shall not have commenced the working of his discovery or invention in France within two years, dating from the day of the signature of the Patent, or who shall have ceased working it during two consecutive years, unless that, in one or other case, he can satisfactorily explain the causes of his inaction."

It would be very easy for us to cite other differences in the nature of these two classes of property ; we shall only refer to one more, which points out how solid is the property in land, and how uncertain and ephemeral the so-called property of invention. Land, considered as property, increases in value from day to day ; there is no invention whose value does not diminish daily.

M. le Hardy de Beaulieu further adds, that " the inventor, in taking exclusive possession of his idea, harms no one, since he leaves all which previously existed in the same condition in which he found it, without in any way lessening the social capital on which he drew." We should require, however, to come to an understanding as to what may be called the social capital; for if the exclusive property of invention had existed from the germination of the idea which led to the construction of the first hut to the making of the earliest weapons, tools, and furniture, it is difficult to know where we should find it. By putting property in invention on the same footing as property in the soil, all that man uses or consumes would belong to the descendants of the first inventors, and every one would require to pay a sort of rent for its use. The inventor of the wheelbarrow would have to pay a royalty to the inventor of wheels, and the maker of the plainest pump would pay an annual rent to the inventor of the lever or piston; there would not, there could not, be any social capital.

But it is wrong to say that the exclusive possession of an idea hurts no one, because it leaves what previously existed in the same condition. I, or my neighbour, might put together ideas to form the basis of an invention; this faculty of combination belongs to each of us; with exclusive possession it belongs only to one. It cannot be said, then, that no one is hurt, and that everything remains in the same position.

After having said that the property of invention is in every respect similar to property in the soil, M. le Hardy de Beaulieu places, nevertheless, boundaries to the extent and duration of the first. He says : "It is not meant precisely that property in an invention ought to extend over the globe, nor that its duration should have no limit in time ; all property, in fact, is bounded by the cost of preservation, maintenance, and working, which it requires, already, long before the limit of space or time when the produce of the property no longer covers the expense, the proprietor does not require to defend it against seizure, and from that time it becomes public property."

It follows that property of invention is not identical with property in land or other material objects. A diamond which belongs to me in any corner of the globe, the cotton stuffs which I have sent to Bombay or Saïgor, are still my property until I have voluntarily ceded them. My descendants, or those of some rightful owner, will cultivate in four or five hundred years or more the field which I may now possess. There is no limit of time nor of space for real property; it remains for ever.

V.

The whole history of humanity protests against this assertion of M. le Hardy de Beaulieu, that inventions " being realisable only on the condition of a just re- muneration, sufficient for the exceptional work which they require, and of a compensation in proportion to the risks they cause, property in them, which alone can assure this remuneration and this compensation, is necessary." Let us remark, first, that by a just and sufficient remuneration he probably means a special, exceptional, and exclusive one.

We will now ask it to be observed that man's most indispensable and useful tools were invented, and were

everywhere in daily use, many years or centuries before there was any question of property of invention.
We shall only cite the hammer, the file, the saw, the
screw, the pincers, the plough, spades, needles, &c.

Did any of the inventors of these tools take out a
Patent? Did he who first put a shoe on a horse claim
a property in the idea?

All the great inventions, with the exception of a few
of the most modern, and for which it was not possible
to take a Patent, date from the earliest times.   Who,
then, invented the art of smelting the ores of iron,
copper, lead, and tin? of making malleable iron and
steel? When did man first invent the manufacture
of glass, of pottery, porcelain, paper, ink, boats, and
carriages?

Railways existed in a rudimentary state in the coal
mines of Northumberland and Durham long before Patents were dreamed of. Printing and gunpowder appeared in the world without the guarantee of Patents;
so also with the tanning of hides, the spinning of thread,
weaving, dyeing, printing, &c. The electric telegraph
is the result of a series of studies, and of the social
capital of knowledge which these studies, and others
foreign to the object as it were, have formed. Patents
or rewards which have since been granted only concern
modifications, more or less ingenious, of the original
principle.

For what are inventors now doing? Without
seeking in any way to detract from the merit of their
labours, we may boldly assert that they modify in a
profitable and economical way the older processes;

instead of welding iron, they roll it; instead of the cold, they use the hot blast, in smelting.

To the tanning of hides they add currying, shamming, graining, polishing, &c. Are these services which cannot be sufficiently rewarded in the free working of the idea? Are they services which exceed by a hundred cubits those rendered by great manufacturers, large capitalists, intrepid seamen, or profound thinkers? And if, carrying out the argument of M. le Hardy de Beaulieu, we should say, credit being necessary to the progress of the community, and being realisable only on condition of a just and ample remuneration for the exceptional labour which it requires, and of a recompense proportionate with the risks incurred, the community ought to grant to the bankers exceptional rewards, or assure to them a special and perpetual privilege,—should we not be going on the premises of the learned Belgian Professor?

No doubt that branch of credit, the issue of notes, is at present allowed in many countries to the great privileged banks; but may not the same arguments apply to discount, the receiving of deposits, quite as well as to the issue of notes?

VI.

To admit, with M. le Hardy de Beaulieu, " that the rights of inventors are useful even to non-inventors," we must allow that the progress of invention would be stopped if the privileges guaranteed by Patents were withdrawn. Now, we have already said that all human history up to a very recent period demonstrates the

K

weakness of the assertion. Man has invented from
the time he began to think and compare, and he will
continue to invent while he exists on this planet.   Invention is nothing else than thought.

If, as M. le Hardy de Beaulieu says—but which we
doubt—there be no fear that property in invention
allows the inventor to exact for his services a higher
price than they are worth, neither need it be feared
that the absence of this right of property would hinder
the inventor from obtaining by his discovery all the
profit which he has a right to expect from it.   This
fear would only be justified in the event of his being
deprived by law of the right of using his own discovery. Now, this right remains intact ; only it is not
exclusive. If the inventor saves labour or outlay, the
inventor will profit by this saving, like his neighbours ;
he will profit by it before his neighbours ; he will
profit by it exclusively so long as he can keep his
secret, and while his opponents are establishing rival
works on the same principle.

M. le Hardy de Beaulieu tells us that the inventor
can never take advantage of his property to hold an
unjust and injurious monopoly.

We will quote one example of a thousand from M.
Louis Reybaud's excellent work on wool. Speaking
of the wool-carding machines, the learned Academician
thus writes : " There may be cited twenty names
engaged in these discoveries, incomplete as a whole,
almost all fortunate in some detail. What is incomplete is laid aside, what is fortunate is so much gain ;
the new comers discriminate and choose. After a

period of twenty years there are only three processes in use—those of Leister, Hellsmann, and Hubner ; of analogous merit, and each having its partisans. Will they strive one with another? No, they compromised. M. Holden gets the assignment, and also acquires, either by purchase or by judicial decisions, the rights of Donisthorpe, Noble, and Croft. Messrs. Schlumberger and Co., the assignees of Heilman, retain only the manufacture of certain machines. We may imagine the wealth of a business established on so many purchases and decisions. M. Holden has added inventions of his own, and *he may be considered the master of wool-carding until his Patents expire.* Nothing is more interesting than the answers he gave on this subject before the Commission on the Commercial Treaties. On his own avowal he is proprietor of 45 Patents, 28 taken by himself, and 17 purchased from others. In these 45 are good, middling, and bad. He works them all *in obedience to the law* and *to guard against lapses.* In the bad, as well as the good, there is an idea to defend and a chance of upsetting; he fears that in abandoning them they might be used against him; *for one machine in constant use there are forty-four which make a pretence of working; he does not hide it—it is his interest to hinder, as much as to work.*

What would it be if, as it is demanded, property in invention, put on the same footing with property in the land, were perpetual? By the present system it may be the interest of one man to fetter improvement, and, having acquired the mastery of it, to mortally

K 2

wound it wherever it appears! Is this not already too much the case?

Must we, then, repeat what reason and experience teach us, that unjust exactions cannot be made under a system of open competition, but always spring up under the shelter of privilege?

VII.

The eminent Professor of the "Musée de l'Industrie Belge" makes a just and well-founded criticism on the diverse laws of different countries relating to Patents. Usually law-makers do not appear so perplexed, nor contradict themselves so frankly; this is because, when we forget what is right, when we leave principles to make a legal caprice, we sail over unknown seas, where no lighthouse guides us, nor compass shows us the right direction.

He attributes to the defective state of these laws "the almost unanimous censure displayed either against the legislation or against property in inventions."

Would it not be more reasonable to acknowledge that if the learned law-makers of the numerous countries in which the principle of property in inventions has been adopted have not been able to frame laws capable of protecting the rights of pretended proprietors conjointly with those of individuals and society at large, it is because the principle is radically wrong, and contrary to the general interests of mankind? The law-giver finds an obstacle at every side in legitimate scruples; he fears to give too much, and he fears to take too much.

At present the censure is almost unanimous, it is acknowledged.   Let us suppose that property in invention were abolished, and what complaints would result from the abolition ? Few or none. When the inventor knew that, placed on the same level as all other workers, he must only rely on his intelligence, his capital, his time, and his right arm he would leave off claiming a privilege and complaining of the insufficiency of his rewards. At present the inventor says to the State : " I have found out a great thing, but I require your protection ; you must place at my disposal your agents and your law-courts ; the first shall enter the homes of my fellow-citizens, shall search their drawers, examine their books and papers, in my interest. By the second, their cause being lost, shall be condemned to ruin and misery.   I am about to bring ruin on such and such manufacturers, to condemn a crowd of work-people to idleness ; but you must grant me a privilege which will place me beyond the reach of all opposition, and allow me to make a fortune, quietly and without much chance of a failure."

What difference do the champions of Patents find between this language and that which was held by the Protectionists ?   They also required Custom-house officers, and law-courts always open, to punish the smuggler ; they further required the ruin of those who traded with distant countries, and the continual inactivity of our mercantile marine and sea-board population.

VIII.   •

The honourable Belgian economist next combats the

opinion of those who, struck by the numerous and weighty inconveniences presented by the Patent-Laws, and their extreme diversitude in every country, have imagined a remedy in the expropriation of invention for the public good.

We shall be far from attaining our object if the reader has not already understood that, renouncing all idea of property as applied to manufacture, we shall not discuss this phase of the question. We will say, however, that we must protest with all our might against the following principle, expressed by M. le Hardy de Beaulieu : "Neither can we admit," says he "the justice of expropriation for the public good so far as it concerns property in inventions any more than in real property. Here also," he adds, "the *right* of one ought to prevail over the *interest* of the greater number."

It is no doubt intentionally that the word *interest* in this phrase is put in opposition to the word "right." But would it not be more correct to say, the *right* of the community ought to prevail over the *interest* of the individual.

Individual right in property is certainly worthy of respect, and cannot be called in question ; but to our thinking, the right of the community precedes and is superior to it. A part cannot be greater than the whole ; no one can place his right above that of mankind, and the individual cannot oppose his will, good or bad, on the whole community.

We belong to no learned corporation—a simple volunteer in the army of economist disputants—and have no other banner than that of the truth ; but we cannot refrain from saying one word in defence of those whom the learned Belgian speaks of among many others in these terms : "The judgment of the Academy of Sciences on the steamboat invented by Fulton may help to form an estimate of the contradiction which experience sometimes inflicts on the best-intentioned verdict of a committee of *savants*."

We assert as a fact that if the steamboat presented to the Academy of Sciences by Fulton were now submitted to the judgment of a committee of machine builders, they would declare unanimously that the boat could not navigate. We wish in no way to seek to depreciate the acknowledgments which mankind owes to Fulton ; but his invention, as all are at starting, was only a sketch, which required half a century of labour to perfect and to make as practical as it now is.

Here there is room for an observation which must be noted.

The advocates for the principle of property in inventions fall into ecstacies before a transatlantic steamer, and exclaim, "Behold, what a crying injustice ! what deplorable ingratitude ! Society has denied the rights of the inventor to this wonder of the sea ! He died in poverty, or nearly so."

Others go further back, and attribute to Solomon de Caux, or to Papin, all the honour ; they forget that between Papin, or Solomon de Caux and Fulton, a crowd of men of genius brought their contributions of knowledge, experiment, and work of every kind ; and that between Fulton and the makers of our day there are so many inventors, so many explorers, fortunate or unfortunate, ridiculous or serious, whose attempts or applications have helped to perfect the steam-engine, that it may truly be said that every one has had a hand in it.

It is the same with the railway, the electric telegraph, and the different machines for spinning, carding, weaving, &c.

IX.

To pretend, as does the defender of the principle of property in inventions, in the ninth paragraph of his work, that the sudden and inconsiderate introduction of a new invention may cause a sensible injury to existing manufacturers, and that it is consequently advisable to maintain the system of Patents, which during a certain time limits their use and hinders production, to prevent the lowering of prices immediately at least; so to pretend is to renew the plea of the protected manufacturers, who demanded that the greatest precautions should be taken to facilitate the transition from Protection to Free-trade. But we do not see clearly what benefit there can be to the community at large in delaying the advantages to be derived from an invention. The misunderstood interests of certain manufacturers may appear to require this delay, but common sense tells us that manufacturers and consumers have every interest in immediately adopting every invention which saves labour, capital, and time.

If we look back, we will see that a delay of this kind would have retarded for an indefinite period the dis-

coveries of Columbus in order to avoid a sensible
injury to the monopoly which Venice had acquired in
Eastern commerce.   We maintain, as indeed experience
proves, that however innovating inventions may be,
displacement of labour occurs gradually.   We will only
cite, in support of this assertion, the well-known instance
of the substitution of printing for manuscript copying.
It may be answered that the substitution of mechanical
spinning and weaving for hand-work caused great
suffering.   We answer, that you should blame the system
of Patents, which, raising inordinately the cost of the
machines, must have restricted labour, although they
lowered the price of the product.   If there had been
no royalty to pay to the inventor, the number of the
machines would have rapidly increased, and a greater
number of workmen would at once have found employment similar to that to which they had been accustomed.

How many enterprising and intelligent speculators
would most eagerly have availed themselves of these
new outlets for their activity, if the course had been
cleared of all these obstructions which the law has
arbitrarily established.

At the risk of being considered by the honourable
Professor grossly ignorant of the laws of political
economy, we do not believe that monopolies will always
exist, as he ventures to affirm.   We know that there
always will be intellectual superiority, unrivalled artistic
ability, or special natural advantages ; but these do not
constitute monopolies, in the proper acceptation of the
term ; and the object we shall not cease to strive for is
that no others shall exist.

X.

It is beyond our province to consider the inquiries of M. le Hardy de Beaulieu as to the best plan of securing to inventors exclusive right in their discoveries. To take up this question is to undertake the discovery of the philosopher's stone, or the squaring of the circle ; several generations have vainly grappled with it, and the different attempts made without satisfactory results in almost every country prove this conclusively.

But the honourable Professor seems to calculate on the improvement of public morals, in order to reach the point where every attempt against the property of the inventor shall be considered as guilty as robbery, or as any injury done to property existing in material shape.

Under the uncompromising Protective system also it was attempted to improve the morals of the public, who would not see the equal guilt of the smuggler and the robber, and always loudly protested when repression was enforced by bloodshed.

    *   *   *   *   *

No reform of public morals will change the nature of these acts ; they will always be received as the appeal of right against abuse ; and we would deeply pity the country where it would be sufficient to say such is the law, and where no conscience might protest against it.

XI.

" Discovery, the appropriation and creation of outlets, is too complicated a work," says M. le Hardy de

Beaulieu, "for the inventor singly, and especially without the aid of capital, to undertake with sufficient chance of success."

Here again we believe the learned economist is in error; he seems to imagine one inventor arriving at perfection either at a jump, or after many attempts—one inventor giving us at once our ocean steamer, or a spinning-mill with a hundred thousand spindles! Inventions go more slowly; when they spring from the brain of the thinker, they are only sketches, and no man in his senses will risk a large capital before making many trials, and that only on a small scale. We do not believe there has been a single invention which, after numerous trials, has not been modified, improved, and perfected.

And how many have at last been thrown into oblivion, from which they will never be recalled?

Also, when we see the defenders of property in invention draw a sad picture of the piercing miseries which inventors of these last have had to endure, we are always tempted to ask them to show us the pitiful account of ruin caused among those who placed faith in their promises and delusions. Every medal has its reverse, and if more than one real inventor has been misunderstood, many of the too-confident have been victims of the mad and inapplicable ideas of inventors who imagined themselves men of genius.

Is the law, which seems to promise an Eldorado to all inventors, to blame for these losses, for these undeserved sufferings?

Bernard de Palissy's saying, "Poverty hinders the

success of the clever man," is often quoted. But this saying will always be true, whatever the law may be. Can we admit that if perpetual property of invention had existed in his time, Bernard would more easily have found the money which he required ?

The success of an invention is secured by the services it can render being easily understood, immediate, and speedily realisable. The capitalist, in dealing with hazardous undertakings—and inventors' undertakings "are always hazardous"—does not calculate on perpetuity. He works for immediate and large profits ; he is in a hurry to realise, because he knows that some other invention may dispossess him of all his advantages. Little does he care, therefore, about the perpetuity.

XII.

In his twelfth and last paragraph the learned Professor answers several minor objections to the system of property in inventions—objections which seem to us not to carry great weight.

However, in answer to the objection taken from the case of two applications for similar Patents, made at intervals of a few minutes only, the eminent economist says that this case occurs only at rare intervals, and making light of the rights of the slower, affirms that it is not worth considering. Does not this denial of a right on account of its infrequency, however, seem to show how arbitrary and artificial is the constituting of property in invention ?

We are among those who believe in the harmony of all economic relations, of all legitimate interests ; and when we see the right of one sacrificed to false exigencies, we mistrust the exigencies. We believe them unjust and contrary to the principles of equity, which forms the basis of all economic science. We should wish to have seen M. le Hardy de Beaulieu more logical in his deductions, claiming, as he has done, for real property [la propriété fonciere] that the right of one ought to prevail over the interest of the greater number, and give a chance of obtaining an indemnity, if he could not be assured of a part of the property [Donner ouverture a l'obtention d'une indemnité si l'on ne pouvait lui assurer une part de propriété].

But we repeat, these questions of the arrangement [organization] of property, which we do not acknowledge, are beyond our province, and if we accidentally touch upon them, it is only to show how little the foundations of this right are similar to those on which rests the principle of material property.

In recapitulation, we reject property in inventions and the advantages claimed for it, because it seems to us that all this scaffolding of legal prescription and Government protection only results in throwing out of their natural course a crowd of workmen who would become more useful to society and to themselves in ceasing to pursue chimeras.

We reject the proposed assimilation of this property to that of the soil, because the privilege sought to be created cannot fail to hinder and lessen the right of each member of the body politic. We reject this privilege because nothing justifies it; the services rendered to society by inventors being nowise different in their nature from those daily conferred by skilful manufacturers, intelligent agriculturists, *savants*, navigators, &c.

Finally, we reject it because history attests that great discoveries were made before there was any conception of such property, and that it could hardly be in operation at this day, except with regard to modifications, or, if you will, improvements [perfectionnements], which do not merit this abstraction from the common right.

ADDITIONAL CHAPTERS (FROM THE MAY NUMBER OF THE *Journal des Économistes*).

The question of granting or denying a property in inventions is of such importance that the discussion raised by the honourable Belgian Professor, M. le Hardy de Beaulieu, ought not to be allowed to drop, and that we should try to renew it.

We believe it to be of importance for the future of manufactures and of progress, and most especially to the security of real property, that whatever is doubtful and disputed in this question be deeply studied, and that all shculd be agreed as to what property is, and if this title ought to be applied to all or any of the inventions which daily start up.

M. le Hardy de Beaulieu pretends that one of the most frequent errors of those whose enlightenment ought most to guard them against it is to believe that property being inherent in matter, is, like it, imperishable, and that property in land especially is as durable as the land itself. He adds that we should beware of it, because this error lays open landed property without defence to the attacks of communists and socialists, who, sliding down the incline of irresistible logic, are fatally led to declare all property illegitimate, to whatever purpose it is applied.

Here, it seems to us, is a misunderstanding which may be easily explained.

We do not believe that property is inherent in matter, any more than we believe that value is confined to any given substance. We believe that property is the result, the consequence, of human labour which has been incorporated in matter. As long as value conferred on land by labour endures, so long the property has a *raison d'étre*, and cannot be contested. It is labour which has allowed the utilisation of the productive faculty of the soil, and productive faculty remains, like the property, as long as labour is bestowed in preserving, improving, and increasing it.

M. le Hardy de Beaulieu adds that he could cite numerous examples of lands abandoned or sold at a nominal price by their owners, either because they had exhausted and rendered them unproductive by an unintelligent culture, or because they had not been able to withstand the competition of more fertile soils, recently brought into cultivation or brought nearer the common centre of consumption by a considerable reduction in the expense of transport.

We do not contest this fact, of which the exactness may be verified any day in the increase or diminution of the value of property induced by the various changes brought about either in the grouping of the population, in the modes of culture, or in the means of transport. There are, however, few lands completely abandoned; to find examples, we should probably have to go back to those fatal times when by force of conquest proprietors were removed or all their means of culture and production were suddenly seized.

But we do not see how this can help the argument of M. le Hardy de Beaulieu. It has small relation, it seems to us, to the question of property in inventions, that—perpetual by law, as long as labour continues and renews it—landed property should sometimes come to an end by occurrences or violence such as we have been speaking of.

However, to state all our thoughts on the subject of landed property, we must confess (and here may be seen in all its clearness the radical difference between placing under culture, or cropping land, and working an idea), the vindication of property is found in the fact that land can only be cultivated by one at a time, must be subject to one will, and under one direction. It would be to my injury and the injury of the entire community that Peter should be allowed to plant potatoes in the field where Paul has already sowed wheat, or that James should open a quarry where John has built a house, and so on.

As we have already said, the power of the lever, the laws of gravity, those of the expansion of steam, the attraction of the magnet, the caloric of coal, the facility of traction imparted by the wheel, the optical properties of glass, &c., may be utilised to the great profit of all, in a thousand different ways, by a thousand individuals at once, without the efforts of any one being diminished, hindered, obstructed, or lessened, as to their useful result, except by the beneficent laws of competition.

" The first cause of property," says M. Matthieu Walkoff,* " is the impossibility of matter being moved in more than one direction at one time, or, to state it otherwise, of its being subject at one time to more than one will." " If matter," says this eminent economist, " were gifted with ubiquity, like ideas, knowledge, or truth, which several may use simultaneously, and each in his own way, property would never have been constituted; and it is even difficult to imagine how any idea on this phenomenon could have arisen in men's minds." " In fact," he adds, " to preserve property in an idea would have required that it should never have been expressed nor practised, to hinder it, being divulged, which would have been equivalent to its non-existence."

We do not go so far as M. Walkoff; we do not affirm that the impossibility of matter being subject at one time to more than one will is the *first cause* of property ; but we say it is the distinctive character of property, and, like him, we cannot see a subject, for property is a shape, plan, or system, which, to see once, as in a spade, the wheel, the corkscrew, is to possess an indelible idea.

Besides, the author whom we have quoted expresses so clearly our opinion on this subject, that we must further borrow from him the following quotation,

---

* Precis d'Economic Politique Rationale, page 44 ; Paris, 1868.

which will not be uncalled for at a time when property itself is threatened. It is of importance that the lawful bounds should be carefully marked :—

" Economists have too much neglected the first cause of the perpetual subjection of matter to exclusive property. They made property to be derived only from a man's original possession ; from himself and his acts ; that which leads to possession of the result of his activity. But this reasoning only establishes the indisputable right of the appropriation of that which he appropriates or produces ; it does not explain why exclusive property in material things is permanent, and does not show how the very nature of things renders this possession inevitable. It is to the incomplete understanding of the causes of property that is probably attributable the contradictions of those economists who, while professing the doctrine of free labour, are still in favour of the establishment of artificial barriers against the free use by every one of ideas, skill, progress, and other products of the mind, conceived and suggested, or realised, by any one."

Let us remark here that in fact the manufacturing community, more liberal in practice than the economists in theory, are eager freely to submit to inspection at exhibitions the processes in use at their different factories.

" To require that an idea be subject to only one will," continues M. Walkoff, " is to require no less an impossibility than to pretend that a material point can obey more than one will—that is to say, that it can be moved in more than one direction at once. It is true that it is not proposed to hinder ideas from being developed ; it is desired simply to convert their reproduction or their material realisation into an indefinitely prolonged monopoly.   But, in order completely to succeed in anything, it is necessary that the object aimed at be in conformity with the nature of things. Now, is it not placing oneself in opposition to everything which is most natural, this denying to every one the use of an idea ?   And even where this interdict is most successful, we soon find, in a manner most unassailable by the law, works copied from those to which the law has guaranteed a monopoly.   The effect of the interdict is here, as in all regulations contrary to the nature of things, essentially demoralising ; it begets fraud, entices to it, even forces to it, in making it useful and often even indispensable.   Forbid men, as was once supposed by the witty author of the ' Sophismes Economiques,' the use of the right hand, after a few hours, there would not remain, in the eye of the law, a single honest man.   It may be boldly affirmed that such a law would be immoral, and all those which recklessly contradict the natural order of things are incontestably such."

In fact, we repeat, the field which I turned into a garden may not be used by my neighbour as a pastureland for his cattle ; where I have planted a vine another may not plant colza or beet-root ; but the steam-engine which I have invented, or the electric power which I have discovered, may be applied to the grinding of corn, or the spinning of cotton, or to the extraction of iron, or to the draining of a marsh, or to traction by land or sea, without the productive force being neutralised, wasted, or lost, like the application of the productive force of the soil to different purposes.

Not only do the various applications of the idea not hinder the inventor in the employment which he may make of it, but if the application made by others is exactly the same as his, he is only subjected to the universal law of competition—a law of progress, if ever there was one.

II.

The Hon. M. le Hardy de Beaulieu asks, "Why the effort which consists in rendering productive some natural agent in which this quality was not formerly recognised, should not entitle to a recompense of property in the value given to the natural agent in rendering it productive, in the same way that labour bestowed on barren land to render it productive, to the profit of all, makes him proprietor of that portion of land who performed this labour ?"

Here is our answer : He who renders productive some natural agent has an incontestable property in that agent which he has rendered productive, but not in all similar or identical agents in nature ; he who converts a certain quantity of water into steam, to obtain a motive force, is incontestably proprietor of the water he employs and of the steam, as well as of the force which he obtains, but the remainder of the water, and of the steam which may be produced from it, and the force which may be derived from it, remain the common property of mankind ; that is to say, each should have it in his power to employ an unlimited quantity of water to obtain the same results. The man who first broke up and sowed a field never could have claimed as property all the ground in the world ; he only retained for himself, and that reasonably and justly, the portion which he had reclaimed and rendered fertile by his labour.

We may add that he who renders productive some natural agent avails himself in this work of all the acquired knowledge and all the work previously done, and he would unduly monopolise it if the community recognised his exclusive right to it.

It is said that Pascal invented the wheelbarrow ; did he not borrow from the social capital both the wheel and the axle, and the two arms, not to speak of the species of box which forms with the other parts the whole wheelbarrow ?

Our learned opponent maintains " the perfect identity between the labour of discovery, and of the putting the soil in culture, and of this same labour applied to other natural agents which did not exist in indefinite quantity ; and he makes the deduction, having the same result, that inventors placing at the disposal of mankind new quantities of gratuitous utility, not hitherto available, deserve the same reward—property in the natural agent, or portion of this agent, whose gratuitous services have been acquired by mankind."

We must allow that we do not know of any natural agent of which the quantity is not indefinite, excepting only the earth ; but steam, wind, light, electricity, magnetism, the force of attraction, that of weight, the

affinity of particles, their divisibility, their different
properties, may be employed in whatsoever quantities,
and still there would be no perceptible diminution or
restraint in the use of them to any one. The only
possible restraint is that which comes from the unre-
flecting action of the law, from artificial hindrances
and obstacles which may be made law.

We believe, with Bastiat, that the greatest service
that could be conferred on mankind would be to
remove the obstacles which stand between his efforts
and the supply of his wants.

How does M. le Hardy de Beaulieu not see that no
one has the right to make burdensome that which is
naturally gratuitous, and that it is just to exact that no
one should appropriate any part of what constitutes
common property ?

That learned Professor of the Brussels Museum
tells us the inventor has a right to say to the manufacturer, " Find out my process for yourself if you
can, search for it as I have done ; but if you wish to
spare yourself this labour, and avoid the risk of
spending it in vain, consent to yield me a part of the
expenses which I save you in simplifying your appliances." And he asks us if we find this demand unjust
or unreasonable.

Not only do we find this demand just and reasonable, but we maintain that it is the only one we can
recognise. But M. le Hardy de Beaulieu forgets
that, according to the Patent-Laws, things are not
thus arranged. The inventor, with the law in his
hand, and the law courts to support him, says to the

manufacturer, " It is forbidden to you to search and
to find ; or if you search and find, you are forbidden
to use the power or the agent when you have found
it : the process which I have invented is my property,
and no one has the right to use it, even if his researches, his labour, enable him to discover it ; even
if he had commenced the search before me, all his
labour is lost. I alone am proprietor of this agent,
power, or process." If this system be right, he who
first rendered productive the most indispensable
natural agent could have confiscated the whole world
to his profit.

III.

M. le Hardy de Beaulieu acknowledges that the
savage who first thought of substituting a hut, as a
habitation, for the cave, has not the right to forbid
the construction of others like it.

This concession is as important as the preceding,
and we shall probably end in agreeing. We must
now inquire where may be found the exact limit
between inventions of which imitation is allowed, and
those in which it is forbidden.

The man who first made a canoe from the trunk of a
tree, either naturally hollow or artificially by fire, or
otherwise,—may he forbid his neighbours to make one
like it ?

If he may, where, then, is the difference between
the hut and the boat ? If not, what is the reason
for this prevention?

From the boat we might gradually go on, up to the
latest Patent, by invisible transitions ; and we have

still to find the exact point at which M. le Hardy de Beaulieu might say, There is the limit!

We do not know whether, in the absence of all positive right which would guarantee a recompense to the inventor of the hut, a natural sentiment of justice would prompt the savages living in that country to make him a present of some useful object as a reward for this service, as M. le Hardy de Beaulieu suggests. We doubt it much; gratitude is an analytic virtue. The savages would probably have a certain respect for this man, whom they would look upon as gifted with superior qualities and faculties, but the presents would only arrive when, the contemporary generations being extinct, cheats and hypocrites would found on the inventions of this man some system of religion.

Yes, we acknowledge the truth and justice of the principle in virtue of which it is said, "Reward for merit." But it must not be abused. Let a cultivator make a thousand trials, a thousand experiments, to give to the potatoes all the elementary qualities, all the nutritive virtue of wheat, and arrive at the object of his researches—to what recompense will he be entitled? According to the system of M. le Hardy de Beaulieu, no reward could equal the service which this individual would have rendered to mankind.

According to the system of non-property in inventions, this man would only have made his trials and his experiments—he would only have risked his advances of money, of time, and of labour—with the view of being able to sell his potatoes at a higher price than before, and, in fact, they would command a higher price, by means of which he would find himself sufficiently rewarded. This man asks nothing of society; he requires neither Patent, nor guarantee, nor monopoly, nor privilege ; because the law has wisely placed beyond the reach of Patents all improvements in agriculture.* Does this imply that agriculture no longer progresses, that the breeder of cattle does not improve, that they remain completely *in statu quo*? It is not from M. le Hardy de Beaulieu that we learn that the want of Patents does not hinder for an hour the progressive advance of agriculture ; quite the contrary.

Establish the same system for all that concerns manufactures, and inventions will follow one another as rapidly as they now do. They will be more serious, for those who are engaged in them will no longer be excited by the allurements which the Patent-Laws dangle before their eyes, and will no longer lose their time in running after useless things and mere chimeras.

We do not wish to prolong too far this answer, but we cannot pass in silence the arguments which M. le Hardy de Beaulieu thinks he has found in the facts relating to the inventor of the mariner's compass, and to the discoveries of Lieutenant Maury. We will simply remind him of the following passage from Bastiat : "He who can gain assistance from a natural and gratuitous force confers his services more easily ;

---

* Unfortunately, this is not true of British law. The illustration founded on it is (like the rest of these papers) admirable.—R. A. M.

but for all that, he does not voluntarily renounce any portion of his usual remuneration. In order to move him, there is required external coercion—severe without being unjust. This coercion is put in force by competition. So long as it has not interfered—so long as he who has utilised a natural agent is master of his secret—his natural agent is gratuitous, no doubt; but it is not yet *common*; the victory is gained, but it is for the profit of a single man, or a single class. It is not yet a benefit to all mankind. Nothing is yet changed for the multitude, unless it be that a kind of *service*, though partly rid of the burden of labour, exacts nevertheless full pay [*la rétribution integrale*]. There is, on one hand, a man who exacts of all his equals the same labour as formerly, although he offers in exchange only his reduced labour; there is, on the other hand, all mankind, which is still obliged to make the same sacrifice of time and labour to obtain a product which henceforth nature partly realises. If this state of things should continue with every invention, a principle of indefinite inequality would be introduced into the world. Not only we should not be able to say, value is in proportion to labour; but we should no more be able to say, value has a tendency to be in proportion to labour. All that we have said of *gratuitous use*, of *progressive community*, would be chimerical. It would not be true that labour [*les services*] is given in exchange for labour [*des services*] in such a manner that the gifts of God pass from hand to hand, *par-dessus le marché*, on the man intended [*destinataire*], who is the consumer. Each one would always exact payment for not only his labour, but also for that portion of the natural forces which he had once succeeded in applying. In a word, humanity would be constituted on the principle of a universal monopoly, in place of the principle of progressive community."— *Harmonies Economiques*, Vol. vi., p. 354.

We think, with Bastiat, that the use of natural agents ought to be gratuitous, and that no one has the right to artificially monopolise in such a way as to exact royalties [*prelever des redevances*], which are not due, and which often are obstacles almost as insurmountable as those which invention ought naturally to remove.

T. N. BENARD.

SPEECH OF MICHEL CHEVALIER,

AT THE MEETING OF THE "SOCIETE D'ECONOMIE POLITIQUE," ON THE 5th JUNE, 1869.

(From the June Number of the *Journal des Economistes*.)

M. Michel Chevalier, Senator, proposed to consider Patents in their relation to freedom of labour [*la liberté du travail*], a corner-stone of modern political economy, and to the principle of the law of property, which is greatly respected by economists and which serves them as guide.

Does the principle of freedom of labour accommodate itself to that of Patents? It may be doubted. All Patents constitute a monopoly; now, it is indisputable that monopoly is the very negation of freedom of labour.

In the case of Patents, it is true, monopoly has a limited duration; but in France this duration generally extends, if the Patent is worth it, to fifteen years; which makes a long time in our day when the advances of manufacturers are so rapid and so quickly succeed one another. A hindrance or an obstacle which lasts fifteen years may greatly damage and seriously compromise important interests.

It would be easy to exhibit by examples the extent and the importance of these disadvantages.

In France the manufacturer to whom a new apparatus or a new machine is offered is always in uncertainty whether the invention proposed is not already the subject of some Patent, the property of a third party, in which case he would be exposed to the annoyance of a law-suit at the instance of this third party. It follows that he frequently hesitates about adopting a machine, apparatus, or method of work, which would be an advantage not only to the manufacturer, but to the community at large, whom he might supply better and cheaper. Another case which occurs to us is that of a manufacturer in whose factory an improvement has suggested itself. He is forced to take out a Patent, and consequently to observe formalities and undertake expenses with which he would rather dispense ; he is obliged, and becomes a patentee, whether he will or no ; because, if he did not, it might happen that the improvement might come under the observation of one of the numerous class of Patent-hunters. This man might take out a Patent, which is never refused to the first comer ; and once patented, he might annoy and exact damages from the manufacturer with whom the invention, real or pretended, actually had its birth.

In France the annoyances which Patents may occasion are very serious. It is well known that, by the French law, the patentee may seize not only the factory of the maker, but also, wherever he may find it, the machine or apparatus which he asserts to be a piracy of that for which he has taken a Patent. He may take it away or put it under seal, which is equivalent to forbidding the use of it. M. Michel Chevalier thinks that this is a flagrant attack on the principle of the freedom of labour.

It can also be shown how, in another way, labour may be deprived of its natural exercise by the monopoly with which patentees are invested. When an individual has taken out a Patent for an invention, or what he represents to be such, no one is allowed to produce the object patented, or use it in his manufacture, without paying to the patentee a royalty, of which he is allowed to be the assessor, and which sometimes assumes large proportions. The result is, that the produce manufactured can only be offered in foreign markets at a price so augmented that the foreigner refuses it if some other producer, residing in a country where the Patent is not acknowledged, establishes competition. Thus, for instance, France, which worships Patent-right, cannot export the "Bessemer" steel to Prussia, because there this product is not patented ; whereas in France, on the contrary, it is subject to a heavy royalty, on account of the Patent.

The same thing may be said of velvets, which have been very much in fashion, and for which a French manufacturer took out a Patent. The effect of this Patent was, that French manufacturers of this stuff were shut out from the foreign markets, because outside France they had to encounter the competition of Prussia, whose manufacturers were not subject to any royalty, the Patent not being acknowledged there.

In our day, when export trade excites so great an interest among all manufacturing nations, and has so much influence on the prosperity of internal commerce, M. Michel Chevalier believes that the observation he is about to make ought to be taken into serious conside-

ration. At least it follows, according to him, that
before approving and continuing the present system of
Patents, it would be necessary that they should be
subjected to uniform legislation in every country.
Now there are manufacturing nations—Switzerland,
for instance—which absolutely refuse ; there are others
where Patents are subjected to so many restrictions
that it is as if they did not exist ; such is Prussia.

From the point of view of the right of property, it
is contended that Patent-right should be respected,
since it only assures property in invention in the
interest of him to whom the community is debtor.
M. Michel Chevalier sees in this argument only a
semblance of the truth.   We must first inquire whether
an idea may really constitute an individual property—
that is, exclusive personal property.   This pretension
is more than broached.   A field or a house, a coat,
a loaf, a bank-note, or credit opened at a banker's,
readily comply with individual appropriation, and can
hardly even be otherwise conceived of ; they must
belong to an individual or to a certain fixed number of
persons ; but an idea may belong to any number of
persons—it is even of the essence of an idea that once
enunciated, it belongs to every one.

Besides, is it certain that the greater part of
patentees have had an idea of their own, and that they
have discovered anything which deserves this name ?
Of the great majority of patentees this may be doubted,
for various reasons.

The law does not impose on the individual who
applies for a Patent the obligation of proving that he

is really the inventor. Whoever has taken out a Patent may very easily turn it against the real inventor; this has occurred more than once.

Besides, the law lays it down as a principle that it is not an idea that is patented, and constitutes the invention valid; and thus it excludes from the benefit of patenting the *savants* who make the discoveries, of which Patents are only the application.

It is by the advancement of human knowledge that manufactures are perfected, and the advancement of human knowledge is due to *savants*. These are the men prolific in ideas; it is they who ought to be rewarded, if it were possible, and not the patentees, who are most frequently only their plagiarists.

M. Michel Chevalier does not desire systematically to depreciate patentees. Among them there are certainly many honourable men. The inventions, real or pretended, which they have patented are supposed to be new and ingenious uses or arrangements [dispositions], by help of which we put in practice some one or more specialities of manufacture; true discoveries are always due to the *savants*. But in general these arrangements, represented as new, have no novelty.

In the detailed treatises on Mechanics, Physics, and Chemistry, in books of technology, with their accompanying illustrations, such as are now published, we find an indefinite quantity of combinations of elementary apparatus, especially of mechanical arrangements, and very often the work of professional patentees consists in searching through these so numerous collections for uses and arrangements, which they combine and group. What right of property is there in all this, at least in the greater number of cases ?

Against the pretended right of property alleged by the defenders of Patents there will be much more to say. There exists in the greater number of cases much uncertainty about the inventors, even when true and important discoveries are in question. Is it known with certainty who invented the steam-engine, who invented the aniline dyes, or photography, even ? Different nations are at variance on these points, as formerly they were on the birthplace of Homer. The fact is, that the majority of inventions are due to the combined working [*collaboration*] of many men separated by space, separated by great intervals of time.

On this subject M. Michel Chevalier repeats what he heard from an eminent man who was Minister of Finance at the time when Daguerre received the national recompense which had been awarded him with the acclamations of all France. One of the Government clerks brought to this eminent personage proof that he too had made the same invention ; and also there were the labours of M. Niepce de Saint Victor, analogous to those of M. Daguerre.

[M. Passy, the chairman of the meeting, confirmed the statement of M. Michel Chevalier on this fact.]

M. Michel Chevalier, in continuation, remarked that in our time industrial arts are subject to great changes in the details of their operations.

Independently of the general alterations which from time to time completely change the face of any given

M

manufacture, there is no important workshop where some useful notion is not occasionally suggested by some mechanic or overseer, which leads to minor improvements [*un perfectionnement de detail*]. It would be an abuse to grant, during a term of fifteen years, or even a much shorter, exclusive use of any particular improvements to any single individual. It would not be just, for it is quite possible that the idea might have occurred to another at the same time, or that it might occur the next day. It would even be against the general interest, for it would fetter competition, which is the chief motor in the progress of the useful arts.

But it is said inventors are useful to society ; we must therefore recompense them. To this M. Michel Chevalier answers that it may be too liberal to confer the flattering title of inventor on men who, when a veritable discovery has been made by *savants*, push themselves forward to appropriate the profits, in securing by Patents the various special applications which may be made of it. Besides, there are different sorts of recompenses ; there are other than material rewards, and these are not the least coveted. The *savants* who are the greatest discoverers are satisfied with these immaterial rewards—honour, glory, and reputation. The example is worthy of recommendation ; not but it is quite allowable for a man to extract from his labour [*travaux*] whatever material recompense he can. But, in many cases at least, the Patent is not necessary for this purpose. The authors of some useful discovery would often have the resource of keeping their secret and working the invention themselves. That would last for a time. Even under the system of Patents several inventors have thus sought and found an adequate remuneration.

Thus the famous Prussian steel manufacturer, M. Krupp, has taken out no Patent, and yet has made a colossal fortune ; also M. Guimet, of Lyons, inventor of French blue. Their secret remained in their own hands for more than fifteen years, the maximum duration that their Patent would have had in France.

Lastly, in the case of some truly great discovery it would be natural to award a national recompense to the inventor. If James Watt, for instance, had received from the British Parliament a handsome sum, every one would have applauded it. These rewards would not impoverish the Treasury, since similar cases are of rare occurrence.

In recapitulation, Patent-right may have been allowable in the past, when science and manufactures had not yet formed so close and intimate a union. It was advisable to attract towards manufactures, by means of exceptional inducements, the attention of those who made a study of the sciences. But now that the union is consummated, Patent-right has ceased to be a useful auxiliary to industry. It is become, instead, a cause of embarrassment and an obstruction to progress. The time is come to renounce it.

Another speaker at the meeting, M. PAUL COQ, thought that, on a question so delicate and controverted history furnishes instruction which directs to a right solution. Notably Franklin, a genius eminently practical, declared himself unwilling to avail himself, as to his numerous discoveries, of any Patent. The refusal of this great man is founded upon the principle that every one receives during his whole life ideas and discoveries from the common fund of knowledge by which all profit, and therefore ought, by reciprocation, to let the public freely benefit by every invention of his. This, with Franklin, was not a mere sentimental truth, but a practical conviction, based upon reasons worthy of the author of "Poor Richard." There is in the bosom of society a constant exchange of beneficial thoughts and services. Every one stimulated by the efforts of others ought, in the spirit of equity, to make the community participants of the improvements and useful applications for which he has in a manner received payment in advance. On this system, equality, competition, and freedom of industry find their account in the law of reciprocity; whereas, on the footing of privilege established and defined by the theory of Patents, there is created an artificial property, along side of that rightful property which has in it nothing arbitrary or conventional, and depends simply for its existence on civil law. These circles, thereby traced round the inventor and his discovery, are so many hindrances and so many obstacles to the expansion of forces, in the way of continuous progress. Under pretext of maintaining individual rights, improvement is in reality paralysed by superimposed difficulties, and especially litigation without end, on account of which nobody dare touch, either

far or near, what has been appropriated. The numerous actions at law, raised with a view to ascertain
whether such and such a process constitutes a per-
fectionation, a new application, or merely an imitation,
are my proof. There is another proof in the distinction attempted to be made between matters patentable
and methods scientific which may not be patented.
All this, as it affects progress, the free expansion of
forces, is infinitely grave. Franklin has found for his
precepts, already alluded to, more than one adept
pupil. One modest *savant*, whose name deserves to
be better known among us for his numerous services
rendered to science as well as to the arts—Conté—
honoured to replace in France the pencils of England,
the importation of which was not possible in time of
war—not only supplied by his new process the want
of plumbago with success, but made it better than the
English. To him are due, besides black-lead pencils,
which make his name celebrated, the crayons of
various colours, which have been so serviceable in the
arts of design. Well, like Franklin, he presented his
process to industry, and contented himself with being
first in the new manufacture. It must be remarked
that he who thus opens the way easily maintains the
first rank which the date of his invention assigns him,
and which public confidence assures him. . . .

Before concluding, M. Paul Coq adverted to the
distinction between the right of property generated by
a creation of a work of art or of literature, and factitious property decreed in the interests of industry.
The skilful painter, who should copy faithfully line for

line, tint for tint, a *chef d'œuvre* like the picture of
Ingres, which every one knows, "The Source," in
order to expose it for sale and pocket the advantages,
not merely lays hold of the property of a great artist
who lives by the fruit of his talent, but perpetrates,
in all points of view, an action mean and vile. To
inventions in the domain of the useful arts, processes
and operations do not carry the stamp of personality,
which is the glory of the artist and author, and which
of itself constitutes a protection equal to that which
protects right of property.

The invention is something *impersonal*, like a service
rendered and returned, which is not exchanged or
paid by services of equivalent weight and description.
There is, therefore, no plausible objection to maintaining unimpaired the common right, which, by its
freedom of movements, its equality, and its recipro-
cations, alone efficaciously favours the result of which
these are the indispensable corollaries.

EXPERIENCE IN FRANCE.

The following observations were published in the AVENIR COMMERCIAL, *November* 1, 1862, *and June* 28, 1863, *have been kindly translated and presented by the Author :—*

THE RESULTS OF A BAD LAW.

I.

WHEN you walk along a public road, if you find a watch, a diamond, a note of a hundred or a thousand francs, and, far from seeking the owner to give it back, you apply it to your own use, moral law and civil law take hold of you and condemn you without hesitation. It matters not whether he who lost what you found be rich or poor, his carelessness, his negligence, or the accident that caused his loss, give you no sort of right to use it and make it yours.

There are not two opinions on that point : the laws of all countries condemn the man who enriches himself with what chance throws in his way.

But if a scientific man—seeking some impossible discovery, finds a clue to an idea—meets with an interesting phenomenon—indicates, in some way, new properties belonging to some bodies—announces the results of some new chemical combination – it is only a scientific research. This or that other skimmer of inventions can get a Patent for the application of the idea, of the discovery, of the method ; and the law guarantees his pretended right not only against all reclamations of the scientific man who has discovered the whole, but against the whole world, deprived of all possibility of making use of the discoveries of science !

And not only the law forbids every one to use this or that produce, except if made by the patentee, but it also prohibits the use of any similar produce made by different means.

Then, to prevent all inventors to approach the ground that the patentee has chosen, he takes immense care to have his Patent made of formulas so wide and elastic, that all inventions in the same course of ideas will be infringements in the eye of the law.

To these observations it is answered that industrialists or scientific men are equal before the law, that all have an equal right to its protection, but on the express condition that the invention be put in use.

We see very well where is the privilege of the chance patentee, who has made the discovery of the scientific man his own, but we do not see where is its justice or equality.

We see very well where is the privilege of the man who has had nothing to do but to apply the idea deposited in a book by a scientific man—an idea that, in fact, was at the disposal of the public, since the discoverer did not claim its proprietorship ; but we do not see why the law gives a monopoly to him who has only borrowed that idea.

But we are told, the law is quite equitable, for it says, "To every man his due. The scientific man discovers a body, glory be to him. If he will add to it some profit, let him indicate the properties that may be used industrially, and let him take a Patent for his discovery. But he must hurry, because if industry forestalls him, industry will get the profit."* It is exactly as if this was the law : A millionaire drops a 100-franc note. It will not make him much poorer. If he wants to get it back, let him return where he came from and seek along the road. Let him hurry, for if this note is found, he who will have got it may keep it.

Common sense and equity would join to say that when a scientific man indicates a discovery or an invention, that invention or discovery remains at the disposal of every one if the finder does not claim the exclusive right to work it. But the law is different, and the results are soon made apparent.

In 1856 an English chemist, of the name of Perkins, was seeking the way to make artificial quinine. In the course of his experiments he discovered in the laboratory of M. Hofmann the property residing in aniline of producing a violet colour by the action of bi-chromate of potass.

Perkins got a Patent for this discovery. The attention of the scientific and industrial classes being called to this property of aniline, and to the possibility of extracting from it divers colouring matters, several French and other chemists and manufacturers got Patents for many more new processes.

In 1858, Hofmann, continuing to study aniline, discovered the red colour. He sent a memoir to our Académie des Sciences, in which he gave the exact method to produce this magnificent crimson red.

---

* Extract of a paper on the subject in the *Propriété Industrielle*.

Hofmann took no Patent ; it seemed as if he wanted to present gratuitously to tinctorial industry a new and beautiful produce.

Six months after, a manufacturer, who as early as 1857 had tried to get patented in France the patented discovery of Perkins, sold to a manufacturer of chemical produce a process copied from the discovery of Hofmann, by which the red of aniline could be manufactured by the reaction of the bi-chloride of tin. The Patent was granted, and the produce manufactured. But very soon after, in France and abroad, more advantageous and more scientific methods, preferable to the patented one, were found.

All the French manufacturers who tried to use any of these new processes were prosecuted and condemned for infringement on the right of the patentee. It then followed that one kilogramme of red of aniline was sold abroad for £12, and the monopolisers sold it for £40 in France.

This could not last, particularly after the treaty of commerce, by which printed and dyed goods could be introduced. Manufacturers threatened to give up work, and the patentee thought proper to reduce his prices.

But another result, no less fatal to French interests, soon followed.

The most intelligent manufacturers of colouring-stuffs, those who were at the head of that branch of industry, and had concentrated in Paris, Lyons, and Mulhouse the fabrication of the finest and most delicate dyes for the home and foreign market, went to establish new factories across the frontiers.

The existing Patent prevented them from satisfying the demands of their customers abroad, who required some aniline colours, and they were obliged to carry their industry to foreign parts.

The following is the list of the manufacturers who have founded new establishments beyond the reach of the monopolising Patent :—

A. Schlumberger, of Mulhouse, new factory at Bâle (Switzerland) ; Jean Feer, of Strasburg, new factory at Bâle ; Peterson and Seikler, of Saint Denis, new factory at Bâle ; Poirrier and Chappal, of Paris, new factory at Zurich ; Monnet and Dury, of Lyons, new factory at Geneve.

Five other establishments, raised by Swiss people but under the direction of Frenchmen, are being founded at Bâle, Zurich, Glaris, and Saint Gall. Then there are still to be founded, the factory of M. A. Wurtz, brother to Professor Wurtz at Leipsic ; another, by M. O. Meister at Chemnitz ; a French factory at Elberfeld ; three, also French, in Belgium ; and three others in Switzerland.

It is, in fact, a general expatriation, like the one that followed the revocation of the Edict of Nantes. It is worthy of remark that in Germany there are twelve Patents for making colours or dyes from aniline ; in England there are fourteen, in France (thanks to the interpretation given to the law) there is *one*. " *Et nunc caveant consules.*"

T. N. BENARD.

II.

In our number of November 1, 1862, we published on this very same question an article in which we stated that about twenty French manufacturers had been forced to go abroad to escape the unheard-of exigencies of the law of Patents. We were answered by insults that we disdained ; but the facts that we had revealed were not contested.

A volume just published on the legislation and the jurisprudence of the law of Patents enables us to show another side of the question, and to prove how injurious it is to manufacturers and inventors, and how profitable to certain gentlemen of the Bar who have the speciality of cases for infringement on Patents. We say it openly and fearlessly, if it was not for the lawyers who swim freely amongst the windings of that law, it would not have a supporter. Manufacturers and inventors are shamelessly made a prey to a group of pleaders who defend right and wrong with the same deplorable alacrity.

What an immense number of law-suits have arisen from the 54 articles of that law ! The volume we have in hand has been written with the intention of giving to the public a view of the jurisprudence adopted by the Courts in the interpretation of each paragraph. A summary of the trials that have taken place since its promulgation in 1844 follows each article of the law.

Article I. is as follows : " Every new discovery or invention, in all kinds of industry, ensures to its author, under the conditions and for the time hereafter determined, the exclusive right to work for his benefit the said discovery or invention. This right is established by documents granted by the Government, and called Patents."

The first trial that we find in the list took place in 1844. The question was, Whether the words *all kinds of industry* could be applied to things that are not in trade? The Court's decision was for the affirmative.

The second trial was raised to know if, when a working man is only executing the orders given to him by another party, with the indications and in the interest of this last, the working man may be reputed the inventor, and if the results of his labour may have the character of an invention, so that he may claim [revendicate] its ownership by a Patent. The Court decided for the negative.

We pass four other suits running on the interpretation of this first article, that seems so innocent, so inoffensive, and come to the eleventh trial. In conferring by Article I., under the conditions that it determines, on the author of new discoveries or inventions the right of working them exclusively for his own benefit, did the law intend to deprive of all rights those who were using the same means of fabrication prior to the delivery of the Patents? The question was, in other terms, to know whether the Patent is good and legal against every one except against the party who, having worked it for a certain period anterior to the granting of the Patent, might be kept in possession of his industry? On March 30, 1849, the Court of Cassation decided for the affirmative in the case of "Witz Meunier *versus* Godefroy Muller." You fancy, perhaps, that the affair is all right and settled; the Court of Cassation has spoken, and every inventor who will not have taken a Patent may work out his invention without fear of prosecution from a patentee coming long after. You are greatly mistaken. You do not know how keen, and ardent, and clever, and anxious are the seekers of Patents. Previously to that the Court Royal of Paris had declared in May, 1847, in the case of "Lejeune *versus* Parvilley," that the Patent can be put in force against the manufacturer working the invention before it was patented, if he has not published it before the patentee, and if the patentee is the first who has introduced it in commerce. But in 1847 the Court Royal of Paris did not know the opinion given in 1849 by the Court of Cassation. We see how unsafe are the things of this world. Say if you can ever be sure of holding and knowing the truth.

On August 19, 1853, the same question was brought again before the Court of Cassation in the case of "Thomas Laurent *versus* Riant," and the Court decided that the Patent can be put in force against whoever possessed the invention before it was patented. There is at Lyons a manufacturer who for a great many years fabricated a dye for which he has not taken a Patent, but the secret of which he carefully keeps to himself. If, by some manœuvring, by some doubtfully moral means, an industrialist—as there are too many amongst the patentees—contrived to worm out this secret, and got a legal Patent, he could work the discovery and oblige the Lyonese manufacturer to cease all productions of the same kind. Would it not be an admirable example of legality ?

The contradiction that we have just noted between two verdicts given by the same Court upon the same question gives us the right to say that the magistrates ought to show a little more indulgence to those they condemn. When there is a law like that relative to Patents, common mortals are very excusable if they make a mistake in interpreting in a wrong way this or that expression, since we see the highest Court in the country giving sometimes one interpretation and sometimes another. .

The first article of the law has given rise to fifteen different suits, inscribed in the pages of the volume we hold. These fifteen suits have been tried before the Civil Courts or the Court of Cassation. People may well be frightened at the mountain of papers that must have been used and destroyed by the attorneys, counsel, barristers, &c., before the public could have any clear notion of what the legislators meant.

The second article is as follows : " Will be considered as new inventions or discoveries—the invention of new industrial produce ; the invention of new methods or the new application of known methods to obtain an individual result or produce." This article. we may say, is the main beam of the edifice, consequently it has given occasion to no less than 104 suits. One might fancy that the multitude of judicial decisions given by the Courts has thrown the most brilliant light on the interpretation to be given to the three

paragraphs forming the second article. Alas! these
paragraphs are just as obscure as before. For instance,
the Imperial Court of Paris decided on August 13,
1861, that the "change in the form of a surgical
instrument, even when there may result an advantage
or greater facility to the operator, cannot be patented."
But on July 26 of the same year it had decided that "a
production already known—a straw mat, for instance
—may be patented when its form, its size, and its
length are new." So, again, the Court of Cassation
decided, on February 9, 1862, that "the production
of a new industrial result is an invention that may be
patented, even if it is only due to a new combination
in the form and proportions of objects already known."
On the contrary, the Correctional Court of the Seine
decided on December 24, 1861, that a modification of
form, even when it procures an advantage, is not of a
nature to constitute a patentable invention. Can we
not say with the poet :

> "Deviner si tu peux, et choisis si tu l'oses ?"

The lawyers of Great Britain are accustomed to
celebrate certain anniversaries by a professional dinner.
The President of the party, after having proposed the
health of the Queen and the Royal Family, calls upon
his brethren to join in a toast to the prosperity of the
profession they follow. This traditional toast is characteristic enough. It is as follows : " *The glorious
uncertainty of the law !*" We think the facts we have
related give to this toast a right of citizenship on this
side of the Channel.

T. N. BENARD.

IMPORTANT MESSAGE FROM THE SECRETARY OF THE CONFEDERATION, COUNT VON BISMARCK, TO THE NORTH GERMAN FEDERAL PARLIAMENT.

Berlin, December 10, 1868.

In the presence of the manifold and well-founded complaints concerning the defective state of legislation on Patents in Prussia and Germany, the Royal Prussian Government deems it important to have considered without any further delay what course might best be adopted in the matter.

At the same time, however, and with a view to the position long since taken by Government in regard to the question, it must not be omitted in the first place to decide whether henceforth Patents should be granted at all within the boundaries of the Confederation. The frequent polemics on the principles of Patent-Laws, to which the repeated attempts at reform have given birth during the last ten years, and more particularly the discussions in the late German Federal Assembly, have enhanced the questionability of the usefulness of Patents.

After taking the opinion of the Chambers of Commerce and the mercantile corporations, the Prussian Government, on the occasion of the German Federal Assembly Session of 31st December, 1863, gave utterance to the doubt whether under present circumstances, Patents for inventions may be considered either necessary or useful to industry. Since then the

N

Royal Prussian Government has taken the question once more into serious consideration, and feels bound to answer it in the negative on the strength of the following arguments.

From a theoretical point of view, it may be taken for granted that the conferring of an exclusive right to profits which may be derived from industrial inventions, is neither warranted by a natural claim on the part of the inventor which should be protected by the State, nor is it consequent upon general economical principles.

The right of prohibiting others from using certain industrial inventions, or bringing certain resources and profitable means of production into operation, constitutes an attack upon the inalienable right which every man has, of applying each and every lawful advantage to the exercise of his profession, which is the more obvious, as there exists a prevailing tendency to free industrial pursuits from all artificial restrictions adherent to them, and the time-honoured practice can only be upheld by a thorough vindication and a practical proof of its fully answering the purpose. To demonstrate this should be the chief aim of all arguments against abolition.

To an argument which has repeatedly been urged— *i.e.*, that the granting a temporary exclusive right is indispensable (so as to secure for the meritorious inventor a reward adequate to the mental labour and money expended, as well as risk incurred, in order that there be no lack of encouragement to the inventive genius)—the objection may be raised that the remark-

ably developed system of communication and convey-
ance now-a-days, which has opened a widefield to real
merit, and enables industrial men promptly to reap all
benefit of production by means of enlarged outlets for
their articles, will, generally speaking, bring those who
know how to avail themselves before others of useful
inventions to such an extent ahead of their competitors,
that, even where no permanent privilege is longer admissible, they will make sure of a temporary extra profit, in proportion to the service rendered to the public.

It is, in fact, in the peculiar advantage produced
by the early bringing into operation of a fresh suggestion of their minds, that the remuneration of those
lies, who, through cleverness and steadiness of purpose, succeed in satisfying existing wants in a manner
less expensive and superior to what previously was
the case, and notwithstanding do not obtain any
monopoly. Not of less account are the practical
impediments which stand in the way of every effort
to bring about an improvement of the Patent-Law.

It is generally admitted by the promoters of Patent-
right, that the system of inquiry or examination, as it
is now working in Prussia, cannot possibly remain in
its present condition, and the experienced officers
appointed to decide upon Patent matters and make
the necessary inquiries, unanimously confirm that
opinion. Though provided with relatively excellent
means of ascertaining, the Prussian Technical Committee for Industry had to acknowledge as early as
1853 (*Vide* Prussian Trade Archives of 1854, Vol. ii.,
page 173, ff.) that the question whether an invention

submitted for being patented might not perchance already have been made or brought into operation elsewhere, was almost an unsolvable one. Since then, inventions have augmented yearly in steadily increasing proportion. The main difficulty, however, not only rests in the impossibility of mastering the matter submitted, but equally so with the upholding of firm principles relating to the criterion of originality. If the inquiry do not altogether deviate from its primitive object by patenting any and every innovation in construction, form, or execution, which is presented, we fall into such uncertainty when sifting actual inventions from the mass of things which are not to be considered as undeniable improvements—owing to the continually increasing and diversified combinations of generally known elements or material and altered constructions or modes of application—that it is hardly possible not to be occasionally chargeable with injustice. Every day shows more clearly how annoying a responsibility grows out of such a state of affairs, and it is highly desirable that the authorities no longer be conscious of doing injustice in their duties on account of rules which cannot properly be put into practice.

As for the often much-commended so-called "application system," it would by no means really answer the purpose; even without considering the theoretical objections which might be raised against it. Its practical results have been far from giving satisfaction wherever it has been adopted. The complaints of the abuses and impediments industry suffers under, and which are brought about through the overwhelming mass of Patents, for the most part taken out with a view to swindling speculation, the unpleasant experience acquired by those who take all legal means so as subsequently to contest and defend Patents granted without previous inquiry being made, have led to a reaction of public opinion in favour of abolishing the system.

The unsatisfactory and quite abnormal state of all matters connected with Patents in England and France had, years ago, claimed the most earnest attention of the legislators, and led to practical deliberations on the necessity and the means of effective improvements. The French Government introduced a Bill in 1858, to the effect that the hearing of objections to Patents applied for might, as much as possible, take place previous to the same being granted. A similar system which is in force in England has, however, proved inadequate in that country, and the commission which, in 1863, made a detailed statement as to the merits of the existing Patent-Law, recommended the adoption of official inquiry.

Under the circumstances, it can hardly be the question at all, for the North German Confederation, to admit of the mere "application system." Nor can the imposition of high taxes [on patentees ?] (not taking into account their inconsistency with the real object of Patents) be considered a sufficient corrective of the system, after the experience acquired in England on this head.

Both the inquiry and application systems having proved defective, the conclusion is arrived at, that the difficulties cannot be overcome by means of altering certain details in the institution, but rather arise out of constitutional infirmities of the institution itself. The Patent system makes such distinctions necessary as are now practically inadmissible, and the impracticability of which is by no means removed through merely transferring the evil from one side to the other. It must be granted that if artificial contrivances be at all required to adequately remunerate an inventor for the services rendered to society, they cannot be hit upon in this direction without hurting all important interests.

That the final step of repealing Patents altogether should not yet have been taken anywhere, in spite of the leading theoretical and practical authorities having urged it, may be easily explained by the fact that we have to deal with an institution which very long ago has taken root in the usage of the industrial nations, and to which tradition ascribes most of the immense progress industry has taken during its existence. To this may be added the apprehension lest the country which would take the lead in the matter might find itself at a disadvantage with the remainder.

Generally speaking, the anticipation of a profitable use to be made of an invention for one's exclusive benefit is, no doubt, a powerful incitement for the inventive genius, and equally is it admitted that to temporary Patent-right we owe the successive improvements on many a useful invention.

Experience has, however, taught that in most instances Patents do not fulfil their mission ; that on the whole they have not proved an actual benefit,

either to the proprietor or the public ; that the profits
have gone just as often into the pockets of strangers
as into those of the able inventor. When chiefly
ascribing the progress made by industry through
technical improvements in many of the countries
where extensive regulations of Patent-right are provided, to the incitement consequent upon the protection afforded by Patents, the fact is overlooked that
the great inventions made in old times, as well as the
scientific discoveries which in the modern era paved the
way for industry, have perfectly done without any
such incitements. Against the stimulating influence
of monopoly upon individuals, we must, however, in a
period so extremely favourable to industrial progress,
not underrate the very important point, that it also
checks the quick and fertile development of a new
thought, which, when totally free, might be expected to
spring up in a higher degree from the competing
labours of all. Of course, it is impossible to say
whether in England, Belgium, France, and the United
States, industry, if supported by other favourable
stipulations, might not have taken an equal development without the protection of Patents ; but we have
at all events an illustration of this being the fact in
Switzerland, where the absence of Patents has not at
all been found prejudicial to the public at large. The
records of the latter country may dispel all apprehension lest the abolition of Patents should place national
industry on an unequal and disadvantageous footing
with foreign. If Germany be foremost in the indicated direction, we must, it is true, be alive to the

very likely occurrence of her standing, at least for some time to come, isolated on her platform. A favourable result of the movement in either England or France can hardly be looked for at a very early date, considering the state of public opinion prevailing in those countries, as well as the large individual interests at stake, owing to the wide scope for protection arising out of their Patent system, while at the same time it is yet a fact worthy of remark, that neither England nor France have been able to make up their minds as to reforming a system the numerous defects of which are universally recognised. In Germany the same difficulties do not present themselves to the same extent, the less prolixity of our Patent institution not affecting the industrial part of the nation in nearly the same ratio. The whole system in this country has been less active in all directions ; proof of this is given by the statistics of Patents, as compared with those taken out abroad. The actual items in 1867 were as follows :—

For Prussia	103 Patents.
,, Saxony	179 ,,
,, the Thuringian Union	33 ,,
,, Brunswick	32 ,,
,, Hesse	20 ,,
,, Oldenburg	12 ,,
,, Bavaria	214 ,,
,, Würtemberg	139 ,,
,, Baden	46 ,,

Whereas, in 1866, there were granted—

In England (including the provisional
   protections) 3,453
In France . . . . . . about 4,400
In Belgium . . . . . .   „   1,700
And in the United States .   „   9,450

In Prussia, on account of the rigidly adhered-to pre-liminary inquiry, 87 per cent. on an average of the Patents applied for during the last ten years have been non-suited, and only from 50 to 100 requests a year were granted.   Besides, it is scarcely subject to a doubt that even of these only a small number has been turned to practical use.   Again, the amount of privilege the Patent ensures is less in Germany than abroad, as in conformity with the clauses of the Treaty of 21st September, 1842 (and which provisions should be kept in force under any circumstances), a Patent does not confer upon its proprietor (not taking into view machinery or instruments) a prohibitory right against the importation, sale, or consumption of foreign articles.*

The anticipation that the abolition of Patents might cause the results of new inventions to be lost to the nation through the respective inventors turning themselves towards the protection-affording countries, is not confirmed by the experience acquired on this head in Switzerland.   The industrial who has invented a new process will, in most instances, be influenced by other

---

* This mighty difference from our British practice is in harmony with what I have shown is the scope of the original English Act, and with our common law.—R. A. M.

motives to bring the same into operation where he has his factory and his already acquired customers. Nor can much importance be attached to the apprehension that, should the Patent-Law be repealed, inventors might show more disposition towards keeping new inventions secret from the public ; for, even assuming the aboli- tion to be an incitement to keeping inventions secret, yet it cannot be admitted that any prejudicial change from the present state of things would take place. Even now, under the rule of the Patent-Law, it is a recognised fact, that to such methods of fabrication and resources as admit of being kept secret, the very secrecy affords ampler protection than the Patent itself. By thus drawing the conclusion that those inventions which might eventually be kept secret are so at the present time as well, no actual prejudice will be caused by one measure being in force rather than the other.

The Royal Prussian Government, therefore, thinks that by completely abolishing the Patent system within the limits of the Confederation (a resolution recommended by economical theory, and which public opinion has been sufficiently prepared for), instead of making any further and necessarily unsuccessful attempts at reform, the circumstance of the Confederation preceding other important industrial nations cannot be considered an actual impediment, although it would be far preferable that the South-German States should join in the measure, so as to extend the innovation to all countries comprised in the Zollverein.

The undersigned is of opinion that previous to fur- ther inquiring into the particulars of the Patent-Law, the North German Confederation ought first of all to decide whether henceforth any protection by means of Patents should be afforded at all within the boundaries of the Confederation. Assuming this, and also considering that the Confederation shall have to take a decision as to the attempts at reform, the undersigned moves : " That the Federal Parliament appoint the Committee on trade and intercourse, to deliberate on the question proposed, and report on the same.

(Signed) " Von Bismarck."

PROPOSITION FOR THE ABOLITION OF PATENTS IN HOLLAND.

SECOND CHAMBER OF THE NETHERLANDS LEGISLATURE, SESSION OF 21st JUNE, 1869.—DISCUSSION ON THE ABOLITION OF EXCLUSIVE RIGHTS IN INVENTIONS AND IMPROVEMENTS OF OBJECTS OF ART AND INDUSTRY—(PATENTS).

M. VAN ZINNICQ BERGMANN was not sufficiently prepared for the discussion while the project was in Committee. He feels much sympathy for all such measures as tend to do away with impediments to trade and industry. At the same time, people ought to discriminate between the kind of protection which is a hindrance to industry, and may be called monopoly, and the one to which property is entitled on the part of the State.

At this part of his speech the hon. member indulges in extensive remarks on the right of property. According to Roman law, the right of property was a "*jus quod natura omnia animalia docuit.*" But that definition is not a correct one, as the right of property is especially maintained in civilised society.

After that, the hon. member launches himself into allegory. Try, quoth he, to drive the lion from his den ; he will defend it until his last drop of blood ! Look at the boy who snatches the young and tender bird from its nest; the mother will pursue the robber, and not leave him. Now, he should like to know whether an artist,

an inventor, an author, has, or has not, a right of property
in his work which entitles him to the benefits to be
derived from it?   This question he answers in the affirmative, and refers to Soy, Massé, and the "Assemblée
Constituante" of France in December, 1791.   And why
should there be no right of property?   Perhaps on
account of an article in the Civil Code, which says,
"*possession vaut titre*," or of a restriction to a greater or
smaller lapse of time?   We are continually referred to
England and the United States.   But what is England?
England is a country at the same time emancipated and
in course of emancipation.   Duly considered, England
will be found to be, internally, in about the same state in
which the Netherlands were before 1795, or before the
end of the sixteenth century—(laughter)—but, the
hon. member adds, always accompanied by such improvements as rulers have successively granted with regard to
Patents.   England may have had its commotions; but,
nevertheless, charters have never been otherwise but
granted, and the privileges, exacted though they may
have been, were received at the hands of the King.   And
what have we been doing?   We expelled our Stadholder,
and got annexed to France; the principles of 1798 have
taken root in our country, and continue to be the basis
for present action.   The hon. member further argues
that Patents are granted to emancipated slaves, but
free citizens take out "brévets d'invention."   He is of
opinion that it is a wrong impression that Patents are to
be placed upon a line with the abolition of guilds.   There
is no connexion whatever between these institutions, and
this he demonstrates by reference to French authors.

Even taking Michel Chevalier's doctrines for granted, he asks, "Could such difficulties not be obviated through a *reform* of the Patent-Law ?" Once at a time, Alex-ander made himself famous by cutting through the Gordian knot. That was a despot's doing; he might have deserved more fame had he succeeded in disentang-ling the knot. Such should be the final aim the legislator ought to strive to reach. Finally, the hon. member puts forward the question, whether the passing of the law now before the House might not involve the country in international troubles ; for, Switzerland alone excepted, every country in Europe has its Patent-Law. Besides, we are aware that, as far as literary right of property is concerned, a neighbouring country has, against its will, been compelled to maintain it. We, at our turn, might once have to come back to what we want at present to repeal. Let us, therefore, be cautious.

M. HEEMSKERK AZN remarks that continued allusions are being made to reaction. Generally speaking, such allusions are made out of personal motives; but he should very much like to see a real live reactionist, who would like to repeal what progress has brought us. There may possibly be people extant who would wish to do so, but as for him, he is not aware of any reactionary plots against our institutions, or the effects of science and progress ; yet this very project now before the House, which *he* considers to be *reaction*, has been most favour-ably received in Committee. Should the Netherlands Legislature sanction it, *then* he shall have to believe in the existence of reaction. For it is an easy thing to find evidence of reaction in the project under discussion. M.

van Zinnicq Bergmann has already more or less demonstrated it. He (M. Heemskerk) will add a few more particulars. Where, the hon. member asks, lies the origin of Patents? In the cultivation of a free spirit, and the ennobling of labour; and of these, the right of protection existed since time immemorial. Deviating from the civil rights, the Stuarts, through favour or arbitrary motives, granted "privileges;" but the Free Parliaments saved Patents, that protect inventions. Moreover, this principle has been adopted in the most freedom-advocating of constitutions—viz., that of the United States. The same may be said with regard to France. On the 31st December, 1790, the "Assemblée Constituante" resolved that the right [of property] in inventions should be guaranteed, and in this resolution originated the first French Patent-Law. The Netherlands would be the very first country on earth (with one exception only) to deviate from the principle of a right of property in inventions, in a moment, when public opinion, dissenting thereby from a few economists, everywhere declares in favour of Patents. He reminds the House of the immense influence inventions have had on history and society, such as the invention of printing, of the compass, steam, gas, &c. And would it be fair to withhold from those who promote progress that protection which is legally due to them; whereas there is no end of provisions in the code protecting mere material property, such as the right of inheritance until the twelfth degree, lotteries, stock gambling, and the like? Government has evidently been aware of the circumstances standing in the way of the project, as is proved by page 1 of the

Memorial of Explanation; but it shrinks from the logical consequences. The Patent system is based upon the principle that nobody should enrich himself by another man's property. This has also lately been argued at length in Savornel Lohman's pamphlet. The hon. member gives it as his opinion that in this matter an author is in exactly the same position as an inventor. If Patents be abolished, we shall logically have to come to repealing Copyright as well. A counterfeited edition is nothing else than the imitation of an object of industry; the writer is an author, but the inventor is no less an author. Amongst others, he refers to a speech from Lamartine (as reporter of a Committee in the French Legislative Chambers, which consisted of the then most eminent economists) on the Patent-Law of 1844, which is still in force. He insists that the justice of his system of maintaining the right of property is proved beyond a doubt by the ever and again recurring circumstance of an inventor lacking capital for a practical application of his lucubrations. Still, he often obtains the requisite means; and now everybody will be enabled to imitate the result of his thoughts and labour, and to reap the profits to accrue from the same. He points to Professor Visvering's work on practical economy, who also recognised that, if no exclusive Patents be delivered, still inventors had a right to a remuneration of some kind. Those who oppose the Patent-Law contend that an inventor is not entitled to a reward; he admits that no reward should be expected, but most assuredly the inventor may lay claim to remuneration for the labour expended on the invention.

We are referred to Switzerland, where no Patents are given. But what of that? In the first place, most of the industrial Cantons of Switzerland are clamorous for a Patent-Law; secondly, the Swiss, as a body, equally want the measure to be put through; and, in the third place, the hon. member points to the large benefits which, according to Klosterman's recent work, Swiss industrials derive from foreign Patent-Laws. It is alleged that the number of Patents which are being delivered [in Holland] is but small. But, says M. Heemskerk, foreigners, on the contrary, claim that the number is large. There exists apprehension of law-suits; but can that be brought to bear upon the repeal of the Patent-Law? In that case, landed property would be the least tolerable, as the proverb says—" *Qui terre a, guerre a.*" Moreover, no three law-suits are known to have sprung up from Patents in this country since the law has been in force. In Belgium, it is true, much action has of late been taken in order to do away with Patents; but there, as well as in Prussia, the movement is rapidly decreasing. The hon. member refers to the " Nederlandsche Industrieel," a periodical which, though strenuously in favour of abolition of Patents, nevertheless mentions in its issues of 14th and 21st of February, and 20th of June, what has lately occurred in this respect in Germany and elsewhere. In Great Britain also the question has lately been discussed in Parliament, but the member who moved it did not even take the votes upon it, but quietly dropped the matter; such was the impression made upon his mind by the arguments brought forward [!]. The subject has

equally engrossed the attention of the "Société Econo-
mique" of Paris, when eminent economists, amongst
whom Wolowski, declared in favour of Patents. This
is mentioned in the *Economistes* of June [see page 164].
For all these reasons the hon. member recommends
to the serious consideration of the House that, for
the time being at least, the rash Act be not consummated. Do not throw such a stain upon your
Legislature, he emphatically exclaims. Do not step
backward; beware of relinquishing the protection of
any description of property. Do not cripple the law by
ignoring a principle which protects the fruit of human
intellect. Beware of laying violent hands upon property,
of whatever kind it may be. Let us do better than that;
let us reject the bill. Persuade Government, there
being no haste whatever, to propose to the Chambers
that the subject be deferred until next Session. At all
events, nothing would be lost by it. Meanwhile Government would be enabled to reconsider the subject, and to
make inquiries abroad as to the state of legislation on
this head. No prejudice would be occasioned by deferring the matter; for the hon. member expresses his
firm belief that a dangerous measure is about to be
adopted with regard to a subject with which the utmost
caution should be observed.

M. DE BRUYN KOPS would not enter into all particulars, the matter having been treated at length in the
sundry documents relating to it; but he would restrict
himself to a refutation of M. Heemskerk's arguments.
He is in a position to place himself on a very simple
point of view. The law of 1817 is generally disliked, in

principle as well as in its details. It has been admitted
that it does not give the inventor any guarantee, and
this on the ground of the issue of some law-suits which
have sprung up from it. So Patents, far from giving a
security, hinder the general public and impede industry.
It is a fact worthy of notice, that the leading industrial
organs, such as the Chambers of Commerce and Factories, the Industrial Society, the Union for Promoting
Mechanical and Manual Industry, and the Nederlandsche
Industrieel, unanimously have declared against Patents;
so have a score of industrials. Are these not facts
worth more than a few considerations about a right to
special protection? Add to this the circumstance that
in those countries where Patents do exist difficulties are
gradually increasing; as, first of all, the question arises,
whether the invention is really a new one; and to
ascertain this is very often a most arduous task. Then,
again, Patents are being asked for mere trifles. Within
a short period, 126 Patents for improving bicycles have
been taken out in England. It thus becomes necessary
to make a minute inquiry into the usefulness of the
matter. This has been the cause that in France they
have gone to the other extreme—granting Patents
" without guarantee by Government." Patents are not
consequent upon the recognition of man's, or inventors', rights; they are the remainders of the guild
system, and of protection to national industry in
exclusion of foreign. It cannot be a question of
right of property, for, if such were the case, Patents
would not be granted for a fixed term of years. If
invention means right of property, why, then, that

arbitrary restriction? Originally the idea may have been a good one, but in the sequel it has proved a failure. There are examples of different persons having made the same invention without having any knowledge of each other. It is consequently becoming almost a matter of impossibility to ascertain priority. The hon. member says that all endeavours to bring about a practical result out of an originally elevated idea have utterly failed; that the guarantee of the right is, as has been proved by means of the report in England, at best uncertain and unsatisfactory; and that when the project shall have been made law, he will rejoice at his country having been foremost in leaving the wrong track.

Session of Tuesday, 22nd June.

The President reads an address from the Board of Directors of the Union to Promote Mechanical and Manual Industry, of Rotterdam, in which they support the project now pending before the House.

The discussion on the subject is continued.

M. van Houten observes, that M. Heemskerk has given the epithets of " reactionary " and " ruinous " to the measure proposed by Government. By opposing the project, that deputy did *his* duty, but at the same time it more than ever becomes the duty of those who strenuously support it openly to express their convictions, and to show that they know what they are about. His opinion is that M. Heemskerk's arguments have been tested, and did not stand the test. M. de Bruyn Kops having refrained from arguing on the ground of theoretical considerations, he (M. Van Houten) will say a few words in that direction. The main question is this : Is prohibiting the imitation of an invention lawful, and shall it or shall it not be upheld? Those who want to let things remain as they are talk of rights acquired; but on what are these so-called rights based? Certainly on no very solid basis; for, if a right it be, why is only a temporary protection granted? A right is permanent, and cannot be taken away but through expropriation for the common weal, and even then in consideration of an indemnity only. M. Heemskerk argues two points : 1st, The inventor has a claim of priority, as the first who takes possession. 2nd, The imitator enriches himself at the expense of the inventor. But, says the hon. member, M. Heemskerk loses sight of the fact that first occupation can only take place of " corporeal " effects ; not of an invention which may be made, and is often being made, by others at the same time. Besides, he contends that it is not the imitators, but the public, who enrich themselves and benefit by the invention. He is of opinion that the Patent system remunerates where no labour has been expended ; whilst claiming Patents has become an industry prejudicial to the general public. It has been urged to frame a " good" Patent-Law ; but that the hon. member holds to be impossible. Whatever might be its provisions, monopoly must needs be created by it. And if this is such an easy matter, why did M. Heemskerk not introduce a bill for a new law? It is alleged that if everybody is allowed to imitate, the inventor works for nothing. But how is it with so many gratuitous appoint-

ments? Is that a question of right? Certainly not.
As M. Heemskerk, in his speech, invoked Providence,
he should like to know whether it can be supposed that
Providence intends enriching an individual or society at
large? On that ground, we may safely set the public's
right against the inventor's. Hereupon the hon. member
considers the question from an economical point of view.
In the first place, Patents are useless for such objects as
baffle imitation—like the Krupp guns, for instance; and
then objects emanating from the inventor direct are, as a
rule, preferred. As for petty inventions, he would say
that, it being the normal course of social development
that every branch of industry should steadily progress,
so it is the case with them. On that field, everybody is
more or less of an inventor; and with regard to petty inventions, Patents not only are superfluous, but noxious.
M. Heemskerk, it is true, has rather spoken with a view
to great inventions, and the hon. member fancies he has
given evident proof that no harm can be done by abolishing Patent-right on the latter. It is these great inventions that the public at large benefits by. He denies M.
Heemskerk's assertion, that in the absence of Patents no
capital would be forthcoming for the practical application
of an invention, for, pending the tests and experiments an
inventor subjects his invention to, no capitalist loans him
money. He equally contests what M. H. said about the
logic of repealing Copyright, should the Patent-Law be put
aside, and that, by doing the latter, violent hands would
to a certain extent be laid upon the right of property.
The hon. member thinks that no such comparison can be
drawn, as the law providing for Copyright does by no

means prevent anybody from applying any published work to further development of science. Copyright in no way interferes with public interests. The member for Gorcum has called the project a "reactionary" measure. This will frighten neither him nor us, for it matters little what is *called* reactionary, but much what *is* reactionary. The project is closely connected with the historical development of society, and the liberation of labour and industry. The Patent system may be placed upon an equal footing with the exclusive right to discoveries and other similar privileges of yore. We have given up all those things. Each and every benefit derived from them becomes a public one, and so ought every new outlet for trade to be. On these grounds, the hon. member advocates the removal of those impediments.

M. GODEFROI said:* I rise to make some observations on three points in the speech, containing so much that is valuable, delivered by M. Heemskerk. These points are, first, the legal basis; secondly, treating the question on the footing of Copyright; and, thirdly, the reference to the practice in foreign countries. The speech of the hon. gentleman who preceded me has made my task with reference to the two first points peculiarly easy, so that I can content myself in a great measure with simply referring to it. His confutation of the legal basis, as laid down by M. Heemskerk, appears to me conclusive. To speak of occupation in a non-material sense, to say that the *primus occupans* can maintain for himself or make over to another, on certain conditions,

---

* For this translation I am indebted to the Foreign-office, to whose reports I have been politely allowed access.

does seem to me an untenable position. We must take into consideration what the preceding speaker has already proved, that occupation from which a claim can be made, and which one can consider as equivalent to the right of possession, is inconceivable when the right is of a temporary nature. But this is not all. How can any one acquire by occupation anything that another at the same moment may occupy in precisely the same way? How is it possible that two persons at precisely the same moment (and this possibility is here not to be denied) can by occupation be possessed of the same right? I shall say no more on the first point. The second point, treating the question on the footing of literary property, or Copyright. I freely admit that, if I were convinced, in case of our consenting to pass this Bill, we should be pronouncing the abolition of Copyright, I should recoil from giving my vote in its favour. But the preceding speaker has, in my opinion, most clearly shown the points of difference between industrial and literary property. I think I may be allowed to refer, for further confirmation of the view I am taking, to the observations of a man held in general consideration, and of especial weight in this case, inasmuch as he was President of the Commission appointed by the British Government to inquire into the question of the retention or abolition of the "Law of Patents." I refer to Lord Stanley, who, in a debate in the House of Commons on the 29th May, to which the hon. member for Gorinchem appealed, expressed himself with regard to the difference between Patent-right and Copyright in a manner so clear and distinct that I cannot even now

see how I can improve upon his distinctions. Lord
Stanley said, speaking of the distinction : " The analogy
seemed a plausible one, but he thought that, on being
looked into, it would not hold water. The difference
was simply this : he did not rest it on any abstract
ground as to the distinction between invention and discovery, but on the obvious fact that no two men ever
did or ever would write, independently of one another,
exactly the same book ; each book, be it good or bad,
would stand alone ; whereas it might happen that two or
three men, quite independently of one another, would
hit upon the same invention. That alone established a
distinction between the two cases." And he was perfectly right. While it is impossible for two men,
independently of one another, to write the same book,
it is not only possible, but such a case *has* occurred,
for two men to make the same discovery—to light upon
the same invention. There are examples of this in the
history of French industry. Daguerre and Niepce
both pursued that line of thought from which
photography took its rise, and the fact is so
well ascertained that when the French Academy
of Sciences had to come to a decision about
assigning a reward for the invention, they divided
the reward between Daguerre and the children
of Niepce, then deceased. In a report made by the
present Minister of Public Works in Belgium, M. Jamar,
with reference to property in drawings and models
of machinery, the question of Patents is treated, and
I notice in it one highly important observation applicable to this subject under discussion. It is known—

it appears also in the supplement annexed to the
Official Report—that at the conclusion of the first Great
Exhibition in London, the French Commission brought
out a report, in which the renowned politician, Michel
Chevalier, as the result of conclusions drawn from the
Exhibition, declared himself in favour of unconditional
abolition of Patents. How did Michel Chevalier come
to that opinion? The report to which I refer informs
us, and from it I extract the following passage : "On
seeing at the Exhibition in London, at a few paces from
each other, the same machines, the same tools, new
productions, invented or discovered a thousand miles
apart, by men who arrived at the same result sometimes
by different ways, legislators and magistrates felt themselves bound to ask to what principles of justice and
equity could one of these inventors appeal, that he
might obtain a temporary monopoly rendering abortive
the efforts and experiments on the part of ten other
inventors as persevering, as conscientious, and as intelligent as himself?" When Michel Chevalier, at the
London Exhibition, had seen a few paces from each
other the same inventions, presented as the mental
produce of persons who lived thousands of miles apart,
and knew nothing of each other, he might well say
that it is impossible to recognise an exclusive right.
But here is another proof that industrial property and
Copyright cannot be put upon the same footing. Moreover, Patent-right precludes the possibility of the same
thought being carried out, at least for a time, but
Copyright does not. Lastly, the third point—the appeal
to the feeling in foreign countries. M. Heemskerk, in

his excellent speech of yesterday, made it to appear that the feeling on this subject in foreign countries was that the abolition of Patents was condemned. It is perfectly true that at this moment, in most of the European States, there still subsist laws for conferring Patents. But must we thence infer in foreign countries an overwhelming conviction, that there must be no abolition? I do not think so. There are, in fact, evidences on this point worth attending to, which I shall proceed to lay before the House. How is it in France? The law of 1844 is still in force; but is it approved in France? Certainly not. They are convinced that the operation of this law has given rise to the most serious difficulties. This is a fact; and this fact has led to several proposals for modification which have been pending for some years, and are still pending, although the French Chambers get through their work more rapidly than we do. The proposals have been already for several years pending, because the carrying them out is hindered by the impression which the valuable report of Michel Chevalier has produced, for every day the doubt gains force whether it is a question of improving the law, or whether it is not much rather a question of putting an end to the granting of Patents. England— it is known that two investigations have taken place in that country. One in 1851, by the Upper House; the other in 1862, by a Government Commission, which issued its report in 1865. What was the result of the investigation in 1851? I find the result in the report of M. Jamar, which I just now referred to. I will read the following extract: "The result of this inquiry was remarkable. Lord Granville had been President of the Commission charged with presenting the Bill, which, while it modified the Law of Patents, respected or left untouched the principle. The inquiry so completely modified his convictions, that he did not hesitate to declare, in the sitting of the House of Lords on the 1st July, 1851, that he considered the issuing of Patents was an advantage neither for the inventors nor the public." So the Commission of Inquiry, which undertook the task of discovering what amendments could be made in the law, came to the conclusion that it would be better to abolish Patents. I should occupy the House too long were I to quote all that M. Jamar, in his report, borrowed from this Commission of Inquiry. I will content myself with remarking that, among the witnesses examined, and on whose testimony the opinions of the Commission were founded, there were men perfectly well qualified to form a judgment. They were not only economists, men of science, but also men of business, practical men: Cubitt, President of the Institution of Civil Engineers; Brunel, the celebrated engineer; Ricardo, Member of Parliament; Reid, President of the Committee for carrying out the Great Exhibition of 1851; and other industrial and commercial witnesses, so described in Jamar's report. According to the same Belgian report, the testimony of the English judges was very remarkable. They almost unanimously declared that it was impossible to apply the law, and that they did not ascribe this impossibility to the application of the principle in itself. Lord Granville declared also, in a sitting of the Upper House, on July 1st, 1851, that his opinion was formed from the sentiments of the judges; and he added: "The only persons who derive any advantage from the Law of Patents are the lawyers. Except, perhaps, warrants for horses, there is no subject which gives such an opportunity for roguery as the Law of Patents." And one of the law lords of the Upper House, Lord Campbell, declared, after hearing the speech of Lord Granville, that having been for nine years legal adviser of the Crown, and having had some experience in the matter, he coincided perfectly in the opinion of Lord Granville. The inquiry made by the English Government Commission led to the same result. In the sitting of the Lower House on May 28 of the present year, of which I have already spoken, Lord Stanley distinctly said that he had taken his place in the Commission with the impression that the business before them was not to abolish Patents, but to take measures for the amendment of the English law on that subject. During the inquiry, however, together with those who took part in it he had come to the conclusion that not only the existing law, but every law on Patents, would meet with almost insurmountable difficulties, because these difficulties do not lie in the application, but are inherent in the principle. M. Heemskerk made it appear yesterday that the result of the discussion of May 28 in the Lower House was in favour of the continuance of Patents. I cannot go to such a length in my estimate of that discussion. A motion was brought forward by Mr. Macfie, [an ex-] President of the Liverpool Chamber of Commerce, to declare that the time had now arrived for the abolition of Patents. At the end of the debate the motion was withdrawn by the proposer. Now, the hon. member for Gorinchem has drawn the conclusion, from the course pursued, that the proposer durst not put his motion to the vote, because he was certain of a minority. The conclusion is somewhat hasty, for nobody can tell—we at least cannot—what the vote of the Lower House would have been had the motion been put. Besides, the object of the motion appears in the speech of the proposer. His chief aim was to invite discussion, "to lay a general view of the subject before the House," as he expressed it, rather than to get a decision. In his speech he also gave it as his wish that the subject should be again investigated by a Government Commission. I am of opinion that, from what I have said with reference to England, the conclusion cannot be drawn that the retention of Patents is there the unqualified and prevailing determination. Belgium : The last law on Patents, the law of 1854, is there in operation. I know not if it works well, and perhaps it would have been worth while for the Government to get such information. Meanwhile I have a thick volume here before me, containing a commentary on the law, which I have not read completely through. It contains 300 pages, but I have run through it, and it appears to me that the so-called commentary is in very many respects a criticism on the law, and affords a proof that it by no means works so extremely well. Last of all, Germany : M. Heemskerk spoke yesterday of the unanimity of the Germans on the subject of maintaining Patents. I should not like to admit that unanimity so unreservedly ; there are facts, at least, opposed to that assertion. This fact, for example, which we have extracted

from an article in the *Nieuwe Groninger Courant,* just sent
to us, a proposal for the abolition of Patents made to the
North German Bund; and if this is carried out, no more
Patents will be granted in a great portion of Germany.
Another fact: so far back as 1864 the Prussian Government asked the opinion of the Chambers of Commerce on
the question whether or not Patents should be maintained, and of the 47 there were 31 for the abolition and
16 against it. I scarcely venture to speak of the
economists, otherwise I would appeal to the German
Economic Congress of 1863, which pronounced Patents
injurious to the national welfare. But there is one argument which has more weight with me than any other.
I am thoroughly persuaded that a good law on Patents
is an impossibility. It is, indeed, matter of regret that
the hon. member for Gorinchem, when he was in the Ministry, did not try to present a good law to the Legislature.
He was the right man for it. He will, however, do me
the justice to believe that, when I say this, I do not mean
to censure him; what I do mean is to express my regret.
He is open to no censure, for during the time he held
office he attended so assiduously to his duties that even
his most violent political opponents were compelled to do
him honour. But yet it is to be regretted that when he
was Minister he did not propose an amendment of the
law of 1817. We should then have seen whether it was
possible or not to have a good efficient law on Patents.
For my part, I have arrived at the conclusion that it is
an impossibility. This is the impression made when one
goes over foreign laws on Patents. There is not a
single good one among them, nor one which does not

give rise to difficulties which hitherto have been found
to be insurmountable.   But there is a further objection.
According to my notions, there is a formidable stumbling-
block which is directly encountered when one sets to
work to frame a law on Patents.   The question at once
presents itself, must it not be proved that the person who
demands the privilege has a right to it?   When
has the claimant that right?   When it is proved
that his invention has for its· object a new industrial
product, or a new operation, or a new application of
an operation already known, to obtain an industrial
result or an industrial product.   The words which I
here employ are taken from Art. 2 of the French Law,
which, in my opinion, exactly express the object of the
law.   I now ask, if a Government is in a position, in
this sense, to examine the claim of an applicant for a
Patent?   I shall endeavour to prove that a Government
is not in such a position, and I cannot do better than
quote the words of the author of the report on the
French Law of 1844, the celebrated Philippe Dupin.
We know that the French Law does not undertake the
preliminary investigation; and, therefore, as we have
been already reminded by M. de Bruyn Kops, when an
announcement is made of articles for which a Patent is
granted in France, the letters S. G. D. G. (sans· garantie
du Gouvernement) are generally added.   Now, hear what
Philippe Dupin says in justification of that principle of
French Law, and to prove the impossibility of a preliminary examination on the part of the Government:
"The preliminary examination would be the establishment of a censorship in matters of industry.   And how

could this censorship be carried out? How, for example, are we to decide that an industrial fact is new, and that it has not been produced in the course of manufacture or in the retreat of an obscure and industrious workman? How are we to foresee and judge the amount of utility in a discovery just made, before it has been developed, before it has been put to the proof? Who will take part in this debate? Who will represent the parties interested? Where are the judges to come from? Who will exercise this jurisdiction by guesswork in the regions of thought and futurity? Shall it be a clerk turned into a judge of what he does not understand? Shall we take a practical man, who is often only a man of routine, to judge a man of theory and inspiration? Shall we invite philosophers? But if they are philosophers, they are not to be supposed to know everything, and they have their preferences, their prejudices, their own sets; and the applicant, perhaps, contradicts their doctrines, their works, their ideas. These are incontestable impossibilities. It has been said, with as much wit as reason, in such matters the only suitable proceeding is experience, the only competent judge the public." So much for experience. But, Mr. President, if a Government is not in a position to decide whether the claimant of a Patent has a right to it, can it be sanctioned in granting a privilege blindfold which establishes a temporary monopoly? According to my view, this is a formidable, almost insurmountable, stumbling-block, which, in my deliberate opinion, will always stand in the way of a good and efficient Law

P

of Patents.   I, therefore, am of opinion that no other
satisfactory course is open to us than to abolish Patents.

M. VAN VOORTHUYSEN will not enter into many details,
the subject having been considered both from a juridical
and an economical point of view.   He will, therefore, restrict himself to a few remarks on M. Heemskerk's speech.
The hon. member acknowledges the satisfaction the
project gives him; it gratifies the feelings to which he
has given vent a great many times.   It has been said that
the measure was a step backward, as Patents have taken
the place of exclusive privileges to guilds.   At the time
the Patent-right was assuredly an improvement on the
then existing system; but we have been progressing so
much since then that at present nothing short of abolition will satisfy the wants of progress.   He also refers
to the conclusion arrived at by Lord Stanley, which point
M. Heemskerk has left unnoticed—viz., 1st, that it is
impossible to reward all who deserve to be rewarded;
2nd, that it is impossible to reward adequately to the
service rendered to society at large; 3rd, that it is impossible to hold third parties harmless from damage.
And, in fact, the alleged instance of the Daguerre prize
having been divided with another who equally proved
his claim to the invention, speaks for itself.   It is doubtful
who was the first inventor of the steam-engine;
there are several, at least, who claim the invention as
their own.   There is another point he feels bound to refer
to.   M. Heemskerk has said that abolishing Patents constitutes an attack upon the right of property, and that
deputy cautions against a first step, perhaps to be
followed up by others.   This being a very serious

inculpation, the hon. member has asked the opinion of an
eminent jurist, whom he will not name as yet, whose
authority M. Heemskerk is not likely to deny, and who
is in many respects congenial with that esteemed deputy.
The hon. member reads that opinion of one of the foremost opponents of Patent-right, who calls it an obnoxious
and intolerable monopoly. And who is that clever jurist?
It is M. Wintgens, who very likely owed to his extraordinary acquirements in law matters his appointment
to the Department of Justice in the Heemskerk van
Zuylen Ministry.

M. Fock (Secretary of State for Home Affairs) will
not have much to say, after all which has been argued in
yesterday's and to-day's Session, in defence of the project.
Nevertheless he will indulge in a few remarks on the
final report. With a view to the same, M. Heemskerk
submits the maintenance of Patents for inventions, but
the repeal of those "of admission." But the Minister
calls the attention of the House to the circumstance that
the Patents for inventions which are being granted may
aggregate to ten a year or thereabout. What should
remain for us to keep? Or else agents here will apply
for Patents on foreign inventions, so that "Patents of
admission" will re-appear under a different denomination.
M. Godefroi has already pointed to instances abroad,
and the Minister can but add that, despite M. Heemskerk's assertion to the contrary, the Prussian Government
is by no means favourably disposed to the Patent-Law.
In December, 1868, Count von Bismarck addressed a
message to the North German Confederation, embodying
the opinion of the Prussian Government in favour of

repeal, and even hinting that Prussia would not mind taking the lead in the matter.* After entering into a few more details concerning the final report, the Minister once more demonstrates that Patents are great impediments to industry and free-trade, and that it is in the public's interest that they should be abolished. The Netherlands, having once been foremost in doing away with the tax on knowledge, must not now shrink from conferring entire freedom on the field of industry. That is no reaction. Is it reaction to break off with an intolerable state of things? No; it is progress, and leads to free development. The Minister concludes with a citation from Michel Chevalier, and declines to take M. Heemskerk's hint of deferring the discussion on the project.

M. HEEMSKERK AZN replies. He tenders thanks for the urbanity observed throughout the discussion. But it is undeniable that his opinion agrees with the existing right and the prevalent ideas in Europe and America. Of course, if revocation is intended, improvement of the law has to be given up. In reply to the Minister, he has no doubt but that the desire for revocation originated in Prussia, but he has said that in Germany the tide has turned in favour of Patents, on the strength of the "Deutsche Industrie Zeitung" and Klosterman's recent work. The revocation of the Patent-Law may have been contemplated, but the Prussian Government is not now disposed to have the idea carried out. He asks but for what the English equally asked for—*i.e.*, a renewed

---

* This admirable document is prefixed, see page 185.

inquiry. What, after all, is foreign experience to the exercise of law in the Netherlands? How does the project tally with the establishment of a new division of industry in the Department for Internal Affairs, the chief occupation of which is the granting of Patents? He will not argue with the Minister on general remarks, but merely on the one relating to the abolition of newspaper stamps. Why has that tax been repealed? If henceforth a larger quantity of paper be covered with print, the tax has most likely been done away with to promote the diffusion of general knowledge. He supposes, however, the Minister will agree with Cicero, who says that fame acquired by means of deeds which are not useful is but vanity. The stamp duty has been repealed in order to be useful. And in the present case, will the Minister deny all benefits to him who does his utmost, so as to be useful? He replies also to the several members who have made speeches; he contradicts M. de Bruyn Kops about a general disposition supposed to exist in France towards revocation of Patent-Laws. Michel Chevalier only has changed his mind, but there is no opinion prevailing against Patents. Quite recently both Joseph Garnier and Wolowski have refuted Chevalier's arguments.

The hon. member further insists upon *his* interpretation of the Parliamentary debates in England, and names several instances of inventors having acquired wealth. He does not admit that there is a difference between Patent-right and Copyright; imitation of articles of fabrication is, and will remain, as immoral as it is unfair. He shrinks from touching the legal side of the question, but

asks whether, because of the Patent-right being restricted
to a fixed time, the conclusion must needs be drawn
that absolutely no right should exist, and that there
should be no plea in equity whatever for an inventor
to get rewarded for his labours? Does the abstract
question of occupation of immaterial things cripple that
hypothesis in any way? He considers it from a more
general and social point of view, and vindicates his
assertion that an inventor is entitled to a certain amount
of protection for his work, by which, at all events, he
renders a service to society; that Patents are incitements
to many useful inventions and to industry, which is
equally M. de Bruyn Kops' opinion, as stated in his
work on political economy. He has been asked why,
when in the Ministry, he did not introduce a Patent
Reform Law. In the first place, he begs to observe
that much was to be done then, and besides, considering
the smallness of our country, he indulged in the anticipation that the idea of an international agreement might
gradually have gained ground. Should he, however,
have lived longer (politically speaking), he *would* most
likely have introduced a Bill for remodelling the Patent-
Law. As for M. Wintgen's opinion, it is almost superfluous to say that one is not bound to have in every
respect homogeneous ideas with one's political friends.
In reply to the question why, as a member of the House,
he does not make a proposal, he accepts the invitation,
and will in September next be prepared to take, as a
member of the House, the initiative of presenting a Bill
for Reforming the Patent-Law, provided the project now
pending be no longer discussed.

M. Van Zinnick Bergmann replies, and maintains his opinion about the justice of the Patent-right.

M. de Bruyn Kops refutes M. Heemskerk's reply, and demonstrates, by means of fresh examples, that the Patent-right is intolerable and most obnoxious. He considers the question now merely economically; MM. van Houten and Godefroi having so ably discussed the legal points. The large benefits acquired by a few are, as taken from his point of view, prejudicial to the public at large, and against these few advantages there are great damages, as large capitals dwindle away in the chase for the snare of Patents. M. Heemskerk himself favours the revocation of Patents on the right "of admission." What is left after that? Nothing but the Patents of invention. Why not try entire freedom and removal of all impediments?

M. Godefroi will add one word more with reference to M. Heemskerk's readiness in accepting the challenge of framing a new project of law, and he must say that, whatever be the nature of such proposal, it can hardly be expected to satisfy those who condemn the principles of Patent-Law. But the orator who is so well posted must certainly have framed already the main points from which the project would have to be formed. By stating and explaining those points, he would have done more service to the House than by mere opposition to those who favour abolition. The hon. member repeats the important query, whether Patents should be granted without previously inquiring into the merits of the case; and then Government would have to give its opinion just as well on an improved chignon as on an improved steam-engine.

M. G̱EFKEN gives his motives for voting in favour of the project. He says, where there is a right of property, it must be permanent, and even transferable to the heirs; but a guarantee for a few years would not do. He consequently does not recognise the right of property, and merely considers the question with a view to usefulness; and, as far as that goes, his experience in administrative and juridical offices has taught him that Patents are not actually useful, and, on the contrary, lead to speculation and impede the development of many a useful concern. He favours free competition.

M. VAN VOORTHUYSEN will not revert to M. Bergmann's remark about his being accustomed to recapitulate the debates, but denies having intended to force upon him the authority of M. Wintgen's opinion. Such is not the case; but the fact of the opinions of two such jurists as MM. Godefroi and Wintgen agreeing has set his mind at rest as far as legal opinion is concerned.

M. HEEMSKERK AZN replies to M. Godefroi, and does not see why he should just now go and sketch his project. Give him time and opportunity, and he will introduce a Bill, provided this project be deferred; and, in fact, what are they making such haste for?

Minister FOCK maintains his sayings about the Prussian Government favouring revocation, and further explains that the new division in his department has no connexion with Patents, but was made so as to concentrate all matters referring to industry. As for the right of property in inventions, he would merely add that, according to our legislation, Patents are but favours, which may be granted or not, as the case may be.

Hereupon the discussion is closed.

With reference to Art. 1, M. Lenting asks, why the date on which the new law has to take effect should be fixed for the 1st January next. He would prefer that the words be, " After the day of the publication of the law ; " then no new Patents would be granted, those already applied for only excepted.

The Minister inserts the amendment, after which Arts. 1 and 2 are passed.

The project is then put to the vote, and passes the House by 49 ayes against 8 noes.

Against it voted MM. Bichon, Blussé, Vader, Hofmann, Heemskerk Azn, Van Wassenaer, and Van Zinnick Bergmann.

FROM THE DUTCH GOVERNMENT MEMORIAL.

The project of law, which is accompanied by an extensive memorial of explanation, contains the following stipulations :—

Article 1.—From and after the 1st of January, 1870, no fresh Patents for inventions and improvements, or the first introduction of objects of art and industry, shall be granted, those only excepted for which application shall have been made previous to that date.

Article 2.—The term for Patents formerly granted or deliverable within the provisions of Article 1 of this law may be extended in accordance with the law of 25th January, 1817. (*Vide* "*Staatsblad*," No. 6.)

The memorial says, *inter alia* :—

" In order to let Netherlands industry and Netherlands people reap the benefit of the bulk of improvements in industry, the best course to take appears to be the repeal of the Patent-Law.

" The first requisite of a reform of the existing legislation on Patents would be to more completely guarantee their rights to inventors, they being by no means sufficiently protected by the provisions of the law now in force.

" Considering, however, the consequences of any kind of Patent-Law, the means that are to be employed and the expenses to be incurred, so as to render all parties interested quite familiar with the Patents granted ; the fact that, in consequence of the development of industry, the number of Patents is increasing, the result of which is more and more to burden the exercise of the sundry branches of industry with a larger portion of obstructive privileges, besides the abuses and wrong practice to which they lead ; in one word, the price which the public have to pay, compared with the very few inventors, whose advantage is even at best uncertain—considering all these points, there can hardly be a doubt as to the choice the Netherlands ought to make, placed as they are between the dark path leading to more obnoxious privileges and the highway where freedom of movement prevails."

We subjoin the following, with which we have been favoured, on the same subject :—

The project of law to repeal the Act of 1817 for granting exclusive rights on inventions and improvements of objects of art and industry, has given general satisfaction in four Committees of the House, and many have received it enthusiastically. By introducting this Bill, Government has satisfied a desire which of late was frequently manifested by members of the House. The memorial of explanation, with its vouchers, gives full particulars of the objections raised against the Patent system. Most members, in fact, simply gave their adhesion in substance, without considering it necessary to "motivate" their opinion.

A few Members of one of the Committees did not agree with absolute repeal, and even held such a measure to be at variance with justice and equity; they recognised the law of 1817 to be defective and in many cases impracticable; they granted that when a reform might be arrived at " Patents of admission " ought not to remain in force; but they did not see why, on account of the insufficiency of the law in this country, " Patents for invention " should be abolished as well. There are a good many industrial inventions which cost the originator vast mental labour, sometimes even heavy pecuniary sacrifice. By means of his invention he renders society a service which entitles him to enjoy, for a fixed period at least, the exclusive benefit of bringing it into operation. Should this benefit be denied him, it would be but fair that the State should give him a reward; this, however, is subject to difficulties of a peculiar nature.

The opinion that the repeal of the law would leave intellectual property altogether unprotected, may be refuted by the fact that the principle of intellectual property cannot possibly form the basis for a Patent-Law. Although it was emphatically proclaimed in the French Legislature of the first years subsequent to the Revolution of 1789, it will not stand the test of sound criticism. Could right of property be admitted in this case, it ought to be permanent, and not temporary. Yet no Legislature ever dared to extend the so-called right, even for the inventor's lifetime; the terms were generally ten, twelve, fifteen, and, at most, twenty years. Another circumstance, which is in downright contradiction with the notion of right of property, is the fact that everywhere Patents are granted only on payment of a certain sum.

If Patents are to be defended at all, better try to do it on a principle of utility. Some appearances are in favour of the plea that anticipation of reward and pecuniary benefit originates useful inventions; but pecuniary experience has taught that although every now and then this may be the case, still the very existence of a strict Patent-Law, is, on the whole, a decided hindrance to industry; that the inventor's benefit from his Patent is, in most instances, but doubtful, whereas by doing away with this artificial encouragement, inventions will not, on this account, remain in the bud undeveloped.

A strict Patent-Law is subject to strange drawbacks, which have been chiefly demonstrated by the inquiry in England; whilst in Holland the well-known decision of the Supreme Court of 1846 has well-nigh vitiated it.

Under the circumstances, no choice was left our Government but between a stricter law than before and complete freedom. Very justly it has declared in favour of the latter, and, as it states, chiefly Switzerland in its eye, where very many branches of industry are in a most flourishing condition, ascribable, in part at least, to the very absence of Patent-Laws, with their escort of drawbacks and law-suits. There the manufacturer goes upon his own errand, avails himself of inventions made by others, and, if he cannot at once get at the bottom of the same, tries to arrive at them through his own exertions and his own ponderings.

The step taken by Government deserves the more approbation, inasmuch as no legislation can sufficiently guarantee to the real inventor *that* exclusive right which is considered a reward for the service rendered to society. Not seldom it happens that the inventor is a scholar, who makes the fruit of his labours public, leaving to others the deriving pecuniary benefits from it.

Some persons, adverse to Patent-Laws, cannot yet make up their minds as to the new system being in accordance with morality, and perhaps be an encouraging of the dishonesty which lies in the appropriation of another man's invention, thereby reminding the Netherlander of Güttenburg. To this we may bring forward the argument that, as far as the deed ascribed to that German falls within the limits of theft, or of violation of contract between master and servant, nobody will defend it; but in the circumstance that Güttenburg, having once mastered the art, applied it to bring it into operation, and by exerting his intellect, raised it to a much higher pitch of perfection, there lies nothing dishonest. If these proceedings be incriminated, then the principle ought to be transferred to another field—that of trade. Then the merchant who takes advantage of a new outlet or a new branch of commerce inaugurated by another, ought to be reprobated; but if so, farewell to all competition—nay, to the very principle of free-trade.

A few of the supporters of the Patent-Law ask whether Copyright does not rest upon the same basis as the exclusive right to inventions, and whether the new law will not be followed in its wake by the iguoring of literary property. But against a few similarities we have a material difference in substance.

If not all, yet most literary productions bear such a marked stamp of individuality, that intellectual property cannot be contested. However it may be, the different subjects have each their own laws, and both authors and publishers we quite leave out of the question.

OPINION OF THE LEADING JOURNAL OF HOLLAND, THE "ALGEMEEN HANDELSBLAD."

In the history of the Netherlands economy, the 22nd June, 1869, will be long remembered. Whatever shall be the decision of the First Chamber, the fact of the Law [Bill] having passed the Second Chamber by 48 yeas against 8 noes is a highly gratifying occurrence.

The chief feature in the opposition on the part of the Conservatives was the able speeches made by their leader, M. Heemskerk, in order to prove that invention confers a right of property. Without going into the merits of the case, we cannot help recording that, in the opinion of those that side with M. H., it must be a suggestive circumstance that, despite all the earnest pleading of the honourable gentleman, 48 out of 57 representatives, of men of the highest moral and intellectual standing, did vote for abolition, and still did not intend despoiling anybody of his own.

Invention is the effusion of thought, and just as thought cannot but be free, so invention must be the same.

We hope that the Netherlands will not long remain alone in this instance. At any rate, we may be proud of the overwhelming majority of men able to understand the real means of progress.

EXTRACT FROM AN OBLIGING PRIVATE LETTER.

Amsterdam, June 28, 1869.

. . . In some respects, the rather powerful arguments of the members who were favourable to the
continuance of the system of Patents—and who contended that an inventor, the same as an author, has a
right to protection of his individual mind-work—were
defeated, principally by the pretty general opinion of
the majority that it would be next to impossible to
adopt any new Law on Patents efficient to protect one
inventor without at the same time injuring not only
some brother-inventor, but also the public at large.

FROM THE "FRANKFORT JOURNAL," JULY 21.

The abolition of the Patent-Laws in the Netherlands will, it is
evident, not remain without influence on the decision which other
European States, and in particular those of Germany, will form in
regard to these laws. Of the two countries, one of which is in possession of the sources of the Rhine, and the other of its mouths—the
former the most industrious country in the world, never had a Patent-
Law; the latter, eminent for its foresight, dispenses with those
laws. Through this act are intensified the unsatisfactory circumstances which the existence of these laws produces, and the want of
confidence which is felt in their advantage to inventors and the
public. The number of their defenders is constantly declining.
People are daily more and more becoming convinced that these
laws belong to the same category as the Usury-Laws and the Corn-
Laws, and other similar excrescences introduced by bureaucracy, and
that they should be thrown into the lumber-room of laws which effect
the very reverse of what they profess to do. They stop progress.
Inventions of importance can always be made useful to the inventors
without Patent-Laws. Great inventors might perhaps be indemnified
by Government on behalf of a nation, but as for the innumerable
herd of small inventors who prosecute inventing as a trade, they
cause the consumer severe injury instead of benefiting him. Since
Patents for inventions in Germany do not extend to protection
against dealing in foreign articles patented here, we may consider
the abolition of Patents in the Netherlands a reason why Patent
monomaniacs should now ask themselves whether the cost is likely
hereafter to yield a good return.

PROCEEDINGS IN LIVERPOOL CHAMBER OF COMMERCE.

At a meeting of the Council on July, 1869, E. K. MUSPRATT, Esq., rose and spoke to the following effect :—

Mr. President,—I rise to call your attention to the late debate on the Patent-Law. This Chamber has frequently expressed its dissatisfaction with the working of the present law, and after the issue of the Report of the Royal Commission on the subject, endeavoured to bring about an inquiry into the policy of granting Patents for inventions. I cannot but think the time has now arrived for further action in this matter. The late debate upon the motion of Mr. Macfie has re-awakened public interest in the subject, and it is gratifying to note, both in the debate itself and the subsequent discussion in the newspapers, that the formerly very prevalent idea of a natural property in inventions has been tacitly abandoned. In some of the arguments used the old fallacy seems to lurk, for the *Pall Mall Gazette*, in a very able article, says : " It is plausible to say that if there were no property in invention every one would get the benefit of all inventions ; but this appears to us to have some analogy to the notion that if there were no property in land every one would get the benefit of the crops." There is, however, a very great difference, because an invention cannot possibly yield all the benefits which society can derive from it until it becomes public property ; whereas all experience proves that land, in order to yield the greatest results, must become and remain individual property. Let us discard, therefore, all comparison of property in invention with other property, and discuss the subject as one of expediency. Is it the interest of the community at large that Patents should be granted for inventions? I am not prepared to say whether or not inventors should be remunerated by the State; but, after mature consideration, I have come to the conclusion that, in the interests of the nation and of all engaged in industry, Patents for invention should be abolished. A Patent is a monopoly, a patentee a monopolist. When the Protectionist system was in vogue, Patents which were in full harmony with that system could be justified; but in these days of Free-trade all monopolies which act in restraint of trade should be abolished. Some of the arguments used in support of the system of Protection to inventors by granting to them a monopoly of manufacture are, to my mind, very similar to those used in former days in support of other monopolies. Before the repeal of the Navigation Laws, it was said that without them our marine would be destroyed, and no more ships would be built, because there would be no inducement to build them. Without Patents, say the defenders of the system, there will be no inventions, because there will be no special inducement to make them. We maintain, however, that under a freer system invention would be stimulated, and not restrained. As was well pointed out by Sir R. Palmer in his able speech, "Bounties and premiums might be adapted to a rude state of the arts and an early stage in the progress of commerce ; but when a nation had reached so high a degree of progress in all ingenious arts and discoveries, and in trade and commerce, as we had, he thought that in this department, as well as in others, the system of bounties and premiums was much more likely to be mischievous than useful." He then very clearly showed how the Patent system worked ; how, in the place of securing the reward to great and meritorious inventions, it gave a monopoly to the first claimer of those minor improvements which he classed as unmeritorious Patents, and which improvements would necessarily be made in the ordinary progress of manufacture. As an example of this, I may mention the manufacture of artificial manures. The modern history of manures dates from the publication of Liebig's book in 1840, in which the conversion of insoluble into soluble phosphate of lime is recommended. This suggestion has been perhaps more fruitful in results than any other of modern times, and forms the basis of the enormous manufacture of super-phosphate and other artificial manures. It was patented in 1842, not by Liebig, but by Mr. Lawes ; and since that period various improvements in the manufacture have been patented, but the real inventor has never been rewarded. There can be no doubt that without a system of Patents all of the subsequent minor improvements would have been made in the ordinary course of trade ; and one of the main objects of the Patent-Law, to secure a reward to the inventor, has, in this instance, as in many others, failed of accomplishment. Then, on the other hand, all these minor improvements, being patented, stand in the way of further progress, and if the manufacturer wishes to adopt a new process, or to improve his manufacture, he must do it at the peril of litigation with some unknown person, who at some time or other has thought fit to claim for himself a monopoly. No matter whether his claim be good or bad, it stands in the way of improvement until it is either disclaimed by the patentee himself or pronounced invalid in a court of law. As an example of how, under the present system, a patentee may create a virtual monopoly and embarrass manufacturers even when his claims are, according to his own showing, to a very great extent invalid, permit me to draw your attention to a Patent, No. 12,867, A.D. 1849, for compressing peat for fuel, making gas, &c., and with which I unfortunately became acquainted, because the patentee, under another Patent (connected, however, with the first), endeavoured to make my firm pay him for the use of a substance in the manufacture of sulphuric acid. Now, the patentee, Mr. F. C. Hills, finding, I presume, that in its first state his Patent was invalid, filed what is technically termed a disclaimer, in 1853 ; and on comparing the original specification, which is very long and consists of about 230 lines, I find at least one-half is disclaimed. This Patent secured to Mr. Hills the monopoly of the purification of gas by means of oxide of iron ; and although, owing to the exertion of the Liverpool Gas Company, he failed to have it renewed at the expiration of fourteen years, by a subsequent Patent for the use of the said oxide (after it has been used in the purification of gas) in the manufacture of sulphuric acid, he continues virtually to enjoy that monopoly, and to prevent chemical manufacturers having access to what, under certain circumstances, may be a cheap source of sulphur. And this I would wish you to bear in mind, although the second Patent is undoubtedly invalid. It would detain you too long were I to enter into full detail on the subject, but I may mention that our firm used some 2,000 or 3,000 tons of this gas refuse from the Liverpool Gas Works, when pyrites was high in price ; and it was only because of the annoyance and waste of time which a law-suit would have cost that we relinquished its use in our manufacture when the price of pyrites fell. But this case is but a sample, and I have no doubt every manufacturer has experienced similar loss and inconvenience from the action of the Patent-Law. When we consider that there are at the present moment 11,369 Patents in force, most of them as invalid as that to which I have referred, and acting as a restriction on manufacturers, we may form some idea of what the community at large has to pay for the luxury of a Patent-Law. But it may be said these objections are due to the imperfections and mal-administration of the Patent-Law. I would refer you, then, to the Report of the Royal Commission, which, in conclusion, says that "these inconveniences are, in their belief, inherent in the nature of a Patent-Law, and must be considered as the price which the public consents to pay for the existence of such a law." There is, however, another aspect of the question which must not be lost sight of. The Lower House of the States-General of Holland has, by a large majority, voted the abolition of Patents.   In Switzerland they don't exist ; and in Prussia, owing to a very strict preliminary examination, faithfully carried out, they are very few in number. We in this country have to compete with the manufacturers of these countries ; and is it fair, I would ask, that we should be thus weighted in the race ?   I beg to move that a petition be prepared for presentation to the House of Commons, praying for the appointment of a Committee to inquire into the policy of granting Patents for invention.

(The motion was unanimously adopted.)

CORRESPONDENCE.

The subjoined letters, with which I am favoured, will be read with interest and advantage :—

FROM SIR WILLIAM ARMSTRONG, C.B.

As to the cost of the system to the public, I don't see how it could be calculated, for it consists not merely of the licence fees, but also of the loss resulting from the stamping out of competition, which would cheapen production and, in most cases, lead to improvement. My great objection to our indiscriminate Patent system is, that it is scarcely possible to strike out in any new direction without coming in contact with Patents for schemes so crudely developed as to receive little or no acceptance from the public, but which, nevertheless, block the road to really practical improvement.

Nothing, I think, can be more monstrous than that so grave a matter as a monopoly should be granted to any person for anything without inquiry either as to private merit or public policy—in fact, merely for the asking and the paying. Amongst other evils of this indiscriminate system is that the majority of Patents granted are bad, and yet such is the dread of litigation, that people submit to a Patent they know to be bad rather than involve themselves in the trouble and expense of resisting it. So that a bad Patent, in general, answers just as well as a good one.

One of the most common arguments in favour of Patents is, that they are necessary to protect the poor inventor, but it is manufacturers and capitalists, and not working men, who make great profits by Patents, and that, too, in a degree which has no reference either to the merit of the inventor or the importance of the invention. One rarely hears of a working man making a good thing of a Patent. If he hits upon a good idea he has seldom the means of developing it to a marketable form, and he generally sells it for a trifle to a capitalist, who brings it to maturity and profits by it. He could sell his idea just as well without any Patent-Law.

May 13, 1869.

FROM ANOTHER HIGH PRACTICAL AUTHORITY, LIKEWISE A NOTABLE INVENTOR.

I would not for one moment deny that instances could be named in which the absence of a Patent-Law might have proved a hardship to a real inventor, but I feel quite satisfied in my own mind that whatever may hitherto have been the case, the time has now fully arrived when infinitely less injustice would, upon the whole, be occasioned by the absence of all Patent-Laws than by the best Patent-Law that could be devised. All Patents for inventions must be considered as founded upon expediency and not upon the idea of any inherent right which the inventor possesses beyond the right of using his invention, or keeping the secret of it to himself. A community may consider it to their advantage to protect inventions by means of Patent-Laws, but a man can have no abstract or natural right to the exclusive benefits of his invention, for such an idea would imply that nobody else could have produced it. The question is, therefore, entirely one of expediency, but not one of right. Again, a very common argument used in support of a Patent-Law is that an inventor is as much entitled to an exclusive right to his invention as an author is to the produce of his pen, but there is really very little resemblance between the two cases, and I believe it would be very inexpedient to utterly abolish Copyright. "Paradise Lost" would never have been written but for Milton; but with the utmost respect for Bell, Fulton, and Stephenson, who would pretend to believe that without them we should still have to be dependent upon the wind for our movements at sea, and the common road ashore? A man who writes a book does not interfere with me in the slightest degree, but the inventor, or more probably the so-called inventor, backed by the Patent-Law, may most unjustly involve me in much trouble and expense. I should be very glad to see a good round sum set apart by Government for the purpose of being awarded to real inventors by competent and impartial authority. Then the poor inventor might have some chance. You will certainly, in my opinion, have done a good turn to this country if you can only get every vestige of Patent-Law swept from the statute-book, and with my best wishes for the success of your motion, I am, &c.

FROM ANDREW JOHNSTON, ESQ., M.P.

MY DEAR SIR,   7th July, 1869.

I am glad to hear that you intend printing the results of your inquiries as to the operation of the Patent-Laws, as the conclusions at which you have arrived tally entirely with my own experience as a manufacturer.

I had no opportunity of speaking in the recent debate on your motion, and will therefore put down one or two points which have specially presented themselves to my attention.

I am not biased, I believe, by self-interest, as the business with which I am connected has profited to a considerable extent by the purchase of patented inventions ; but it is my firm conviction that the commonwealth would benefit by the refusal of the State in future to grant Patents.

Nothing can be more superficial than the objection that the intelligent working man benefits by the present system. For one such who really benefits by his invention, ten sell theirs for the merest fraction of its value ; ten others who may get a fair price are led, by the possession of the capital sum so obtained, to give up regular employment, and generally " muddle away " all the money in seeking to " invent " afresh, while the remaining seventy-nine reap nothing by their invention but disappointment, privation, and misery.

Abolish Patents, and these men would stick to regular work. They would choose the service of employers who had a name for liberally rewarding their workmen for ingenious and profitable inventions, and also for the insight necessary to decide whether inventions were so or not. Employers would vie with one another in getting such a name, and the whole tone and level of the artisans would be perceptibly raised, while useful invention would proceed faster than at present, because the certainty of moderate rewards would stimulate men more than the remote chance of large ones.

No doubt you want facts rather than opinions. I can testify to this much as to another branch of the subject: when there is an infringement of a Patent, or supposed infringement, and an appeal to the law is in prospect, it never occurs to either party to consider whether the Patent-rights in question are good, bad, or indifferent. It is too well known that the longest purse will win, and that whichever party is prepared to spend most money will defeat and probably ruin the other.

Make any use you like of these notes.

Yours, very truly,

ANDREW JOHNSTON.

R. A. Macfie, Esq., M.P.

ON THE DISTINCTION BETWEEN COPYRIGHT AND PATENT-RIGHT.

The following is reproduced under a conviction formed by hearing, in the recent debate, so much stress laid on the resemblance of Patent-right to Copyright, that superficial views are very generally held and require to be met :—

Extract from " The Patent Question under Free-Trade," 1863.

We may now, in order to clear away what has been to some a stumbling-block—the argument from analogy founded on the case of literary property—notice certain distinctions between the subjects respectively of Patent-right and Copyright. Those things that belong to the province of Patent-right are in their nature capable of being independently discovered or originated, in the same identical form, by a plurality of persons. Of this character are the principles of mechanism, processes of manufacture, and forms or methods accordant thereto. Such, indeed, are, as a rule, actually discovered or invented by several persons, and this very often almost simultaneously. It is otherwise with things that belong to the province of Copyright— literary and artistic combinations, books, pictures, musical compositions, involving any degree of elaboration. Such, at no interval of time, have ever been produced by even one other person except a copyist.

This ground for differential treatment is connected with others. In particular, the literary or artistic compositions of any person are perfectly distinguishable from all those of every other. Hence the Copyright privilege is conceded in the absolute certainty that the grantee is their true and only originator, or first producer or creator. No second person can come forward, after the Copyright privilege is secured to an author or artist, and allege that the poem or picture he composed also. To infringe Copyright means to slavishly or meanly copy the work of another. To constitute infringement it is not sufficient that the second person's book has the same subject and the same purpose in view, and is written in the same spirit as the first; the "matter" must be the same, and in the same form. And so with pictures, the subjects may be the same; the ideas may show great correspondence. *Exactness* of "matter" and of arrangement is everything. Patent-right, on the contrary, may be infringed where there is no such exactness, and no copying whatever, but complete originality. Disregarding form, it forbids the embodiment and use of *ideas*, even of ideas entirely one's own.

We have thus the inconsistency, or paradox, that the exclusive privileges which have for their province only material objects—which engage only our bodily frame and those senses merely that have their exercise on matter apart from mind (and this is all that patentable inventions do)—carry prohibition into the region of ideas; while those other exclusive privileges, in whose province matter serves only as a vehicle or excitant of things immaterial—conceptions, memories, tastes, emotions—and as an instrument to set the mind a-working and affect the higher senses and faculties—make no such incursions, keeping entirely clear of interference with any man's practical use of ideas.

Literary and artistic Copyright has for its province visible, tangible works, intended only for the eye or the ear, or inner man through these senses—objects to be looked upon, listened to, thought of; not things to be worked with or employed, nor things consumable, nor mere modes of doing a thing, like the subjects of Patent-right. It has no regard to processes, operations, implements. Therefore, unlike Patent-right, it interferes not with manufacturers, artisans, miners, farmers, shipping. Its sphere is in finished productions, works of art in their completed state — objects that are permanent and unmistakable. Infringements, therefore, are necessarily both manifest and of set purpose, whereas infringements of Patent-right are often doubtful, even when the subjects or results can be exhibited, and when the facts of the case are assented to by all parties; and if it is a question of processes, its infringements are often undetectable after the fleeting moment during which they are alleged to have taken place. Further, as before said, contraventions of Patent-right may be, and not unfrequently are, done unconsciously or unwittingly.

MODIFICATIONS OF THE PATENT SYSTEM.

The following paper on Patent Monopolies is reproduced from the *Liverpool Courier*, partly for the sake of presenting a past phase of opinion with respect to the means of mitigating the injurious influence of the exclusive privilege contained in Patents :—

At the Social Science Congress at Sheffield, in 1865, Mr. Macfie read a paper on the following subject : "Long Restrictions on the Use of Inventions, and Obligation to make heavy Payments to Patentees, incompatible with free and fair trade." He said :—

That the inventor has a right of use or property in his invention we do not dispute ; what we dispute is his *exclusive* right. To give one inventor such a right is to subvert the principle by denying the right of other inventors, who may be as original, and have worked as hard, and spent as much, but who, owing to a desire to perfect their achievement a little more, or because they live in the provinces,—a day's journey further off,—come some hours behind, and so are only second or third applicants for the coveted privilege. The State ought not, and cannot in strict justice, give a right of exclusive property ; that is, power to meddle with others, and forbid them to use their valuable knowledge ; except in cases where *common* use and enjoyment would diminish public wealth or harm a previous possessor. If the land of England were constituted common property, its productive value would be lessened, and the present possessors would be harmed ; therefore, it legitimately is property. Knowledge may be, with the greatest benefits to mankind, common. God has drawn this distinction between things material or measurable (in which classification I include labour), and things mental : between land, ploughs, and the like, and the art or knowledge how to manage or make them,—that the one cannot be appropriated, and the other cannot be unappropriated, without loss to our race. *En passant*, do we conform to the spirit this constitution of nature may be held to commend to man ?

I will not detain you by controverting the arguments of those plansible reasoners who class Patent-right with Copyright. Both, indeed, are creations of enacting law. But there is this obvious and broad dis-

tinction between them : that to grant exclusive privileges to an author
interferes with nobody else's compositions, whereas to grant them to an
inventor continually conflicts with what others have done and are doing.
Nor shall we spend time in discussing the *merits* of inventors. These, we
allow, may be great, and deserve public acknowledgment. What ought
rather to be discussed is the *kind* of acknowledgment that is most
expedient. At present a very primitive mode of rewarding inventors
is alone the rule—monopoly. In old times, when political economy, like
the other sciences, was unknown, it was the easy, but at the same time
costly, way of endowing a court favourite to grant him an exclusive
right to sell or make some commodity. When, in the beginning of the
seventeenth century, all other monopolies were prohibited by law, those
in favour of introducers of *new manufactures* were spared. This exception has been found or made so expansible, that it is ruled to extend
to minute processes or instruments in existing trades, so that what was
intended to promote manufactures is now too frequently a hindrance.
Thus the avowed object of the exception, public good, is on the whole
counteracted. What we maintain is, that, admitting the monopoly attains
to some extent that object, the disadvantages preponderate over the
advantages. We connect this charge with another which is still more
condemnatory, viz., that these advantages, limited as they are, are
obtained by compromise of sound principle and by positive acts of
unfairness, such as cannot be alleged against our view of the case, which
is, that these exclusive privileges should be abolished.

The title of this paper says almost all I care to occupy your valuable
time with. It speaks of *restrictions* in the use of inventions. Patents
impose restrictions, nay, prohibitions. They give an absolute monopoly. Nobody but a patentee has a right to use a patented invention.
It speaks of *long* restrictions. Patents impose their restrictions,
or rather prohibitions, for the long period of fourteen years, with occasional prolongations of the term. To be denied the use of an invention for such a length of time is, now-a-days (whatever it may have
been of yore), much like being denied it altogether. The title speaks
of *payments* to patentees. These are made in all cases where the
patentee allows others to use his invention. It speaks of *heavy* payments, because he has the right to make them heavy, and he, in practice,
makes them as heavy as he can. It speaks of an *obligation*, and
rightly, because a manufacturer who uses a patented invention is under
the necessity to pay whatever the patentee demands or a jury awards,
and competition may frequently compel him to use it, under penalty of
losing his profits of trade, or his trade itself. It speaks of the payees
as *patentees*, not as inventors ; because in many cases (how large a pro-

portion I cannot say) the rights are conferred on mere importers or appropriators of other people's inventions. The title further speaks of *free-trade*. This freedom, which is something different from mere *libre échange*, ought to extend to manufacturing and all kind of labour, as well as to commerce, for, according to the great lexicographer, trade is "employment, whether *manual* or mercantile." Of course it does not so extend when labour is not free, but restricted and burdened. And it speaks of *fair* trade—fairness is about as important as freedom. Will anybody say it is fair to tax one manufacturer and let another go free? Yet this is what Patents do. Those whom the patentee favours, or fears, or forgets, he does not tax, or taxes lightly, while on others he lays a heavy hand. But, worst of all, under the open competition to which the British manufacturer is now exposed with all the world, he often has to pay heavy Patent fees—often four, and sometimes, as I know, five, and even six, figures deep—while his foreign rivals wholly escape. How can any statesman, or member of a Chamber of Commerce, defend or palliate such gross and grievous inequalities? Unfortunately, the start that the United Kingdom has got in manufactures and shipping has done much to blind us, and keep us from seeing the strides that neighbouring nations are making, and has emboldened our legislators and financiers to make treaties, in which we consent, as a nation, to run the race of manufacturing industry weighted. The wise will call this *im*policy, perhaps *conceit*. Let us not deceive ourselves ; peculiar burdens on British traders are incompatible with free-trade ; more, and worse, they are flagrant inconsistencies, subversive of our character for good sense, incompatible with reasonable ground for expecting manufacturing prosperity. The cry and principle so popular this day is belied when there is not a fair field, and there is the opposite of favour. The cause of all these evils and wrongs is the sticking to the exploded and illogical system of monopoly, as if that were the best, instead of being, as we believe, the very worst form in which acknowledgment can be made. We say enough in condemnation when we characterise it as *despotic*, inasmuch as it hands over British manufacturers, absolutely and without appeal, to the exactions or prohibitions of patentees and assignees of Patents; as *erratic*, inasmuch as in one case it occasions not gain but loss to the favourite, in another it ·overpowers with enormous profit, frequently the ill-luck falling to the most ingenious, and the extravagant remuneration to men of slender claims ; as *retarding*, inasmuch as it often causes great delay in the introducing of inventions into use; as *preposterous*, inasmuch as it hinders the perfecting of new inventions by preventing the combination of the further improvements that others than the patentee devise or might devise; as *illogical*, in this among other respects, that through the far larger share which capitalists or purchasers of Patents often get beyond the pittance that may or may not reach the poor inventor, its action is but indirect and small compared with its cost as a means of rewarding and stimulating inventors; as *inquisitorial*, for it justifies the hiring of informers to report who and where are infringers; as *unnatural*, for it takes away a person's attention from his own legitimate business, and divides it with the businesses of other people whom he must watch or teach; as *cruel*, for the unhappy patentee is continually liable to be engaged in costly, often ruinous law pleas, far away from home, in order to establish the validity of his Patent and to prevent infringements; as *extravagant*, because it gives patentees, or rather costs the public (for it is but a small proportion of the burden imposed that is the nett profit of the patentee) much more than a better system would. It is also *partial*, as has been stated, for its incidence is not equal on all British manufacturers, and it inflicts on them the hardship of peculiar burdens not borne by rivals abroad; and in this respect, as in the rest, it is *irremediable*, for equal treatment is morally impossible at home and abroad. It is quite out of the question to expect rectifying amendment in this particular, seeing only some States grant Patents at all. Among those which do, some grant sparingly or only to their own inhabitants; and to take Patents in all places where they are granted would involve the command and risking of so very much capital that few indeed, if ever any, would embrace the whole field; and, if perchance they did, the labour of superintending a business so vast, in languages so diverse and many, would require superhuman powers. The right to demand "compulsory licences" as a mitigation was suggested at the Liverpool Congress. They would be an improvement, and should be practicable, seeing something of that nature exists elsewhere, although the Royal Commission has reported against the plan. But it would be a serious mistake to anticipate from their adoption as a reform any very important relief. I hope it is possible to propose some substitute which will not be liable to these reproaches, one which will give rewards having proportion to merit, which will give them within a reasonable period, which will entail little trouble or distraction on the nation's assumed protégé, the inventor; one which, being regulated by fixed principles and controlled by officers who will sift the wheat from the chaff, will satisfy the yearnings after awards having some proportion to merit, which now are disregarded; and which, above all, will elevate the inventor from what you will surely allow me to call his present equivocal position—that involves little or no honour, and too generally something approaching the very reverse—to a position that implies merit and gives status. I do not speak of mere honours, whether in the form of certificates or medals, or trifles, although all of these I recommend. What I have submitted already to the association, in a paper to be found in the Edinburgh volume, I repeat as still in my opinion practicable and expedient—viz., to grant national rewards in money. I would allow these to be claimed immediately after inventions are specified. It would be the duty of a competent board, after due consultation and inquiries, to award each a fair sum, within certain limits, such as prudence, combined with liberality, would prescribe for their regulation. Or, the patentee might prefer postponement of the adjudication for three years. This should be allowed, or even encouraged, in order that time may be gained for practical expression of the benefit conferred by actual use of the invention. In that case, the reward should be ampler.

This system, I am persuaded, would be found in practice much less expensive to the nation than the present system. So slight are the merits of the majority of Patents that the State would have comparatively little to pay; but the relief to manufacturers and the gain to commerce would be very great; for, however unprofitable a Patent is, it may be very effectual as a restraint and a burden. Such a system would sweep away every hindrance to the immediate enjoyment by every one of every invention, and to the combining with it every cognate improvement; a great emancipation and stimulus would at once be felt to operate. If other nations adhere to the antiquated Patent system which they have borrowed from us, we would be happily invested, in competition with them, with the immense advantage which the Swiss, for instance, enjoy over their rivals, that of being free from Patents, yet knowing the inventions of all other nations. But they would not adhere; on the contrary, they would either totally free themselves from the encumbrance, and leave us to pay the rewards, or (and this is more probable and would be more honourable) they would join in international arrangements, in virtue of which, every State contributing a little, inventors would receive large emolument, and trades would rejoice with them in the advent of an invention millennium, in the bliss of which workmen would share,—on whose interests, by preventing them from benefiting by use of the knowledge they acquire, Patents, I apprehend, act unfavourably.

I am aware that to persuade Government and Parliament to adopt national grants would involve indefinite, perhaps long, postponement of the happy year of release. Therefore I repeat another proposition, also already submitted to you. It is this : To grant Patents much as heretofore (not resisting any reformation that may appear expedient); but to enact that, on the demand of any manufacturer, after three years of monopoly, any invention may be valued—not, of course, on the basis of the return which it might bring—but on that of its originality, the cost incurred in working it out, its advantage, &c., whereupon it shall be lawful for a Patent Board to extinguish the grant in any of the following circumstances : 1. If the patentee's books (which he should be obliged to keep in all cases where his fees from any individual exceed £100 per annum) show that he has already received in fees the valuation price. 2. If manufacturers and others interested unitedly pay as much as will make the price up. 3. If the State pay the remainder of the price, purchasing the invention for the nation. And I would include a condition that any one may obtain exemption for himself or his firm, by paying, say, a tenth of the price.

And now, a kind word to the amphibious class of persons whom we style inventors (we are most of us inventors, more or less, in some form or other). Try to meet the legitimate demands of manufacturers ; act in consonance with the spirit of the age and the requirements of the time ; and remember how, by resisting conciliatory propositions, the great agricultural, sugar-producing, and shipowning interests had to succumb to enlightened doctrines, and accept a settlement far less accordant with their pretensions. Manufacturers (with whom, as in like manner liable to be affected, I class miners, farmers, shipowners, &c.) who employ inventions in their businesses on a right system, ought not to regard the patentee, still less the inventor, as an intruder and an obstacle in his path. Yet that they in general do so regard these reputed benefactors and auxiliaries is, I fear, too true. It is the fault of the system. Let us be well disposed to a better, in which the interests and feelings of both sides—for opposite sides they appear to be —shall harmonise. Either of the plans I sketch would, partially at least, bring them into unison. The only objection that I anticipate is that the amount to be received will not reach the often, it must be admitted, extremely high ideas of inventors. In so far as this objection is well founded, in consequence of the rare merit of any particular invention—a case that does not arise every year—it can be met by special votes, which I would be far from excluding.

It may be regretted that the investigations of the recent Royal Commission to inquire into this subject (most significant against the present system is their report) were not more extensive and radical. This arose from the purposely defective terms of appointment. The Liverpool Chamber of Commerce has consequently asked Government, through the Board of Trade (that department calculated to be so very useful, but somehow in these days jostled aside, and scarcely seen or heard of in deeds), to appoint a fresh commission which shall inquire into the *policy* of Patents. This request has had the honour of public endorsement (either in that form or in the form of a Parliamentary Committee) by no less an authority than the Right Hon. Chairman of the Commission, who also stated to the House the remarkable and most encouraging fact, that doubts like his own had sprung up in the mind of that eminent lawyer, Sir Hugh Cairns, the very member who, almost in opposition to the late Mr. Ricardo, a decided opponent of the monopoly, moved the address to the Crown for the Commission. On the other side of the Speaker's chair we have law officers of the Crown, if I mistake not, impressed with the same dislike, and among the Radicals we know that equally opposed were Mr. Bright and the late pure and noble patriot Mr. Cobden. It is within my own observation that candid inquirers, preimpressed though they may be in favour of inventors' claims and monopolies, reach the same conclusion. As to the Continent, M. Chevalier, Swiss statesmen officially consulted, and the German Congress of Political Economists, have strongly declared that they are utterly opposed. The Social Science Association can, and I hope will, as in the past so in the future, lend important aid to the cause. Nobody is better fitted to reconcile those interests that unnecessarily conflict, and to emancipate productive industry from trammels so hard to bear, while also promoting invention.

R

The reader is also referred to the following lapsed

Scheme submitted to the International Association for the Progress of the Social Sciences at Brussels in 1863.

1. The principal States of Europe and America, with their colonies, to unite and form a Patent Union.

2. Every capital to have a State Patent-office, in correspondence with the offices in the other capitals.

3. Every invention patented in one of these offices to be protected in all the associated States.

4. Each State's Patent-office to receive copies of Patent specifications lodged in the Patent-office of every other State, and to translate and publish within its own territories.

5. The Patent to confer exclusive privileges for three years.

6. With these privileges is conjoined the right of granting licences.

7. An agent or assignee, fully empowered to negotiate for the patentee, must reside in each State.

8. Commissioners shall appraise each invention at the end of the second or third year (or later, if deemed advisable).

9. In estimating the value, the Commissioners shall be entitled to claim the advice of practical men, and may take into view all circumstances affecting value—such as the originality of the invention, and its importance; the probability of its being soon made by another; the expense and hazard of preliminary experiments and trials; the benefit it is calculated to confer ; the gain which use and licences during the three years will bring the patentee.

10. If the patentee resign his monopoly before its term expires, this concession to the public shall be regarded in the price.

11. The Commissioners shall adjudicate in what proportions each State shall pay the price fixed, on the basis of population, revenue, or commerce.

12. They may recommend a further grant, as an *honorarium*, in special instances of singular merit.

13. Their valuation and grants must be framed on the basis of a total yearly expenditure on inventions of not more than one million pounds sterling at the utmost, from all countries of the union, of which sum, however, no one country can be called upon for more than £100,000 in one year, nor more than £1,000 for one invention.

14. The Commissioners shall be entitled to recommend for honorary medals, ribbons, or certificates, real inventors of strong claims, especially such as voluntarily shorten, or never exercise, the exclusive use of important inventions.

OPINIONS OF THE PRESS ON THE DEBATE IN PARLIAMENT ON THE PATENT QUESTION.

Leading Article from the " Times," May 29, 1869.

Public attention has for some little time been withdrawn from the consideration of the Patent-Laws; but, if we may judge from the discussion upon the subject in the House of Commons last night, the day is at hand when this branch of our legislation will be wiped out of the statute-book. It is impossible to withstand the weight of authority and reason advanced yesterday. It was all on one side. Mr. Macfie, the newly-elected member for Leith, introduced the subject, and, incited apparently by injuries he had himself suffered through the operation of the Patent-Laws, argued very vigorously against them on theoretical and practical grounds. He was not left unsupported. Sir Roundell Palmer, who, had he consulted his private interest, would certainly have been among the first to uphold a system productive of such immense pecuniary benefits to the practitioners in the courts, seconded Mr. Macfie's motion for the unconditional abolition of the Patent-Laws in a speech of the closest reasoning, supported by a vast array of facts which had come within his own personal experience. He was followed by Lord Stanley, who confessed that, against all his early prepossessions, he had been convinced, when acting as Chairman of the Patent Commission, that the abolition of the Patent-Laws was demanded on grounds of justice and of sound policy. Two of the foremost representatives of law and of statesmanship thus enforced the reform demanded by Mr. Macfie as a spokesman for manufacturers. It is true that others followed who opposed, or attempted to oppose, the arguments of Sir Roundell Palmer and Lord Stanley. This was inevitable. Men who have not looked into the question are in the same position as Lord Stanley says he himself was when he first began to consider it. They are under the influence of impressions they have never thought of questioning, and are biased by supposed analogies, drawn from cognate subjects, the unsoundness of which they have not investigated. Hence they protest, not without vehemence, against an amendment of the law which is in conflict with their own habits of thought, but they do not reason upon it. Analyse the speeches delivered last night by Mr. Howard, Mr. Mundella, and, we must add, the Attorney-General, and the residuum of argument contained in them will be found to be very small indeed. They are all satisfied the Patent-Laws have been useful to the nation, as people were once satisfied that the Corn-law was the secret of our greatness. They insisted that the abolition of the Patent-Laws would be a blow to our national pre-eminence, just as their predecessors agreed in predicting not so long ago that with the abolition of the Corn-laws Old England would dwindle and decay.

The first point to be borne in mind with reference to the Patent-Laws is, that if we retain them at all they must be retained in their present form. The amendments admissible in their machinery are not important, and the recommendations of the Royal Commission some years ago were so slight that it has never been thought necessary to carry them into effect. What is the scheme of the Patent-Laws A man discovers, or believes he discovers, a new process of accomplishing some useful result. He registers his supposed invention, and acquires a provisional right to its exclusive use for a definite number of years. After a time he finds some other person using his invention, and applies to the courts of law to prohibit him. The alleged infringer of the Patent says that the assumed discovery was no discovery at all, or that it was of no public benefit, or that he is not making use of it, and the questions arising on these issues are then tried. This is a condensed statement of the whole working of the law as it stands. No substitute for it can be recommended that will bear examination. It is sometimes said that an inventor should be required to prove the originality and utility of his invention at the time he makes his application to be registered. But who could examine such a claim? A court of law may, after much trouble and caution, declare that a claimant is entitled to a piece of land, because the claimant, by exercising rights of ownership over it, gives notice in a very palpable way to all other claimants of the property, though even then the court takes extreme pains that the rights of absent or infant persons may not be abridged. But, when a man claims an invention, by what possible process could notice of his claim be brought home to every man in the kingdom? Whoever will consider the matter will be forced to the conclusion that all the State can do is to tell an applicant that he shall be protected in the use of his invention provided he shall be able, whenever occasion arises, to establish its originality and utility against any one who may arise to contest them. The same considerations which negative the suggestion that a claimant could receive an indefeasible title, also negative the proposal that the claimant-should be compensated by a money grant at the outset. If the originality of his claim cannot be proved, payment for it cannot be made, even if there existed at that incipient stage any means of determining its value.

The present system of Patents must be retained if Patents are to be preserved, and the evils of the system flow directly from it. It is impossible to diminish appreciably the litigation attendant on Patents. Sir Roundell Palmer referred to the paraffin oil case, which occupied the Court of Chancery fifteen days. Nor could this be avoided, for the novelty of the process of distilling paraffin was the point contested, and to decide this it was necessary to examine the exact stage of discovery to which a dozen different investigators had advanced, all of whom were trying simultaneously, but independently of each other, to distil paraffin oil so as to make it a commercial product. The expense and uncertainty of Patent litigation being unavoidable, the cardinal defect of the system, that the reward it offers hardly ever goes to the right man, follows. The inventor is at one end of the scale; the transferee or licensee of the Patent is at the other, and while the latter reaps enormous gains, the inventor often has the reflection that it was he who made the discovery for his sole reward. The second great fault of the system of the Patent-Laws is an effect equally inseparable from it. These laws constantly inflict the most grievous injustice on innocent persons. Mechanical and chemical discoveries are not made by unconnected jumps. The history of science and of invention is one of gradual progress. A hundred different persons are pursuing their investigations on the same subject independently of each other, and are all nearing a particular goal, when some one man reaches it a few days before the others. The law which gives him a monopoly denies to the rest the fruit of their exertions. It is needless to refer to the numberless instances in which inventions have been discovered so nearly simultaneously that the real inventor cannot be ascertained; and it is impossible to deny that to give a monopoly to the man who is the most prompt to register his claim often inflicts a grievous wrong on the investigators who accomplish the same results in perfect independence of him. So far we have spoken only of primary discoveries. The secondary Patents, as they may be called, were rightly denominated by Sir Roundell Palmer unmitigated evils, and, according to the same high authority, they exceed in number Patents of importance in the ratio of a hundred to one. A person suggests some small improvement in the course of an elaborate manufacture, and takes out a Patent for it. Henceforth he blocks the whole trade. He cannot be got rid of, and it is not easy to deal with him. He is quite conscious of the obstacle he creates, and in the end he is probably bought off by some great manufacturer in the line of business affected by the discovery, who, by accumulating in his hands the inventions, good and bad, connected with his occupation, monopolises that particular branch of trade throughout the country.

The strength of the existing Patent-Laws lies in the vague belief of those who have not considered the subject that it would be unjust to deprive a man of the benefit of his discoveries. Those who are impressed with this elementary notion may be asked to reconcile it with the undeniable fact that the Patent-Laws do deprive, in the way we have shown, many men of the benefit of their discoveries ; but a little reflection will convince them that their argument rests on a pure assumption. No man would be deprived of the benefit of his discovery because he did not receive a monopoly of its use. His own discovery would be his own discovery still. As long as he is allowed to employ his own inventions in any way he thinks proper he cannot be said to suffer any deprivation of a right. The truth is, that the Patent-Laws are a voluntary addition to our legislation based upon no such obligation as underlies the ordinary laws of property ; and they must be justified, if they can be justified at all, as gratuitous creations of the Legislature, by proof that they produce some national benefit. It is from this point of view that we see the difference between the laws of Copyright and of Patents. They agree in being added on to what may be called the body of natural law, but the reasons in support of each are not the same, and the objections which apply to the law of Patents do not apply to the law of Copyright. The monopoly granted to an author does injustice to no one. The monopolies granted to patentees do injustice to many. Patents are creations of positive law, and must be judged accordingly. The Attorney-General approves them because they are designed to multiply inventions, although he admits that the multiplication of Patents is a serious evil. A sounder judgment will condemn them because of the evils necessarily attendant upon them ; and we have no fear of what would happen to the course of invention or the progress of the country if they were abolished, and the inventor allowed to make such use of his invention as he may be advised. Inventions co-exist with Patents, but the experience of Switzerland is sufficient to show that they would abound if Patents did not exist, and the decline of commercial greatness with which Mr. Howard threatens us should Patents be abolished may be treated like so many other prophecies of evil which have been happily neglected and remain unfulfilled.

Leading Article from the "Economist," June 5, 1869.

It is probable enough that the Patent-Laws will be abolished ere long, though the full force of the real objections to them was perhaps not brought out in the debate last week on Mr. Macfie's motion for their abolition. Sir Roundell Palmer was too metaphysical. The supposed distinction between the copyright of a book and a Patent— that no two men will hit upon the same composition even in substance, while they will hit upon the same idea for an invention—does not prove anything. If a case of general utility could be made out, the abstract justice of giving a man the monopoly of an idea, should he be the first to come upon it, would not be much considered. Lord Stanley, who avoided this mistake, dwelt too much upon such minor points as the practical failure of the law to secure a reward to the inventor and the frequent disproportion between the reward and the service rendered, which are points of *no* consequence so long as the public is generally a gainer by the law. Lord Stanley, however, touched upon the true reason when he referred to the injury of third parties, which the present law occasions, by reason of Patents being granted to only one out of half-a-dozen persons who come upon the same inventions, or to one of a series of inventors who improve upon each other's work, and by reason also of the general interference with manufacturing. What we should have liked to see fully stated was the peculiarity of the present circumstances of the country in which these things are true. The statements in fact amount to this—that there is a large number of inventions which Patents are not required to encourage ; that these are made as ordinary incidents of business ; that invention, improvement of mechanical and chemical processes, is itself a part of a manufacturing business ; and that in this way the granting of Patents only impedes manufacturers to whom inventions would naturally come. The full force of these facts cannot be felt unless we recognise that a change in the character of invention has taken place. The Patent-Laws were intended to apply to different manufacturing circumstances from those which now exist, and were based upon different notions about invention; the objection to them is that they either are, or are becoming, out of date. A little consideration will show how true this is.

Let us look first at the notions still customary about inventors and inventions which are derived from past circumstances. The popular idea of an inventor is of a man who makes an immense addition to the real wealth of the world—who invents the steam engine, or the spinning jenny, or the Jacquard loom, or the hot blast—almost revolutionising the material powers of mankind. The idea associated with his work is in any case that of great novelty in means coupled with great accomplished results. Now there are various reasons why these should not be the .haracteristics of modern inventors and inventions, as we see they are not. It might be true that there are still as many inventions of real novelty and magnitude as ever, though we doubt if there is; and yet there would be circumstances which prevented a legislator regarding them as most important. One of these circumstances is certainly the exaggerated importance of minor improvements, in consequence of the great development of machinery and manufacturing. A single improvement to save 10 per cent. in fuel for the steam engine would probably add more absolutely to the real wealth of this generation than the invention of the steam-engine itself added to the real wealth of the generation in which it was invented. A recent invention just spoken of—the feathering of the blades of screws, increasing the facilities of using auxiliary steam-power in ships—might compare on the same footing with the most substantial invention of a poorer age. Just as the refinement of the machinery of credit, and the extent of its development, cause the least disturbance to be widely felt, so the least improvement in mechanical or chemical knowledge, applied to manufactures, may have great results. A revolutionary invention— owing to the difficulty of introduction—might not tell so quickly even as a minor improvement in an existing groove; but, in any case its effects will now be matched at the first start by these minor improvements.

These improvements again, as well as the great inventions themselves, are usually come at in recent times in a different way from that of the old inventor. Formerly the inventor had almost nothing before him—every department of industry had to be built up from the foundation. Now a man must build upon extensive knowledge of what has been accomplished, and must have great means at his command. What Mr. Mill has just been explaining in his new book in regard to original authorship in the present day is equally true of invention : "Nearly all the thoughts which can be reached by mere strength of original faculties have long since been arrived at; and originality, in any high sense of the word, is now scarcely ever attained but by minds which have undergone elaborate discipline, and are deeply versed in the results of previous thinking. It is Mr. Maurice, I think, who has remarked, on the present age, that its most original thinkers are those who have known most thoroughly what.

had been thought by their predecessors; and this will henceforth be the case. Every fresh stone in the edifice has now to be placed on the top of so many others, that a long process of climbing, and of carrying up materials, has to be gone through by whoever aspires to take a share in the present stage of the work." That is—when we speak of invention—the inventor must be a man who is closely associated with capitalists, or be a capitalist himself. In no other way can he have the means of knowing the thousand improvements of machinery and processes which have culminated in the present factories and machines; and in no other way can he find means for experiments on the necessary scale. "Poor men," says Sir William Armstrong, "very often come to me imagining that they have made some great discovery. It is generally all moonshine, or if it looks feasible, it is impossible to pronounce upon its value until it has passed through that stage of preliminary investigation which involves all the labour, and all the difficulty, and all the trouble." How is a poor man to get this preliminary investigation undertaken, when the subject is an amendment of a complicated manufacturing process? The complaint, in fact, was made before the Select Committee on Technical Instruction, that English manufacturing was suffering from foreign competition, because there is less room now than formerly for the play of "untaught invention." The machine is too perfect for the workman to meddle with; and thus the foreigner, supposed to be more technically instructed, has room to excel us—our peculiar power having been "untaught invention."

Such having been the change in the character of invention, it is easy to see why the Patent-Laws are not only not needed, but are obstructive. The inventor, in the first place, is not in the position of an old inventor. To give him scope he must be employed by a manufacturer or capitalist—that is, his skill must be already highly valued, the manufacturer naturally employing those who can introduce amendments and improvements, and keep him abreast or ahead of competitors. "I believe," says Sir William Armstrong, again, "that if you let the whole thing alone, the position which a man attains, the introduction and the prestige, and the natural advantages which result from a successful invention and from the reputation which he gains as a clever and able man, will almost always bring with them a sufficient reward." And again: "I think that absolute discoveries are very rare things; nearly all inventions are the result of an improvement built up upon a preceding one. A poor man who has the ability to make really practical improvements is almost sure to rise in the world without the aid of Patents." And if the inventor may be thus indifferent to a Patent-Law, the question as to the inducement to capitalists to take up inventions may be settled by their general objection to Patents. Though there are one or two manufacturers who have monopolised a number of Patents in their trade, and so turned the law to account, it is from them that the greatest complaints come—men like Mr. Platt, or Mr. Scott Russell, or Mr. Macfie, who has just moved the abolition of the laws. The truth is, capitalists are now in a position to obtain a profit without a Patent—just as they can sometimes disregard a Patent for a long time till competition forces it upon them. Patents, then, are not required as an inducement either to inventors or capitalists, and the reason of the law fails.

But this is not all. The complaint of manufacturers at the obstruction of the present law would not be enough by itself, but it is a very serious matter when invention is part of the business of manufacturing. The law of Patents, in short, interferes with what has become the normal process of invention. Mr. Platt states : " I think that there is scarcely a week, certainly not a month, that passes but what we have a notice of some kind or other of things that we have never heard of in any way, and do not know of in the least that we are infringing upon them." Sir William Armstrong complains of a personal grievance : " The necessity which I am under of taking out Patents, not for the purpose of obtaining for myself a monopoly, but simply for the purpose of preventing other persons from excluding me from my own inventions." And much similar evidence was given before the Royal Commission, of which Lord Stanley was chairman. Thus the present law is not wanted to promote invention, and it is injurious to a kind of invention which would go on luxuriantly without it. The gradual nature of most inventions is a sufficient security that it will proceed under the law of competition. Perhaps the practice of Government is the best indication of the necessity for the abolition of Patents. A few years ago the manufacturing departments of Government found themselves so hampered by Patents that they resolved to try whether they were bound or not, the result being a legal opinion that they were not bound. But Government is only a great manufacturer, its work in some departments being less than in many private businesses. Is there any reason why Government should be released, and individuals bound to patentees ? As to the supposition that invention will cease, the mere interest of the Government in paying for anything worth having is found a sufficient stimulus to invention in the things which it requires; and so it is assumed will be the interest of competing manufacturers.

There is a universal agreement, moreover, that no Patent-Law should cover all the inventions which are now covered. It happens that the strongest condemnation of things as they are before the Royal Commission came from witnesses who wished a change, though none suggested anything which commended itself to the Commission. The idea seemed to be that a separation could be made between substantial inventions and the improvements or amendments which are now so important, but are admitted to be unsuitable for Patents. It was thought that Patents, instead of being granted indiscriminately, should only be granted in cases of proved novelty and utility. But no working plan of a court to do this could be devised, or one which would not probably discourage inventors as much as the abolition of Patents altogether.

We come, then, to the conclusion that it is for the general interest that Patent-Laws should be abolished, and that their abolition will do no great harm to any one—least of all, to the great mass of inventors or improvers. Perhaps we may point out that, if the circumstances are as described, this country has a special interest in abolishing such laws. As the leading manufacturing country in the world, a Patent here is likely to be worth more to its holder than anywhere else; consequently our manufacturers are more exposed than any others to the interruption and worry of Patents. It may well be that other countries which are less tempting to patentees will find the balance of competition weighted in their favour in consequence. Looked at another way, the more that invention falls into the hands of great capitalists, the more likely is it to strengthen the manufacturing of a country which is already most powerful. The normal condition of things is all in our favour, and we should do nothing to thwart it.

Leading Article from the "Spectator," June 5, 1869.

Those who doubt whether there are subjects upon which no conclusion is possible, which baffle the ablest and most judicial minds possessing the best attainable information, should read the debate which has just taken place on the proposed abolition of the Patent Laws. The most remarkable fact of the debate was the uncompromising attack upon these laws by Sir Roundell Palmer, his eager advocacy of the opinion that they should be at once abolished; but the most significant speech was made by Lord Stanley, who exhibited perfectly the incapacity of reasonable men to come to a wholly satisfactory judgment upon them.　In fact, there is a real balance of considerations which were almost exhaustively stated by Lord Stanley. If you look at one set of facts, you see good reason for conceding Patent rights; if you look at another set, you find innumerable mischiefs arising from the concession; and there is hardly any means of measuring which set of arguments preponderates.　The motive of granting Patents is *primâ facie* very simple and unobjectionable. You wish to encourage inventions, by which the wealth of the world is so much increased, and you therefore promise inventors a temporary monopoly of their use, on the single condition that the inventions shall be made public.　But for some such guarantee, it is said, many inventors would have no temptation to rack their brains, and capitalists would be afraid to help them in putting their ideas into a complete shape.　That invention, as a matter of fact, is to some extent encouraged, is certain, though Lord Stanley hardly touched upon the point.　On the other hand, hardly any Patent-Law can do what it professes, while it is certain to do much harm ; and this is, at least, the character of our own law.　The rewards with which it tempts inventors are too often delusive, and they at least would have small real cause to complain of its abolition.　No Patent brings its holder any immediate pecuniary right.　He can only sue people who infringe his Patent, and the costliness of Patent suits is such that he is seldom able to protect himself.　To make the property worth anything, a capitalist must take it up ; but the capitalist, in doing so, stipulates for the lion's share of the profit. Probably in ninety-nine cases out of a hundred the reward was obtained by such speculators, and not by inventors.　This, of itself, we believe, would not be a sufficient argument against conceding Patent-rights ; but it would certainly be sufficient, if inventors could be induced in some less costly way to surrender their ideas to the public. Another reason against Patents, stated by Lord Stanley—that the reward is usually out of all proportion to the service rendered—is also a strong one, if a better plan can be thought of ; but the main reason, the injury to third parties, is most serious.　There is a great mass of well-founded complaints as to Patents being traps for manufacturers.　Improvements and amendments in the details of machinery and manufacturing processes, which would inevitably be come at by the manufacturers themselves, are appropriated beforehand by inventors who do not possess in reality any particular merit.　Manufacturers are afraid to make

slight alterations, for fear an inventor comes down upon them ; but
they never know but what they may have to encounter an action for
"something they have always done." Even inventors themselves
suffer in this way. It commonly happened that half-a-dozen men
competing in the same line of business would come almost simultaneously upon the same discovery; but if A was a week or a fortnight
before B, the latter was excluded from his own discovery. The
Patent-Law, then, not only does little real good to patentees themselves, but a great deal of mischief to other people. Who is to decide
whether the balance of advantage to the public, through encouraging
invention by offering a rather delusive reward, exceeds the disadvantage of impeding manufacture and preventing people from using what
they themselves discover ?

Lord Stanley, though only recommending the matter for the " particular handling" of the Government, inclines, on the whole, to the
view that the Patent-Laws do more harm than good ; and we are
quite disposed to agree with him. The decisive consideration appears
to be the unavoidable abuse of Patents for inconsiderable inventions,
or inventions of simultaneous discovery. The hardship of excluding
B from a discovery of his own because A had patented it a week
before, is such as to demand the clearest proof of the expediency of
the general law which deprives him of the fruit of his labours.
Where B is a manufacturer, led up to the discovery by the
necessities of competition and suddenly laid under contribution
by a stranger or a rival, the hardship is especially severe.
We are not sure but that to make any Patent-Law tolerably
just, special provision should be made for proof of simultaneous discovery, and either compensation to all the discoverers by the patentees,
or full liberty to them to make use of their discovery. It is of
equal importance, however, that the amendment of manufacturing
processes in detail should not be checked ; and perhaps the fact that
the great majority of Patents now only apply to what may be termed
details is a main reason for abolishing them. It is a simple mon-
strosity, to quote the case given by Mr. Scott Russell, that every conceivable shape of a boiler should be patented, so that the most obvious
change of form, which some particular exigency obviously suggests
when it arises, should not be permissible to a manufacturer unless he
pays black mail to somebody else. If it is said that details are often
important, the answer is that manufacturers and inventors have a
sufficient stimulus with regard to them without a Patent-Law. The
pressure of competition and the large scale of manufacturing, which

make details important, are sufficient inducements to those interested to find out something new, or encourage others to find out something for them.   Just because invention must usually come in the way of great manufacturers, who can recoup themselves without Patents, Patents are no longer necessary.   Men like Sir William Armstrong and Mr. Scott Russell, who are themselves considerable inventors, do not care for Patents, except to guard themselves against the interference of others who might take advantage of the present law to reap where they have not sowed.   They are quite content to let others alone, if they are let alone themselves, deriving their profit from general excellence of manufacture, of which any single process which might be the subject of a Patent is only one out of many details, and perhaps not the most important.   Nor do such inventors conceal their detailed improvements, so that they are in no way tempted to do anything for the advantage of the public by the present law.   It was observable in the debate that the defence of the present law rested exclusively with representatives of probably the least important inventors.   Mr. Mundella's assurance that working men are attached to the present law, and that inventors of the working class would either not be tempted to invent, or would be deprived of the reward of their industry, was, in truth, the only argument in its favour.   But it was plainly insufficient.   It would be necessary also to show that such inventions are overwhelmingly valuable, so as to compensate for all the injury a Patent-Law must do ; but this was not, and we believe could not be, attempted.   The special case of poor inventors might be met by an organised system of voting rewards to those whose inventions had been largely adopted and used ; but we should not frame an entire law, which the public do not require, and which would work a deal of harm, in order to suit their peculiar circumstances.

Such being the nature of the discussion, it is, of course, not worth while saying much on the particular defects of the present law.   But there is hardly a single point where some alteration is not called for.   In particular, the Courts for trying Patent cases could be very much improved ; and additional obstacles might be interposed to frivolous or entrapping Patents.   One of the main reasons for total abolition, nevertheless, must always be the impossibility of suggesting an amendment for some defect which is not itself open to equivalent objections.   Nothing, for instance, seems so obvious at first sight than that the present law might be amended by compelling patentees to grant licences.   Yet the Royal

Commission which reported in 1865 was decidedly opposed to this suggestion, after hearing all that could be said for it. There is no means of saying beforehand what should be the maximum charge for licences, while the moment this principle is introduced the special use of a Patent as a stimulus to inventors is tampered with—the prospect of a complete monopoly of which they are to make as much as they can. Similar objections apply to any suggestion for cancelling Patents which are not used in a year or two to some material extent. The best inventions, requiring the greatest changes in manufacturing machinery, are often the slowest to come into operation. For the same reason, it would also be impracticable to compel patentees to grant licences at fixed maximum rates after their Patent had been two or three years old. It might be just as impossible then, as at first, to say what the licence fee should be. If we are to have a Patent-Law, then we can have no substantial improvement upon the present one; and it is so bad that it can hardly last. Perhaps there is at present a deficiency of evidence on the subject—the workmen not having been heard before the last Commission, and the information presented as to the Patent-Laws of other countries and their working being very deficient; but though this may be a good reason for having another inquiry, we anticipate that it will only confirm the verdict of impartial judges against the present system.

Extract from the " Saturday Review," June 5, 1869.

If the interesting debate on Mr. Macfie's motion proved, what scarcely needed proving, that our existing Patent-Law is extremely unsatisfactory in its working, it equally proved that the arguments against having any Patent-Law at all are not less unsatisfactory. If it were practicable to discriminate between true and sham discoverers, and to ascertain with accuracy to whom the merit of every new invention really belonged, and if it were at the same time easy to secure to the man who increased the common stock of useful knowledge the fruit of his own brain, no one would dream of questioning the moral claim of an inventor to this peculiar kind of property, any more than we now question the justice of giving to an author a copyright in his own work. But when it is found, or supposed, to be extremely difficult to do justice to one man without causing much inconvenience and some occasional injustice to a thousand others, there is a strong temptation to sacrifice individual rights to public expediency. The advocates of a total repeal of the Patent-Laws generally insist (as Sir Roundell

Palmer did in his ingenious speech), not only that they do a great deal of indirect mischief, but that the discoverer of the most invaluable invention has no claim to any reward except the consciousness of having enabled a number of other men to make colossal fortunes. That such arguments should be used at all proves little more than an uneasy consciousness that the proposed repeal would work a certain amount of real injustice. Men who are strongly impressed with the expediency of ignoring the claims of inventors struggle to escape the reproach of injustice by stoutly denying the rights which they desire to disregard. We would rather see the subject discussed with more courage and frankness. There are undoubtedly instances in which private claims must yield to public expediency, and any persons who think the case of inventors to be one to which this rule is applicable would do better to say so openly than to try to persuade themselves and others that those who have created the means of making wealth have no claim to share in the fruits of their discovery. Sir Roundell Palmer affected to dispose of the whole difficulty by saying that there were essential differences between Copyright and invention; but a principle is not the less sound because you may illustrate it by a case which is not on all-fours with that to which you apply it. And the distinctions between Copyright and invention are by no means so radical as is sometimes assumed. The Copyright-Laws give an author a special monopoly because it is conceived that the production of a new work entitles him to a return proportioned to its merit, as tested by the demand for it in the market. The Patent-Laws give an analogous monopoly to an inventor on precisely the same moral grounds. To say, as Sir Roundell did, that a book was a new creation, whereas an invention was merely the application of the facts and the laws of nature, which are common property, was to speak like a lawyer rather than like a philosopher or a man of science. Whatever other distinctions may be insisted on between Copyright and invention, this, at any rate, will not bear a moment's examination. It may have a colour of plausibility in the case of a poem, a play, or a novel, though even there it is not altogether sound. But literature includes history, science, philosophy, mathematics, and the like; and every book on these and most other subjects, so far as it has any value, is based entirely upon facts and laws which·are no more the creation of the author than are the facts and laws on which an invention may be founded. In each case there is creation in the same qualified sense. Say that a man creates what he reveals, or what he proves, and the author and the inventor are equally entitled to be called creators. Say, on the other hand, with perhaps more accuracy, that to proclaim a previously unnoticed truth is only to announce what has all along existed in nature and nature's laws, and some more modest title than creator must be assumed by author and inventor alike. The difference between the two cases is not a difference of principle, but of convenience. The thing created, either in the book or the machine, is the thought or the method; but property in a thought or a method is not what the law allows in either case, simply because it would be impossible to give an effect to such an enactment. What the law does is to lay hold of the most profitable mode of using the idea, and say that for a limited time no one but the originator shall be at liberty, in the one case, to print the book or a colourable imitation of it; or, in the other, to manufacture or use the machine or any colourable imitation of that. It is impossible, we think, to deny the abstract right of a real author or inventor, and more palpably impossible to deny it in the one case while you admit it in the other.

Apart from his abstract reasoning, there is much in Sir Roundell Palmer's argument to show wide differences in practice between the cases of authors and inventors. It is undoubtedly true that in a vast majority of instances the patentee of an invention is not the person to whom the largest share of the merit belongs. The rule, equally in scientific discovery and in practical invention, has almost always been found to be that, when a great step in advance is completed, no one man can claim the entire merit. If one wins the race, there are mostly several competitors who get a place. Even Newton had rivals treading on his heels, and his great discoveries would not have been lost, though they would certainly have been delayed, if his marvellous intellect had never been directed to science. The thought of the world, as represented by a little cluster of inquiring minds, was fast ripening for the harvest which Newton was the first to reap. But no one on this account seeks to deprive Newton of his glory. And we do not see why the pioneers of practical invention should be deprived of the reward for which they work merely because what they have done is but to forestal what would have been accomplished, sooner or later, without them. The real vice of the Patent-Laws is that they give a full fourteen years' monopoly to the first inventor who proclaims himself, even though it may be clear that he has not a week's start of a host of competitors. In order to make sure of adequately rewarding a very few real benefactors of mankind, you give an inordinate privilege to a great many who have done nothing at all in proportion to what they receive; and not only do you prohibit every one from borrowing the patentee's ideas, but you actually forbid a second inventor, who has arrived at the same result without ever having heard of the first, to make any use for fourteen years of the conclusions which he has worked out by his own unassisted thought and labour. This, of course, is a gross injustice, and the opponents of the Patent-Laws say that no machinery can be devised by which it can be escaped. Another serious objection to the system, as worked in this country, is the indiscriminate grant of a Patent to any one who claims it, leaving it to future litigation to determine whether the Patent is good or bad. The Law Officers' of the Crown receive an enormous amount of fees for Patent business, and it is their function to determine in the first instance whether a *primâ facie* title to the privilege is made out. It might be supposed that, if the identical invention has been patented or publicly used before, or if, on the face of it, it is no invention at all, the application would be refused. Nothing of the sort happens. No examination of the records at the Patent-office takes place to ascertain the existence or non-existence of earlier Patents for the alleged discovery ; and even when there is an opposition, and it is clearly proved (as in the case of the bullet which Mr. Metford devised and Mr. Whitworth afterwards patented) that there is nothing new in the invention, the Patent is allowed to go, in order that the claimant may have the privilege of a jury to try an imaginary right. This is the way in which the crop of litigation is raised which is so often pointed to as a reproach to the law. The present Attorney-General, it seems, has introduced the innovation of rejecting the claims of patentees where the alleged inventions are palpably frivolous, but something much more decided than this is needed to make the preliminary investigation of any real value. The vast number of worthless and catching Patents taken out merely as traps for manufacturers is perhaps the greatest nuisance incidental to the system, but it is by no means the most difficult to suppress.

All these evils must be cured, or sensibly abated, if the Patent-Laws are to survive; and if this is to be done at all, it can only be by an effective preliminary inquiry. That there are difficulties to be encountered in such a scheme cannot be denied, but it is not yet shown to be so complete an impossibility as Sir Roundell Palmer assumed it to be. With the best machinery a few Patents would slip through which, on closer investigation, would be held to be bad ; but even the clumsiest methods of *bonâ fide* inquiry would have sufficed to weed out some ninety per cent. at least of the existing Patents. A mere search by proper officials at the Patent-office, with the aid of the excellent indexes which they possess, would settle the fate of the great majority of applications, and the opposition of rival inventors or manufacturers would expose a great many more if it were not understood, as it is now, that any opposition before the Law Officers is a mere waste of time. Under the existing system we have a tribunal which is not, as a rule, competent for the work, and which makes no real effort to do it. The Law Officers give up the investigation in despair; but it by no means follows that a scientific tribunal, with all the aids which the Patent-office could supply, might not be found extremely useful. The experiment, at any rate, has not been tried; and it is scarcely fair to inventors to deprive them of all protection merely because a perfunctory inquiry by an unscientific and busy lawyer may have failed to exclude from the list of patentees a formidable body of mere impostors.

We take it to be quite clear that the attempt to do justice ought not to be given up until the impossibility of putting the law on a satisfactory footing is clearly made out. Mr. Mundella is probably as ingenious as most manufacturers, but he says that all the inventions in which he is interested came out of the brains of his workmen, and that they are sharing with him and the public the benefit of their discoveries. Apart from the serious inconveniences caused by the law as it is now administered, no one could desire to confiscate the ingenuity of artisans for the benefit of master manufacturers. As matters stand now, a poor patentee is generally helpless to turn his invention into money without the assistance of a capitalist; but to allow a master, because he is rich enough to use an invention, to pick the brains of a clever artisan without making him any acknowledgment, would be to aggravate the plutocratic tendencies of the age, which most serious thinkers would gladly mitigate as far as possible. The product of invention and thought is a very difficult kind of property to protect, but it is not on that account the less deserving of protection, if any means can be devised for granting it without too grave an interference with the commercial freedom which public expediency demands. The subject requires a more searching investigation than it has yet received. Lord Stanley's Commission scarcely touched the root of the matter, and no attempt has even been made to test the feasibility of such suggestions as the report contained. It is for those who attack the law to make out a conclusive case, not merely against the particular system in force, but against every possible scheme for securing to inventors the benefit of their own work. And this has certainly not yet been done.

EXTRACTS FROM RECENT CLASS PERIODICALS.

Along with some true light and sound sense, the shifts to which advocates of Patent restrictions are put when they venture upon argument, and the boldness with which advances are being made on the path of monopoly in the face of attack, may be deduced from the following extracts picked up at a glance in current periodical class literature :—

A Good Illustration and Bad Argument.

However absurd it may appear, a valid Patent has been for fourteen years granted, which gave a monopoly to one person to make all the pins for all our railways. I should have thought that the use of wooden trenails to fasten materials together, to have been of ancient date, but for this Patent. That existing Patent-rights are, to some extent, obstructive to the " right of way," is just as true as that the right to enclose common land is so. The natural remedy, in both instances, is to reserve " a right of way " to the public, not necessarily a free right, but one open to all, on payment of a reasonable toll in the latter, and of a reasonable royalty in the former case. With more show of justice, might the enclosure of common lands be prohibited than Patent-rights for inventions be refused, for the common lands were not only discovered, but in human use before enclosure, which is more than can be said of any true invention.—*Extract from " English Mechanic," July* 2, 1869.

Growth of Strange Views among Surgeons.

A change in the views of English medical men is perceptible on the question of the propriety of a surgeon taking out a Patent for an instrument he has invented. Although we have always felt it the duty of a physician who subscribed to a fixed code of ethics to abide by its regulations, and therefore have always opposed, on technical grounds, the taking Letters Patent on improvements in surgical appliances, we freely grant that there is no *à priori* immorality in the act. . . . . If we read Dr. Chapman's letter to the *British Medical Journal*, we find that he there says : " I have been informed that soon after Dr. Richardson invented his ether-spray instrument, Her

Majesty's physician, Dr. Jenner, said, if he were Dr. Richardson, he would patent the instrument." And further on we read, "Before I patented the spine bags, I consulted the President of the College of Physicians, Sir Thomas Watson, and the head of the Privy Council, Mr. Simon; and both these gentlemen expressed the opinion that I was justified in doing so." Such quotations, in our humble opinion, show that Dr. Chapman is, in all probability, right, and the majority of the profession wrong, in objecting to his patenting an instrument which is by no means mysterious or secret. We shall not be sorry to see this frank admission gain ground with the profession in this country, and the prohibition of patenting instruments reconsidered. —*Medical and Surgical Reporter.*

WHAT PRELIMINARY INVESTIGATION REQUIRES.

. . . To diminish the period for which he shall be allowed to retain his exclusive right. . . . If a gratuitous privilege of five years' duration be a sufficient price for John Bull to pay inventors for inducing them to make their inventions Patent, I know no just reason why he should pay more in the form of monopoly price for that which he can purchase for the shorter term. . . . To enable an efficient preliminary investigation to be made with facility, either by individuals, or by the official examiners, I propose to compile a history of inventions, discoveries, and processes, for one rather more full and modern than Beckman's would be required. I have long advocated the compilation and official publication of this great work, for it is not nearly enough for this purpose to have only a classified abridgment of the specifications of English or British Patents. In addition to this, besides all foreign Patents, a brief classified description of the million things formerly and now being done and suggested is almost absolutely necessary to enable either official or private investigators to arrive at anything like a probable resolution of the question if a given thing it is proposed to Patent is new.—*Extract from "English Mechanic," July* 9, 1869.

HARD PUSHED FOR A DEFENCE OF PATENTS.

(Extract from Leading Article in "*Engineer*" of July 9, 1869.)

In a civilised state, we say, everything is property that is the fruit of a man's own intellect, and if the law does not make it property, then the law, not the principle, is to blame. Advocates for the abolition of

Patent-Laws consider the following as one of their most powerful arguments: They say that if inventors would restrict themselves to the
initiation of inventions great and good, there might be some plea for
the concession of reward through monopoly or otherwise; but the fact
is otherwise. It suffices to take the most cursory glance at Patent
records, they say, to be made aware that processes great and good
constitute but a very small minority of those on behalf of which Patent
fees are paid and the rights of monopoly claimed.

We readily grant the second clause of the statement. The number
of great and good inventions, by comparison with the obviously trivial
claims, is very small indeed; but we altogether fail to perceive what
legitimate source of grievance this can be to the public. On the contrary, it seems to us demonstrable that under a competent system of
Patent-Law organisation the fees accruing from these claims of trivial
intrinsic import might be utilised and made to fructify. The surplus
thus accruing might be used in diminution of existing Patent fees, in
establishing a museum of inventions creditable to the nation and the
epoch, and in other ways conducive to the development of invention in
general. . . . Our own experience points to many cases like this; wherefore we are assured a proposition of some not wholly averse to Patents,
whereby they would establish courts of preliminary investigation to
determine whether any given process should be deemed worthy of
patenting or not, would be altogether futile.

According to our way of viewing the case, the registration of inventive novelties should be encouraged on other grounds than that
already specified. We hold the record of failures to be of, at least,
equal importance to the record of successes. Anybody who has given
much time to promote invention will, we are sure, coincide in our
opinion, that the knowledge of what others have been unable to
accomplish in some particular line of invention is one of the most likely
conditions of his own success. This collateral value of failures does
not seem to have been heeded by those who are most prominent
amongst the advocates of Patent abolition. From matters of undis-
puted non-success, we pass now to the consideration of others
confessedly of some value, but the importance of which is trivial. In
respect to such it is argued by Mr. Macfie that they much embarrass
the manufacturer by needlessly stopping the way until terms can be
come to with the inventor. The plausibility of this reasoning we fail
to see. Does not the assumed worthlessness of an invention of the
series contemplated bar the need of coming to terms with the inventor
at all? What manufacturer in his senses would treat for the use of an

invention that he knows to be worthless—such foreknowledge being a postulate on which the argument is raised, and on which the objection turns? The national value of a readily-accessible and classified record of invention must be obvious to all. Those who would desire to uphold the Patent-Laws, and those who would wish to abolish them, must alike coincide in this point. We insist upon this part of the subject all the more strenuously from the conviction that the upholding the abrogation or modification of the Patent-Laws will turn, after all, on considerations of public expediency, not on considerations of right and wrong to individual inventors. This being so, the collateral value of Patent-Laws, in establishing a record of inventive progress, cannot be too prominently kept in view.

PATENT RIGHTS AND PATENT WRONGS.

Sir,—On page 279, in speaking of steel rails, you say: "Could a better result than that achieved by Mr. Bessemer, and by those who hold licences under him, have been arrived at under the 'No-Patent' system?" Decidedly not, for it has landed them in wealth; but I will suppose a by no means improbable case. Suppose Belgian manufacturers had secured Patent-rights in England, and demanded a royalty preventing English manufacturers from selling their steel rails, as you state, under 12l. per ton, when without such royalty they could be sold at 9l. per ton. Now, the case would stand thus: the Belgian manufacturers could be supplying the world with steel rails at 9l. per ton, while the English manufacturers were prevented *by their own laws for fourteen years* from manufacturing them under 12l. per ton, although all the materials were lying at their doors, and both masters and men wanting the work. If England wishes to maintain her position in the trading and manufacturing world, monopolies and prejudice must be things of the past. . . .

You will say the inventor has a right to the invention. Granted; there were no laws to prevent him from finding it out, and getting all the advantage he could out of it, and there ought not then to have been a law made to prevent any one else finding out the process or improving upon it. I cannot see the right of giving anyone the power to block the public highway of thought and enterprise. Necessity is the mother of all useful inventions, and if steel rails were required, English manufacturers would have soon found out how to make them, without a Patent Law to help them.   ` R. R. S.
—From the *English Mechanic.*

MOVEMENTS IN GERMANY, BELGIUM, AND HOLLAND.

For the following translation I am indebted to the Hon. J. C. Heustler, of the Legislative Council of Queensland :—

REPORT OF THE CHAMBER OF COMMERCE OF COLOGNE ON THE PATENT QUESTION.

The resolution to abolish Patents on inventions, arrived at by the Chamber of Commerce of Cologne, at their sitting of the 15th Sept., 1863, has been confirmed in a report to the Ministry of Commerce, as follows :—

The Patent is a monopoly, and if it has been said in its favour that it is justifiable and only temporary, it is, notwithstanding, subject to all the disadvantages in its consequences which are common to all monopolies.

Endeavours to compete in the sphere of inventions are suddenly checked by Patents, while, on the other hand, many a patentee, instead of continuing to work with zeal, and to advance in the direction commenced, simply occupies himself to watch with jealousy possible infringements of others on his monopoly during the currency of his Patent.

Consumers pay exorbitant prices during a number of years for the manufacture so patented, or receive the same in a less perfect condition than would be the case if competition had exercised its wholesome influence on the manufacture of the article in question. It may be rejoined, that nobody is forced to buy the patented article, or to make use of the patented invention ; also that the common weal would profit more by the utilisation of an invention, even if burthened for a period of from five to fifteen years, than not have it in use at all.

To this it could be replied, with good reason, that with the constant activity which working minds develop upon all fields of industry, the invention of it would have been made shortly after by B, and by him possibly would have been brought to light in still greater perfection. If the invention of A, however, is patented, the inventive perfectioning of the object by B must rest until the expiration of A's Patent.

The more an invention is to the purpose for general adaptability, the more reasonable appears the supposition that others would have arrived at the same invention.

In spite of the contrary intention, Patents proved themselves an impediment to the progress of human ingenuity, and by each newly-granted Patent an unrelenting "halt" is shouted to the competition in that direction.

On closer reflection, even persons who move in circles which, from personal interest, have hitherto used their influence to give the greatest possible stability to Patent-rights, will come to the conviction that the disadvantages outweigh by far the advantages.

The Patent system, viewed from a standpoint of political economy, produces a similar influence as the Lottery. The "grand prize" dazzles all; however, only one can have it, and the multitude of those who contributed to the solving of the problem lose very often a not inconsiderable stake in uselessly-incurred costs, and lost time and trouble.

Many have been induced by the system to rush after doubtful reward in the shape of a Patent, instead of steadily applying their ability and knowledge to regular industry.

Besides, it is not sufficient to make up one's mind to make an invention capable of being patented; such proceedings lead to a success in the most rare cases. The most important discoveries have proceeded, on the contrary, from those who thoughtfully prosecute their regular avocations. The fear that with abolition of Patents the ingenuity of mankind would slacken, we cannot share, because the germ of progress is embodied in human nature, and because the joy over an invention made, and the satisfaction felt at a new discovery, in themselves are powerful impulses for the employment of energies in such directions. A strong proof of the correctness of this assertion the men of science furnish, whom we have to thank for the most important discoveries, in so far as the application of physical and chemical laws to industry are concerned—which have been always handed over immediately to the public with the utmost liberality. Others have based their inventions on such laws, and managed to acquire for this one or that other a Patent, and thus, to their own advantage and to the cost of the public, made an invasion of territory hardly legitimately theirs. They reaped where others had sowed.

Let us take, for instance, all the lighting apparatuses during the last twenty-five years. The different lamp contrivances during this period for which Patents have been granted by the industrial States of Europe will number several hundreds. Now, if we sift the matter, we will find that all these patented combinations are simply variations of a principle which Berzelius established and applied to his spirit-lamp.

Similar is the experience with the invention of Bunsen, who reduced the costs of the electric battery considerably, by applying a hard sort of coke in place of the platinum in Grove's Battery.

In a still higher degree has Morse acted meritoriously. It is true, Morse, in consideration of the signal importance of his invention, has received a public reward in the shape of money, and this mode of acknowledging real merit in the province of inventions recommends itself for adoption even in individual States.

After the abolition of Patents, apart from such acknowledgments as aforesaid, very soon associations of the various interested parties who, by each discovery, would be equally benefited, will be formed for the purpose of rewarding new inventions made in accordance with indicated problems, the solution of which may be felt to be most important to them.

For State rewards only such inventions should be taken cognizance of as, according to their nature, cannot be kept secret, and are not of a kind that will ensure to the inventor an adequate reward by his own use of them.

Principles, which hitherto have not been admissible for Patents, would be likewise excluded from rewards. There could be also no premiums for new modes of manufacture, such as simpler or cheaper manufacture of materials already known, and in the same manner manufacture of new articles directly going into consumption, because, in the first case, the secret use of the invention would present an equivalent, while in the latter cases the start which the inventor has with regard to manufacturing, as well as disposal, before and over his competitors, in most cases is more than sufficient reward for the merit of having given mankind new means of satisfying human enjoyments and necessities. It was consequently a timely Convention between the States of the Zollverein, which already, under date of 21st September, 1842, acknowledged the principle that the granting of a Patent henceforth could establish no right to prohibit either the import or the sale, nor the use of articles agreeing with those patented, as far as articles of consumption are concerned, and that a right of that nature was only applicable to machinery and tools for manufacturers and artisans.* Accordingly, the granting of rewards would have to be restricted to inventors of useful

---

* I cannot but think the patenting of machinery a great disadvantage to any community. Yet if importing were allowed in spite of the Patent, the exaction of heavy royalties, and of royalties graduated according to work performed (which is the greatest source of evil), would be impossible, and the disadvantage be neutralised.—R. A. M.

machinery and tools, who do not use them solely in their own interest and keep their construction a secret, but, on the contrary, make them accessible to everybody by multiplication.

With such regulations as to Patent-right in force in Germany, it will be observed that here, as in other countries, the great disadvantage arises from this, that by the patenting of an invention its utilisation or trial is prohibited to home industry, while the foreigner is quite at liberty to make use of it and to bring the articles in question to market in the country where the Patent exists.

In this manner foreign industry is actually enjoying a preference, to the detriment of the industry of that country in which the Patent is granted; consequently even the patentee, through such foreign competition, loses the intended reward partially. The example furnished by the Patent on the manufacture of aniline colours in France illustrates the case. On the whole, it is not to be denied that those advantages which the Patent monopoly should guarantee are often not in harmony either with the value or the importance of the patented invention; just as often these advantages do not reach the author of the invention at all, but flow into the pockets of such people as make it a business either to purchase Patent-rights, and so work them for their own account, or in partnership with the patentee, taking care to secure for themselves the lion's share. It is further proved by experience that insignificant and most simple inventions have often brought extraordinary advantages to the patentee, while the discoverers of important novelties (we instance only Reissel, who introduced the screw as a motor in navigation), in spite of Patent-rights, could not find gratitude nor reward for what they accomplished.

We arrive, consequently, at the conclusion, that the partly imaginary advantages of Patents are outweighed by the disadvantages attached, and that, as the industrial condition of Switzerland exemplifies, no further use of such means is any longer required in helping to elevate industry in all its branches to a very high standard, or to keep pace with the development of other countries in that direction.

EXTRACTS FROM M. VERMEIRE.

After most of this *fasciculus* is in type, I am favoured with a copy of M. Vermeire's " Le Libre Travail," Brussels, 1864, from which I subjoin three extracts.

The first, a noble passage quoted by that gentleman from M. Bastiat's "Harmonies Economiques :"—

" C'est la concurrence qui fait tomber dans le domaine commun toutes les conquêtes dont le génie de chaque siècle accroît le trésor des générations qui le suivent. Tant qu'elle n'est pas intervenue, tant que celui qui a utilisé un agent naturel est maître de son secret, son agent naturel est gratuit sans doute, maise il n'est pas encore commun ; la conquête est réalisée, mais elle l'est au profit d'un seul homme ou d'une seule classe. Elle n'est pas encore un bienfait pour l'humanité entière. Si les choses devaient rester ainsi avec toute invention, un principe d'inégalité indéfinie s'introduirait dans le monde ; mais il n'en est pas ainsi, Dieu, qui a prodigué à toutes ses créatures la chaleur, la lumière, la gravitation, l'air, l'eau, la terre, les merveilles de la vie végétale, l'électricité et tant d'autres bienfaits innombrables, Dieu, qui a mis dans l'individualité *l'intérêt personnel* qui, comme un aimant, attire toujours tout à lui, Dieu, dis-je, a placé aussi au sein de l'ordre social un autre ressort auquel il a confié le soin de conserver à ses bienfaits leur destination primitive, la gratuité, la communauté. Ce ressort, c'est la concurrence.

" Ainsi l'intérêt personnel est cette indomptable force individualiste qui nous fait chercher le progrès qui nous le fait découvrir, qui nous y pousse l'aiguillon dans le flanc, mais qui nous porte aussi à le monopoliser. La concurrence est cette force humanitaire non moins indomptable qui arrache le progrès, à mesure qu'il le réalise, des mains de l'individualité, pour en faire l'héritage commun de la grande famille humaine. Ces deux forces qu'on peut critiquer, quand on les considère isolément, constituent dans leur ensemble, par le jeu de leurs combinaisons, l'harmonie sociale.

" Et, pour le dire en passant, il n'est pas surprenant que l'individualité, représentée par l'intérêt de l'homme en tant que producteur, s'insurge depuis le commencement du monde contre la concurrence, qu'elle la réprouve, qu'elle cherche à la détruire, appelant à son aide la force, la ruse, le privilége, le sophisme, la restriction, la protection gouvernementale, le monopole."

The second, portion of an interesting letter by M. Paillottet, editeur-commentateur of Bastiat's works, (written in May, 1863) :—

"Cette connaissance, résultat de son travaile, est pour toujours à lui ; nul ne peut la lui enlever ni ne doit l'empêcher de s'en servir.

"Seulement, comme la nature permet à d'autres hommes de se livrer à la même recherche, qu'elle les y excite et souvent même leur en fait une nécessité, le jour doit arriver où la notion que cet homme possédait seul est aussi possédée par d'autres. Ce jour-là, je dis que le premier inventeur n'a plus seul le droit de se servir d'une notion qu'il n'est plus seul à posséder. Prétendez-vous que je le dépouille du résultat de son travail ? J'ai à vous répondre : Si je dépouille le premier, vous, vous dépouillez le second, le troisième, le centième inventeur peut-être ; si je dépouille le Chinois, vous, vous dépouillez Guttemberg !

"Un mot maintenant sur le droit à la réciprocité de services.

"Je crois fermement, avec Bastiat, que 'la véritable et équitable loi des hommes, c'est : Echange *librement débattu* de service contre service.'

"Si un inventeur me rend service, je lui dois un service équivalent ; Dieu me garde d'en disconvenir. Mas de même que je n'exige pas de l'inventeur ses services et ne l'oblige pas à en recevoir de moi, j'entends qu'il n'exige pas les miens et ne m'impose pas les siens. Entre lui et moi, l'échange doit être précédé d'un libre débat amenant le consentement des deux parties. M. Le Hardy de Beaulieu oublie ou supprime la nécessité du libre débat."

The third, a narrative by my able and ardent Belgian fellow-labourer in this great cause, the Abolition of Patents, M. Vermeire himself, to whose work I refer readers. He will allow me to say I impute it to no deficiency in courtesy on his part that it escaped earlier and due notice. He there gives the Chambers of Commerce of this kingdom credit for opinions which they have not generally embraced up to this hour :—

"M. Eugène Flachat attaque la loi des brevets comme une *lèpre industrielle.* M. Arthur Legrand ne critique pas moins vivement cette législation surannée ainsi que M. Michel Chevalier, que l'on peut considérer, à juste titre, comme le chef des économistes français.

" Quand l'opinion de ces hommes érudits me fut connue je n'hésitai plus et je publiai l'exposé de ma doctrine du *Libre travail* dans l'*Economiste Belge* du 28 Mars, 1863. — Plus tard M. Macfie, président de la Chambre de Commerce de Liverpool, fit connaître ses idées sur la matière et le congrès des économistes allemands réuni à Dresde en Septembre, 1863, émit la résolution suivante qui fut adoptée à une forte majorité :

" ' Considérant que les brevets d'invention n'encouragent pas les progrès des inventions et mettent plutôt obstacle à la réalisation de celles-ci.

" ' Considérant, que les brevets d'invention entravent plutôt qu'ils ne favorisent la prompte exploitation des inventions utiles et qu'ils ne sont pas un mode convenable de récompense.

" ' Le congrès a résolu que les brevets d'invention sont nuisibles au developement de la prospérité publique.'

" Cet avis des hommes de la science a été écouté en Allemagne par les hommes de la pratique ; car sur les 47 Chambres de Commerce que renferme la Prusse, 31 viennent de se prononcer pour l'abolition des brevets d'invention d'après ce que je viens de lire dans les journaux, au moment même où j'écris ces lignes. —

" *Le libre travail* qui fut suivi, de mon *Examen critique de la garantie légale des modèles et dessins de fabrique* provoqua une ardente discussion," &c.

A Belgian *projet de loi* in favour of copyright of models and designs in manufacture, having been defeated, in consequence, as is alleged, of M. Vermeire's efforts through the press and otherwise, we are told—

" This fact demonstrates once more that in Belgium, as everywhere else, opinions in favour of intellectual property within the domain of industry are declining, and that so far from legislation tending in the direction of giving such property increased proportions, it will soon be proposed to demolish entirely the superannuated legislation which interposes so many and so serious obstacles to the progress of industrial operations.

" The tactics of the partisans of such property consist in identifying or assimilating it with material property. This similarity permits the conclusions and deductions to be drawn which form the basis of Patent legislation.

"The pretended identity or similarity has been completely overthrown by M. Vermeire in his 'Le Libre Travail.' His 'Examen Critique de la Garantie Legale des Modeles et Dessins de Fabrique' deals a fresh blow against the confounding of property in a thing and property in an idea."

EXTRACT OF LETTER, BRUSSELS, JUNE 11, 1869.

There is in Belgium, as in England and all other countries, a feeling antagonistic to Patent-rights. It is even shared in by many eminent political economists. I think, however, I may venture to assert that in this country the Government, far from participating in this feeling, would rather be inclined, in the event of a revision of the Patent-Laws, to secure in a more effectual way the rights of inventors.

GERMANY.

EXTRACT FROM LETTER OF AN EMINENT HOUSE IN COLOGNE.

Although we think it rather difficult to form a general opinion on this matter, we still believe that most Industrials would welcome abolition of Patents for Inventions. The Cologne Chamber of Commerce expressed, in September, 1863, its opinion in the same sense. German legislation regarding Patents will probably be reformed. A proposition made in this direction by Count Bismarck to the Bundesrath, contained in the "Annalen des Norddeutschen Bundes," by Dr. George Hirth, 1ster Heft Jahrgang, 1869, page 34, 42, II., would interest you much, as it coincides, we believe, with your motion. The latest publications in German literature on the subject are Klostermann "Die Patents Gesetzgebung aller Lander," Berlin, 1869; Barthel "Diè Patent frage," Leipzig, 1869.

EXTRACT FROM "DIE PATENTS GESETZGEBUNG ALLER LANDER," BY DR. R. KLOSTERMANN (BERLIN, 1869).

A short time since, in the course of the present decade, the public has spoken out, following numerous and important persons who wished the entire abolition of Patents for inventions, because they allege that the existence of such is incompatible with the free-trade movements. They said that such impede industry instead of advancing it; that the claim of the first inventor to a monopoly is untenable; that discovery is not the work of one man, but the ripe fruit of industrial development.

From the difficulty and complexity of the subject, men would do away with Patent-Laws; but the real cause of the agitation against them lies in the enormous development which our international commerce has undergone in the last ten years through free-trade, steamboats, and railways.

As the complete abolition of the "customs-limits," with the German Zollverein [customs-union], was not made without a direct transformation of the Patent-Laws and a positive limitation of Patent protection, so is—through the concluding of the treaties of commerce made during the last ten years between the Zollverein and France, Great Britain, Belgium, and Italy—a *total reform* in the Patent-Law rendered necessary.

All countries, with *the single exception of Switzerland*, recognise by their existing laws the necessity of *Patent protection;* and this case of Switzerland is particularly brought forward by those opposed to the Patent movement. The Commission which was appointed of Swiss experts (and which said that Patent protection is unnecessary and tends to nothing good) was impartial enough to avow that the particular advantages which Switzerland draws from existing circumstances arise from the fact that in all the adjoining countries the protection of Patents does exist, but in Switzerland alone not so. Swiss industry, which is exceedingly small, is placed in the position of imitating all foreign Patents which find a market in Switzerland, and getting the benefit of the discoveries made under the protection of foreign Patents. Switzerland is just in the position of a man who keeps no cats because he can use his neighbours'.

HOLLAND.

I have before me a series of valuable illustrative documents printed by the Government of the Netherlands, which are too long to introduce here .The movement for abolishing Patents in that country, already referred to on pages 196—230, was consummated by a striking majority, in the First Chamber, of no less than 29 to 1 ; the abolition to take effect from 1st January next, existing rights, of course, to be respected.

ON PERPETUITY OF PATENT-RIGHT.

The following observations, abridged from a review, by M. Aug. Boudron, of M. le Hardy de Beaulieu's *La Propriété et sa Rente*, are from the *Journal des Economistes* for May :—

The author assimilates the inventor's privileges to proprietorship of a field. Nevertheless there is a fundamental difference between the two kinds of property. Independently of State privileges, the originator of a discovery may use it as his own, and even to the exclusion of all others, provided he keep it secret, so that he shall have no competitor to encounter ; whereas the owner of a field, if he is deprived of his right, loses all. The advantages of an invention may be enjoyed simultaneously by many persons; the produce of a field by one only. Now for a difference of importance affecting the interests of the public. Give the possessor of a field his right in perpetuity, and you have circumstances the most favourable for its yielding all the produce which it can. Not so with the privilege of an inventor, for it essentially consists in hindering others from bringing the methods or materials that are patented into use. From the time of invention and first *exploitation* the privilege is an obstacle ; it limits the amount of good that society would in its absence enjoy. What, then, is the motive of certain States in conceding this exclusive privilege ? . . . The legislators who have created the right thought that there would in consequence be a larger number of useful inventions and improvements, and that, on the whole, society would be a greater gainer than if there were no Patents. . . . As there are innumerable instruments and processes for which Patents have been and might still be taken, there must, if perpetuity of privilege be granted, be a prodigious number of monopolies, and almost no operation could be performed, nothing done, without people being obliged to pay tribute to some privileged person. There would be a countless host of administrators like receivers of tolls and pontages, diminishing wealth in place of creating it; the world would soon produce too little to sustain the monopolists and their *employés*. We thus arrive at an impossibility. But conceive all this possible, and the world must yet miss a great number of inventions and improvements, that would under the system of perpetuity be prevented. This is seen by the obstacles which even privileges of limited duration throw in the way of new inventions. In actual practice progress is often attained only by the use of previous inventions. But what if

T

these are the subject of Patents the holder of which will not come to
terms or cannot be treated with? Retardation, if the privilege is
temporary; a full stop, if perpetual.

NOTES ILLUSTRATIVE OF MR. MACFIE'S SPEECH.

[Page 17.]

The views taken in the text as to the meaning of
the word " manufacture " receive confirmation from the
following extract from the *Engineer* of June 4, 1869 :—

THE AMERICAN PATENT-LAW.

. . . . . . Accordingly, in the first general Patent-Law
passed by Congress, the subject for which Patents were to be
granted were described as the invention or discovery of "any
useful art, manufacture, engine, machine, or device, or any improvement therein not before known or used." In the next statute—that of
21st February, 1793—the phraseology was first introduced which has
been ever since employed—namely, "any new and useful art, machine,
manufacture, or composition of matter, or any new and useful improvement in any art, machine, manufacture, or composition of
matter, not known or used before the application for a Patent." . . .
We have, then, the following four heads of subjects suitable for
Patents—viz., an art, a machine, a manufacture, and a composition of
matter. . . . . In England, to make a new process the subject of
a Patent, the word "manufacture" would be used, and would have to
be interpreted somewhat liberally. Thus, in some cases, there might
not be a perfect distinction between the thing itself and the art or
process of making the thing. . . . . With regard to the head
"manufacture," we cannot do better than give the] definition which
Mr. Curtis has added as a note to his work. He says a manufacture
"would be any new combination of old materials, constituting a new
result or production in the form of a vendible article, not being
machinery." . . . .

As well as from the following extract from—

HINDMARCH ON "VENDING OR SELLING."

" The sole privilege of making the invention as expressed . . . is
in truth the same in substance as the sole privilege of using and exercising it. . . . By the first section of the Statute of Monopolies,
patents granting 'the sole buying, selling, making, working, or
using of anything' are declared to be void, and the proviso in favour

of inventions contained in the sixth section only extends to 'grants of privilege of the sole working or making of any manner of new manufactures,' leaving the sole buying or selling of anything within the prohibition. . . . The sole privilege granted by a *Patent* for an invention authorises the inventor 'to make, use, exercise, and vend' the invention. . . . And as no one can use the invention except the patentee, no one besides him can lawfully have such articles for sale. . . . Every part of the privilege granted by a *Patent* for an invention, when thus explained (!) is therefore clearly within the meaning of the exception contained in the *Statute*. . . ."

I demur. Is there anything in the *Statute* to prevent a person *importing* articles and *vending* them though the same as the privileged person is alone allowed to *make* or *work?* In point of fact that surely might, when the statute was passed, be done from Scotland and Ireland as to manufactures not patented in these countries, but patented in England.

[Page 18.]

The number of Patents granted in the first fifty years after the Statute of Monopolies was seventy-two, or at the rate of less than one and a-half per annum.

[Page 19.]

The following list of applications for Patents up to the end of 1862, in several classes, is abridged from Mr. Edwards' interesting treatise on, or rather against, "Letters Patent for Inventions:"—

	Oct., 1852, to Dec. 31, 1862.	Before Oct., 1852.	Total.
Railways and Railway Carriages	1,418 ...	630 ...	2,018
Telegraphs	558 ...	109 ...	667
Steam and Steam Boilers	1,293 ...	377 ...	1,670
Steam-engines	1,228 ...	704 ...	1,932
Spinning	1,837 ...	1,120 ...	2,957
Electricity, Galvanism, and Electro-plating	662 ...	38 ...	700
Sewing and Embroidery	352 ...	40 ...	392
Heating and Evaporating	1,108 ...	373 ...	1,481
Fireplaces, Grates	317 ...	169 ...	481
Flues and Chimneys	278 ...	75 ...	353
Fuel	227 ...	129 ...	356
Ventilating Buildings, Carriages, Ships, &c.	392 ...	81 ...	473

[Page 34.]

SUGGESTIVE EXTRACTS FROM DR. PERCY'S WORKS ON METALLURGY.

THE COPPER TRADE.

It would be sheer waste of time even to notice many of the mis-called improvements in copper — something for which Patents have been granted in this country during the last twenty years. Some of the patentees display such deplorable ignorance of the first principles of chemistry, and such utter want of practical knowledge, as would seem hardly possible with the present facilities of acquiring information.

Various Patents have been granted for alleged improvements in the treating of copper ores, of certain products obtained in the smelting of copper ores, &c., which are only worthy of notice as affording, as I conceive, satisfactory illustrations of the defective state of our existing Patent-Laws. . . . . . . That a man who has worked out an original and valuable process from his own brain, and who may have incurred great expenses in bringing it to a practical issue—it may be, after years of protracted toil and anxiety—should have secured to him by law during a moderate term the exclusive privilege of reaping the substantial reward of his own invention, appears to me as just and reasonable as that an author should be protected against piratical and unprincipled publishers. But that the law should confer upon a man the exclusive right of appropriating to his own benefit facts which are perfectly familiar to every tyro in chemistry, and of practising operations which are of daily occurrence in the laboratories of chemists, is as impolitic as it is unjust. And surely, the particular " inventions " above referred to belong to this category. I cordially subscribe to the opinion expressed by Mr. Grove, Q.C.—namely, that the real object of Patent-Law was to reward not trivial inventions, which stop the way to greater improvements, but substantial boons to the public; not changes such as any experimentalist makes a score a day in his laboratory, but substantial, practical discoveries, developed into an available form.

THE HOT BLAST.

It cannot strictly be termed a great invention, for what great exercise of the inventive faculty could it possibly have required for its development ? There was no elaborate working out of a process or machine, as has been the case in many inventions, but the thing was done at once. Without wishing in the smallest degree to detract from the merit to which Mr. Neilson is justly entitled, I may nevertheless express my opinion that the hot-blast was a lucky hit rather than an invention, properly so-called. Whatever opinion may be entertained as to the expediency of Patents, there can be no doubt that such a Patent as this ought never to have been granted. A Patent, even though it may be proved invalid, confers upon its possessor a *locus standi* in the eye of the law, and enables him thereby to involve innocent persons in most expensive litigation, to say nothing of the attendant annoyance and anxiety. The preliminary examination before the Attorney or Solicitor-General is in many cases an absolute farce, and nothing less. The present system, although confessedly an improvement on the old one, is yet in many cases highly obstructive and injurious to national interests.

[Page 50.]

The following passage from the *Engineer* of May 28, proves clearly that the Bessemer Patents do raise prices of iron :—

The present royalty on rails is 2*l*. per ton; on each ton a drawback of 1*l*. is nominally allowed, but the nature of Mr. Bessemer's arrangements with regard to scrap, crop ends, waste, &c., is such that the true royalty on every ton of Bessemer rails delivered to a railway company—in other words, sold—amounts to about 1*l*. 5s. 6d. After the lapse of Mr. Bessemer's Patents in February, 1870, this sum, all but 2s. 6d. per ton royalty on plant, will be saved; and, therefore, in March next year, rails may be bought for at least 1*l*. 3s. per ton less than they cost now.

[Page 62.]

WORKING MEN AS INVENTORS.

Somewhat to my surprise, I am led to apprehend that the interest of working men will be represented as coinciding with retention of invention monopoly. I hope they are too wide awake to believe such a fallacy, and too upright to approve of the continuance of a proved national disadvantage, even though it were not a fallacy. If Patents are injurious to the community by raising prices of articles of consumption and utility, then the operative and labouring classes, inasmuch as they constitute the bulk of the population, must be the chief sufferers. If Patents interfere with labour in any direction, and tend to drive trade away from our island, they, as the mainstays of industry, must be the chief sufferers. The only pretence for such an allegation as I am combating is this: some inventions in all trades, many inventions in some trades, are made by artisans, who therefore will lose this form of reward. True enough; but is the reward to these few individuals a compensation for the evils inflicted on the many—the millions? and is not the reward often so like the gift of a white elephant, or the catching of a Tartar—so much of a delusion, a difficulty, a disadvantage, a snare, a ruin —that their wisest counsellors would warn against its fascination, especially if through their own favour for my propositions there is the choice of fair and satisfactory alternative recompenses? The position of working men in respect to Patents is frequently dealt with in this compilation; their attention and co-operation I respectfully invite.

THE INVENTORS' INSTITUTE.

An Inventors' Institute has been formed for the purpose of maintaining the Patent System, and amending it in such a way as, I fear and am sure, will only make its yoke more galling and its burden heavier. The public will do well to remember that, in spite of the name, this is rather a society of patentees, including in its membership a portion only of those inventors who take Patents, and not including the innumerable inventors who do not take Patents, and who suffer by the system which the Institute is intended to perpetuate, extend, and knit more tightly on us all and in the first place on them. The honoured names who direct that society will do well to consider who are inventors and what are inventions. If they would but reflect that we are almost to a man inventors in the sense in which the great mass of patentees are such, and that the majority of inventions which choke the Patent-office are such as themselves, at any rate, would disdain to claim and scorn to annoy their fellows by patenting, they would probably arrive at the conviction—which is half-way on the road to complete emancipation of trade from the fetters they hug—that the system is so practically bad that rectification is hopeless, and would join in endeavours, not to amend what is, even theoretically, defective and bad, but to devise and introduce a thoroughly good substitute. I hope the present publication will not be in vain, when it endeavours to remove well-meaning prepossessions by force of truth.

[Page 81.]

JUSTIFICATION OF STATE REWARDS.

It is just and expedient that the public exchequer should pay inventors, because—1. The State is entitled, or required, to undertake all beneficent and useful works which, while they ought to be done for or by the nation, yet cannot be so well, or at all, done by individuals. 2. Though individuals, more than the nation collectively, will reap the benefit of these payments, it is manifest that the range of inventive improvement is so wide that on the average of years every portion of the community, and every individual in all portions, will share the benefit pretty equally. 3. The demand for remunerating inventors proceeds from the State, not manufacturers or producers. 4. These last cannot, under the *régime* of free trade, pass over from their own shoulders upon those of consumers—who are the real, because ultimate, recipients of the benefit—the burden of royalties, or other payments to inventors. 5. The charge of £200,000 per annum is, after all, on a population of thirty-two millions but a poll-tax of *three halfpence per head.* On how easy terms would we obtain for the nation a universal, prompt enjoyment of every novelty, and complete emancipation of our commerce and manufactures from an incubus and thraldom which are every day becoming more depressing !

[Page 86.]

THE PATENT-OFFICE ESTABLISHMENT.

The Patent-office in Southampton-buildings, Chancery-lane, is an establishment highly creditable to its organisers, but far too little known. Its free consulting library should be more frequented. The publications there sold at a cheap rate, and presented gratuitously to public institutions which undertake to keep them for reference under fitting regulations, are invaluable. The indexes, manuscript and printed, there kept, are elaborate, and include lists of scientific and practical matter affecting commerce and the arts, culled from periodicals issued in all countries. No change in our manner of dealing with inventions can deprive us of, or supersede the use of, such an accessible storehouse of useful knowledge. The wonder is, that its advantages are not more extensively availed of, and that so few even of our great towns have applied for sets of its specifications and indexes. There is, in spite of the establishment's excellence, room for improvement in several respects, one of which is in the providing better means for connecting itself with the mass of the people in the provinces.

" THE NEW CANADIAN PATENT-LAW.—The Patent Bill which has been for some time before the Parliament of the Dominion, has passed. The hope, to which we alluded a few weeks ago, that the Bill might be modified to enable Americans to obtain Patents in Canada, has not been fulfilled ; and the only effect of the Bill, so far as we are interested, is to shut out American inventors from a larger amount of territory than before."—*Extract from " American Artisan," June* 20, 1869.

NOTES AND EXTRACTS ON ROYALTY IN COPYRIGHT,

WITH ESPECIAL REFERENCE TO INTERNATIONAL
NEGOTIATIONS AFFECTING NORTH AMERICA.

INTERNATIONAL COPYRIGHT.

The present opportunity is availed of to recommend to notice the royalty form of International Copyright as one which might probably be acceptable to the people of the United States. I apprehend there is little or no prospect of their agreeing to negotiate on the basis of the monopoly form of Copyright which is now established in both countries. This has often, but never successfully, been urged on the United States. The advantages to British authors and publishers of so large an extension of area are obvious. There are now in that country near forty millions of people much more able to read and to buy than our thirty millions. It is in the interests of British authors, publishers, and traders, most desirable to get so large an addition to the number of the readers and buyers of English literature. Every year the benefit will be greater, but perhaps less easily attainable. The conscience and generous impulses of the great American nation will naturally incline them to negotiate on a principle which (as I hope they will consider that of royalties does) at once fairly meets the reasonable claims of authors and the equally reasonable claims, or rights, of the public. Authors and the trade would soon become familiar with, and reconciled to, the change in the form of their remuneration. They cannot but admit and feel that it is the duty of statesmen, when constituting Copyright, to take care that its effect is on the whole beneficial—as beneficial as is consistent with fair treatment of authors—to the whole body of the people for whose sake they govern. If I am warranted in anticipating that, whereas now under monopoly a new book of intrinsic value is seldom or almost never possessed by, or even seen in the houses of, the labouring population, there would under royalties be a tendency to cheapness which might be confidently relied on as the means of bringing such works within reach of the masses—not when they are stale, but when they are fresh—can I doubt that the concurrence both of authors and legislators is a matter of hope approaching to certainty? When staleness is suggested as a deterrent from, and freshness as a pleasant stimulus to, the reading of books, this is no more than the practical recognition of a taste universal among men and women, whether it concerns food material or food intellectual. Let us work it for the good of our race. But it is a quality and power unattainable except either by royalties or else by the Chinese system of open literature. That the present system works unsatisfactorily, even in a mere trade point of view, I am convinced, and for confirmation refer to figures I append from a Return on the Book Trade lately laid before the House of Commons. The sale of books at home and the export of books to the colonies and foreign parts, admit of vast expansion. We should legislate so as to accomplish, in regard to books, at the least such an expansion as has been attained in regard to newspapers. While the present form of Copyright remains in force, it would be vain to expect that the existing hindrances will be overcome. Publishers, therefore, may well co-operate. But I appeal with equal directness to philanthropists, especially all those who have the power of representing to their fellows what a folly and mistake it is to write books with a view to the moral, social, and religious welfare of men, and yet to rest satisfied with a system of law and trade that find the recompenses of authorship and of publishing ventures in a limited sale of dear books instead of an extensive sale of cheap ones—of a few good books at a large profit instead of many good books at a small! I could adduce from my own transactions conclusive proofs of the bad working and obstructive operation of monopoly in Copyright. Ireland, in particular, may well exclaim against it; for before the Union the publishers of Dublin used to drive a useful business in reprinting British works which they have, under the present system, been deprived of, to their own loss and the incalculable disadvantage of their countrymen.

The Chinese, it is said, do not recognise Copyright. What the effect is on their literature I know not. But their post-office and custom-house officers should, at any rate, rejoice that, unlike the establishments in enlightened Britain, they are not employed in the interests of private individuals as detectives of contraband literature.

I submit with some confidence a scheme I have sketched. It is one which I hope will at least prepare the way for this important national and international question receiving the earnest attention it merits.

SUGGESTIONS FOR THE AMENDMENT OF THE SYSTEM OF COPYRIGHT FOR BOOKS, BY MR. MACFIE.

(From the *Leith Herald* of — Jan.)

1. The period of exclusive privileges to continue as at present, unless any publisher demand that it shall be shortened, which he may do any time after the end of the first year, provided he intimates to the author or assignee of the author, or their agent, at the Stationers' Hall, or other place duly appointed, that he intends to publish an edition at a lower price within a year, and also lodges there a specimen copy and a statement of the intended price.

2. On such new edition the intended publisher shall be liable to pay in advance [five] per cent. on the retail price of the book.

3. And there shall be impressed on the first sheet of each copy a distinctive stamp approved by the Stationers' Hall, without which it shall be a penal offence to print or vend any copy.

4. Every publisher making such an intimation shall be bound to actually publish, according to his notice, unless the author or his assignee, within six months of his receiving intimation, shall lodge at the Stationers' Hall a bond obliging himself to publish on his own account, an edition at least as good in quality, at a price no higher; such bond to bar any action under the provisions of Article 1.

5. No reprint to differ from the original edition, without the author's consent, either in the way of abbreviation, enlargement, or alteration of the text.

6. If a book is out of print for a whole year, the copyright privilege to lapse.

7. By special arrangements a longer period of exclusive privilege shall be allowed for Encyclopædias, works *de luxe*, &c. [Engravings, photographic illustrations, &c., not to be subject to the condition now proposed in this paper.]

8. Government to endeavour to negotiate international copyright treaties on the principle exhibited in the foregoing, with the United States and other foreign countries, in order to, first—the increase of the area of remuneration to authors; and, second, the removal of all unnecessary obstruction to the exchange of literary productions.

9. On the completion of the above treaty or treaties, all examination and stopping of books by the Custom-house and Post-office to cease.

10. Government to endeavour to persuade foreign Governments to

exempt printed matter from duty, or else to charge duty at a moderate rate by weight, and not *ad valorem*.

The British colonies to enter into the Copyright " Verein " which would be so constituted, but without any import or export duty, except in so far as proximity to the United States may render modification in Canada desirable.

In the event of such international arrangements being negotiated, the author or assignee of any copyright work to have an agent in the capital of each of the united countries, who shall be empowered to receive and give the notices, intimations, and bonds provided for in Articles 1 and 4.

I am satisfied that the system of royalties could be carried out in practice without difficulty. Each author would have a special stamp—call it, if you will, trademark—the use of which, required as a condition of circulation, he would authorise under such superintendence as he may think fit. No copy should be legally saleable without the stamp, just as in France no pamphlet can be sold without the Government stamp.

Strong confirmation of the applicability of the royalty principle to literature reaches me after the preceding is in type, which I subjoin; No. I. being extracts from articles published in 1837 and 1839, by Thomas Watts, Esq., Keeper of the Printed Books of the British Museum ; and No. II., a chapter from " Traité des Droits d'Auteurs," by M. Renouard, Paris, 1838.

I.

(Extract from the Mechanics' Magazine, Vol. 27, 1837.)

This is the last of the new provisions mentioned in the preface, and the only one in the whole bill that seems intended for the benefit of the public. We were in hopes of finding at least one other, to provide for some method of " taxing " the price of new works, as used formerly .

to be done in foreign countries when a Copyright was granted. A limit is proposed to be fixed to the profits of railway companies; why are authors and publishers to be allowed to demand what sums they please? When they find they have a giant's strength, they are too apt to use it like a giant. There is such a thing, not only in theory, but in practice, as laying too heavy a tax on an author's admirers. In the height of Walter Scott's popularity there was no other way of obtaining an early copy of a new poem than by purchasing it in the inconvenient form of a ponderous quarto; it generally, a few months afterwards, appeared in an octavo shape; but in one instance, Sir Walter, finding it desirable to force the sale of an unsaleable periodical with which he was connected, "The Edinburgh Annual Register," inserted one of his poems in one of the yearly volumes, and drove all such of his adversaries as had not bought the quarto to buy a cartload of old news, along with the vision of Don Roderick. Is all this justified by the comprehensive maxim that a man may do what he likes with his own? Since the Copyright of Sir Walter's poems has drawn near the term of extinction, his publishers have thought fit to issue them in editions not only so cheap that they suit the pocket, but so small that they may be put into it. His novels are Copyright still, and the consequence is, that they are still not only dear, but ill got up. What a torrent of Elzevir editions of "Waverley" there would be if it were now public property! At present there is not one edition of it in one volume, the most usual and convenient form for a standard novel—not one edition in Elzevir, the most usual and convenient size. And this is to remain so for the next sixty years!

Sergeant Talfourd might provide a remedy for these evils in the literary tribunal which, though he makes no proposal for it in the present Bill, he is anxious to see established, for the decision of literary cases (and his arguments for which, by the bye, would answer equally well in regard to every other profession). It would provide itself, if a project were adopted for a Copyright-Law, of which we shall now proceed to state the outlines, but without the forlornest hope of ever seeing it tried.

Let an author be empowered to sell the Copyright of his work to a particular publisher for the space of five years only—a term at the end of which nine-tenths of the works now published are completely forgotten. Let it then become public property, in the same way that a play, on being published, becomes public property, since Mr. Bulwer's Act. As a manager now has the right to act any play he chooses, on paying a certain sum to the author for each night of representation, so let any printer have the right to print any work on paying a certain sum to the author for each copy he issues. The main, perhaps the only, objection to the plan would be the necessity of establishing some Excise regulations, with regard to printing-offices, for the prevention of fraud.

The great recommendation, of course, would be, that of every work of reputation we should have cheap and elegant editions ; that such of them as required comment and illustration (and now, when the Copyrights expire, it is speedily found that very few of them do not) would receive it at an earlier period, and that the works of living authors would be much more extensively diffused than they are, while their interest would, it is hoped, be advanced in an equal proportion to their fame.

After all, however, we are afraid that no Copyright Act, however favourable to authors, will exercise a perceptible beneficial influence on literature. Our own at present is frivolous, and it is assigned as a cause that our authors are ill-protected. If this be really the cause, in what sort of a state ought that of Germany to be? It is, however, in the very country where piracy is most prevalent that solid literature is most flourishing. Unhappily, no Act of Parliament can reform the taste of the public.

(Extract from the *Mechanics' Magazine*, Vol. 29, 1839.)

How and why is it that foreign editions take the place of our own? Because, undoubtedly, of the difference in the price of the two, caused by the monopoly which in one case remains in the hands of one publisher. Is it not notorious, in fact, that even those of the middle classes who have a love for literature never, with rare exceptions, purchase a Copyright book, and that for the very good reason that they cannot afford it? Their only way of getting a sight of a new publication complete is by obtaining it from a circulating library ; and particular passages that they wish to have by them, for the purpose of reference or re-perusal, they get possession of, if they get possession at all, by purchasing them extracted in some of the cheap periodicals which subsist on extracts. The effect of this state of things is now manifesting itself in the condition of our literature, which is becoming more and more the literature of circulating libraries—a heavy mass of light reading. How, indeed, can it be expected that an author will take pains when he knows that all his pains will be of no use ; that his history or his travels will only come into the hands of those who will be compelled to rush through them at a certain rate, and return them by a certain hour. "He who runs may read," under the present system, and none but those who do run.

This system has come up under the twenty-eight years' monopoly. Is it likely to be improved under a law which will secure a monopoly for sixty years certain, and perhaps a hundred? We do not think it is. The advocates of the Bill indeed triumphantly refer us to the recent cheap editions of Copyright authors, as proofs of the—we hardly know what; for what do they prove in their favour? The greater part of the works alluded to—the poems of Southey, the novels and poems of Walter Scott, are works of which the Copyright is on the verge of expiring.

The following extract is also from the same volume :

The strangest misapprehensions seem indeed to prevail generally as to this question ; one of the strangest is, that the only parties interested are the authors and the booksellers, and that if the Bill be thrown out, the former will suffer, that the latter may be enriched by the fruit of their labours. The third party, whose interests are not the least among those concerned—the public—is generally quite lost sight of. Thus it has been said, in reference to the often-quoted case of Wordsworth, that the question is, whether the heirs of the poet shall enjoy the profit of his works, or the heirs of Mr. Tegg (the bookseller who is so active in opposition to the Bill). But it is no such thing. Under the present law, at Mr. Wordsworth's death, and the consequent expiration of the Copyright in his works, they would become the property, not of this or of that man's heirs, but of "all England," of the public at large. If Mr. Tegg, or his heirs, reap any profit, it will only be by the exercise of their callings, and Mr. Wordsworth's heirs will have just the same privilege. The notion that the title of the cause now pending is only "Author v. Bookseller," has been worked upon to such an extent, that it would almost seem that the advocates of the Bill see the importance of mystifying the public on the subject, and preventing the names of the real defendants from being seen.

II.
CHAPTER FROM M. RENOUARD'S "TRAITÉ DES DROITS D'AUTEURS."

La garantie d'un droit exclusif de copie sur la reproduction de l'ouvrage est le meilleur mode de salaire de la société envers l'auteur.

Long-temps on a cru que les écrivains et les artistes devaient être payés par des pensions et des faveurs. C'étaient en quelque façon l'Etat et les princes qui acquittaient ainsi la dette du public, et en même temps que l'on ne se faisait nul scrupule d'accepter ces faveurs, on était facilement disposé à rougir du paiement à tirer du public par la vente de son droit de copie sur ses propres ouvrages (1). Une partie des idées a bien changé. Aucun préjugé défavorable ne s'attache à flétrir la vente qu'un auteur fait de ses œuvres. Tout au contraire, une réaction s'est opérée. L'industrie s'est mêlée à la littérature, et a trop souvent pris sa place. Les pensions et les faveurs n'ont pas cessé ; mais elles ont été reléguées à un rang accessoire et secondaire. Les littérateurs n'ont plus comme autrefois une existence à part, qu'ils tiennent des princes et des grands, dont la libéralité leur faisait de paisibles loisirs, et auxquels, en échange, ils donnaient des louanges et quelquefois de la gloire. Les lettres mènent à la fortune, jettent dans les affaires et les honneurs.

L'observateur moraliste aurait à dire sur cette révolution mêlée de biens et de maux. Dans l'ordre actuel, comme dans la vie littéraire ancienne, les passions grandes ou mesquines, les instincts généreux ou cupides, le calcul et le désintéressement ont leur action et leur rôle. Mais, somme toute, les idées sont mieux à leur place. Vivre du tribut volontaire que le public s'impose ne rabaisse aucune position, ne messied à aucun génie.

D'insurmontables difficultés s'élèvent contre tout mode de paiement, qui procéderait par voie de pensions, de traitement fixe, ou même, sauf quelques exceptions très rares, par prix d'achat, une fois payé, achat qui prendrait la forme d'expropriation pour cause d'utilité publique, si l'auteur n'était pas laissé maître de s'y refuser. Avec de telles formes de salaire, la justice distributive serait impossible ; et il n'est pas de trésor qui pût suffire aux insatiables prétentions, aux faveurs capricieuses, aux concussions faciles auxquelles on ouvrirait une large porte. Qui donc si, par exemple, on adoptait le procédé d'expropriation pour cause d'utilité publique, déclarerait cette utilité et apprécierait les travaux? qui calmerait les rivalités? qui ferait justice de la médiocrité? qui inventerait des récompenses dignes du génie, sans soulever l'envie? qui irait au devant du mérite fier ou modeste? Attribueriez-vous au gouvernement l'estimation des ouvrages à acheter dans l'intérêt public? et ne voyez-vous pas à quels périlleux soupçons, à quelles intrigues subalternes, à quelles corruptions habiles, à quels profits honteux vous exposez l'administration, sans parler de toutes les erreurs auxquelles elle ne saurait échapper? Ferez-vous évaluer les ouvrages des écrivains par leurs pairs; et, si désintéressée, si modeste, si impartiale que soit toute la littérature, oserez-vous ne vous en rapporter qu'à elle seule dans sa propre cause? Trouverez-vous dans des magistrats, dans des jurés, les habitudes d'esprit et la spécialité de lumières indispensables pour une si hasardeuse décision? Pour moi, je n'aperçois de toutes parts qu'inconvéniens, qu'impossibilité. Il n'est qu'un seule juste appréciateur du salaire dû aux écrivains et aux artistes: le public. Il n'est qu'une seule appréciation juste: celle que le public, sans la formuler, mesure sur l'utilité et le plaisir qu'il tire d'un ouvrage. Un seul mode de paiement me paraît juste et possible: c'est celui qui attribue à l'auteur, sur chaque édition ou sur chaque exemplaire de son ouvrage, un droit de copie.

Ce moyen est celui que l'expérience a fait reconnaître comme le plus simple; c'est aussi le plus équitable; car, en général l'évaluation la plus judicieusement approximative de l'utilité d'un livre consiste dans le succès qu'il obtient.

Il résulte de l'adoption de ce moyen que le salaire de l'auteur se trouve très subdivisé, et que le prix de chaque exemplaire s'augmente de la part qu'il supporte dans la valeur générale assignée à l'objet de la copie.

Sans doute, ce renchérissement est un inconvénient; car les livres à bon marché sont des propagateurs d'idées plus rapides, plus puissans, plus actifs que ceux dont le prix est élevé. Mais il n'y a pas de paiement pour les auteurs, si l'on n'a, par une voie quelconque, recours au public pour le fournir. Renchérir un livre, parce qu'il faut acquitter le droit de copie, c'est établir une sorte d'impôt. Or, un impôt, quoique offrant toujours en lui-même des inconvéniens pour le public, se légitime par sa destination, lorsqu'il rend, en dépenses générales, en sécurité individuelle, en garanties efficaces, plus que ce qu'il ôte à chaque contribuable. C'est acheter trop cher l'abaissement du prix d'un livre que de ne pas payer l'auteur, que de le sacrifier à ses travaux, que de le décourager et de le jeter dans l'avilissement par la misère. Le livre coûtera un peu plus, mais il verra le jour, mais on ne l'aura pas étouffé avant sa naissance; mais surtout on n'aura pas été injuste envers celui à qui on le doit. Dire que l'on aimerait mieux passer un pont, un canal, sans rien payer, que d'en rembourser les frais par un péage; que l'on aimerait à être gardé par une armée, sans payer les soldats; jugé par les tribunaux, sans payer de juges; instruit ou récréé par un auteur, sans payer son travail; par un libraire, sans payer les frais de vente; par un imprimeur, sans payer les frais de fabrication; par un laboureur, sans payer sa culture et son blé, ce serait la prétention étrange de tout prendre dans la société sans y rien mettre, et d'exploiter nos semblables, comme s'ils n'étaient pas égaux à nous; ce serait le renversement de toute idée sociale.

Cet impôt au profit de l'auteur sur son ouvrage peut se percevoir de deux manières. L'une consiste à interdire à tout autre qu'à l'auteur ou à ses ayant-cause, la faculté de fabriquer l'ouvrage et de le vendre; l'autre serait de laisser à chacun pleine liberté de fabriquer et de vendre l'ouvrage, mais à la charge de payer une certaine rétribution à l'auteur. Le premier système établit un privilège, le second une redevance.

Le second système peut de prime abord séduire. Beaucoup de personnes qui ne renonceraient qu'avec peine à voir dans le droit de copie un objet de propriété, auraient volontiers recours aux redevances, pour conserver par une sorte de suzeraineté qui pourrait indéfiniment s'étendre, quelque image d'une propriété indéfiniment transmissible. Là se place à l'aise l'ordre d'idées qui, faisant deux parts de la partie spirituelle et de la partie lucrative de chaque ouvrage, livre au public la jouissance de la première, et ne retient parmi les biens vénaux et exploitables que la seconde.

Ne nous occupons pas encore des objections qu'il y aurait à faire, soit à la très longue durée, soit à la perpétuité d'une redevance. Ces argumens s'appliqueraient également à la trop grande extension que l'on essaierait de donner à la durée des privilèges. Examinons les inconvéniens inhérens au mode de redevance considéré en lui-même.

Ce qui le rend inadmissible, c'est l'impossibilité d'une fixation régulière, et l'excessive difficulté de la perception.

Peut-être, à force de soins, surmonterait-on les obstacles à la perception; mais, quant à la fixation de la redevance, le règlement en est impossible.

Cette fixation ne peut dépendre ni de la volonté arbitraire de l'auteur, ni de l'évaluation que jugerait à propos de faire toute personne qui voudrait user du droit de copie. S'en rapporter á l'appréciation du débiteur de la redevance est une absurdité manifeste; mais il serait absurde, au même degré, de s'en remettre au prix que demanderait l'auteur. Que seraitce, en effet, autre chose que de lui conférer le privilège d'exploitation? Il vaudrait mieux mille fois lui attribuer franchement le monopole sur son ouvrage que d'arriver au même résultat par cette voie détournée.

Demandera-t-on à la loi de déterminer une redevance fixe ? mais quoi de plus injuste qu'une mesure fixe, rendue commune à des objets essentiellement inégaux ? Prendrait-on pour base le nombre des exemplaires, l'étendue du volume, son prix de vente ? mais il est des ouvrages dont cent ou cinq cents, ou mille exemplaires suffiront à jamais à la consommation, tandis que d'autres se débitent par dix et cent mille : mais l'étendue du volume varie avec tous les caprices de la fabrication : mais le prix est plus variable encore.   Sans parler des hausses et des baisses dont personne n'est maître, sans parler de l'extrême facilité des fictions dans les prix, et de l'impossibilité de les constater, ne sait-on pas que l'on fabrique des Télémaque à vingt sous, et d'autres, qui ne seront pas trop chers, à cent ou deux cents francs ? Avec le texte qui ne varie point, il faut parler du papier, des caractères d'impression, des soins typographiques, des ornemens accessoires de gravure ou autres, objets tous variables à l'infini. Si votre redevance a pour base une valeur proportionelle, chaque Télémaque de deux cents francs produira, pour le seul droit de copie, plus que ne vaudra, dans l'autre édition, chaque exemplaire tout fabriqué ; et cependant ce sera toujours le même texte qui n'aura pas plus de valeur intrinsèque dans un cas que dans l'autre.

Resterait un dernier mode de fixation ; il consisterait, en cas de désaccord entre le débiteur de la redevance et l'auteur, dans un règlement par experts, variable suivant les circonstances. Mais qui ne voit tous les frais, tous les délais, tous les procès auxquels chaque affaire donnerait lieu, pour n'être, la plupart du temps, que très capricieusement décidée ?

Le raisonnement juge cette question comme l'expérience l'a tranchée. L'exclusion de tout autre système acceptable conduit, par la logique, à l'adoption de privilèges destinés à garantir le monopole d'exploitation, soit à l'auteur seulement, soit à l'auteur et à ses ayant-cause. Toutes les législations actuellement en vigueur en adoptant ces privilèges ont voulu qu'ils fussent temporaires. Les motifs pratiques de cette opinion ont été indiqués par la haute intelligence de Napoléon dans une discussion du conseil d'état (1).

Privilèges, monopoles ; ces mots sonnent mal : les mots de propriété littéraire recommandent bien mieux une opinion.   Si je disais que cette différence dans les mots n'a pas été sans influence sur le succès divers des deux systèmes, les lecteurs sérieux trouveraient cette remarque bien futile ; elle est futile en effet ; mais elle est vraie, et des personnes, tenues pour graves, s'imaginent qu'elles argumentent parce qu'elles s'écrient : Quoi ! vous attaquez la propriété au nom du privilège et du monopole ! Je n'aurais point entendu ce propos que j'y aurais cru d'avance. Que d'opinions se déterminent par des mots !

J'ai defini la propriété. Quant à la définition du privilège, tout le monde la connaît: c'est une loi privée, *privata lex*. Ai-je besoin d'ajouter, d'une part, qu'il existe des privilèges parfaitement légitimes ; et, d'autre part, que souscrire au dogme de la propriété littéraire, c'est décider, d'un mot, que le monopole des productions de l'intelligence sera concentré, à perpétuité, entre un petit nombre de privilégiés.

EXTRACTS ON INTERNATIONAL COPYRIGHT.

I refer to the following extracts, wishing they accorded more with the views I myself espouse. It is about twenty years since Mr. Cobden told me he was opposed to Copyright. Whether the philanthropist, statesman, and patriot changed his opinion, I do not know, but I trust my propositions are such as many profound admirers of his will find consistent with his policy and principles :—

EXTRACT FROM THE COBDEN CLUB PRIZE ESSAY, BY DR. LEAVITT, OF NEW YORK. 1869.

When the people of these two nations shall all read freely the same books, and when the audience of both English and American authors shall be the whole English-speaking public throughout the world, the petty jealousies, the trivial misapprehensions, the unhappy distrusts, which dishonour the intelligence of the age, will be known no more. . . .

The proposed International Copyright has an important bearing in this connexion. The object of this copyright is to give to the authors of books, or their assigns, the exclusive right of publication in both countries, in order to keep up the price in both. That this enhancement of the price in one country of books produced in the other will have a tendency to limit the mutual circulation of current literature, will not be questioned.

Whether the proper encouragement of authors requires this to be done, is the point which the two Governments should first settle.

Copyright does not exist, except as created by law, for it begins only when the steps are taken which the law prescribes, and it continues only so long as the law extends it. There is, therefore, no natural right involved. A man's thoughts are his own only so long as he keeps them to himself. When he has uttered them they become the thoughts of all who receive them, and who thenceforth use them at pleasure. The title to a thought by original invention is no better than the title to an asteroid by original discovery. The clothing of a man's thoughts in language no more entitles him to their exclusive publication, after they are gone forth to the public, than a man's careful study of the clothing of his person entitles him to forbid the imitation of his garb and gait as he walks the streets. The law creates Copyright on the assumption that the public good will be promoted by the encouragement thus granted to authors to publish their works. . . .

The pecuniary return realised from their publications is neither the only nor the chief encouragement by which authors of merit are induced to publish their works. The good they may do to mankind, the reputation they may acquire, and the satisfaction of seeing their thoughts widely diffused and received, and made a part of the mental wealth of their country and age, outweigh a thousandfold, to an enlarged and generous mind, the value of the material silver and gold yielded by their Copyright. And it cannot be doubted that these higher returns are directly increased by freedom of publication unrestricted by Copyright; because cheapness of price, and variety in the forms of publication, are prime elements in the widest circulation of books. . . .

It is impossible to exaggerate the value of this international exchange of ideas through the medium of books, as a means of that general assimilation of thought and life which is the highest guaranty of political and commercial intercourse and permanent friendship between the two countries. While each nation, for the most part, buries its own literary trash, and each retains the exclusive circulation of books adapted specially to its own use, the whole volume of the best thoughts of one country have now their widest diffusion through their freedom of publication in the other.

The present is a favourable time for the consideration of this important question. The following extract from the editorial columns of the *Bookseller*, of May 1, is confirmatory and encouraging :—

An English author has no rights whatever in the United States; this should be thoroughly and clearly understood. He may make any arrangement he may think proper with regard to the publication of his works, but can acquire no Copyright in any way. He may wish Brown and Co. to be his sole and only publishers, but cannot prevent Jones and Co. bringing out rival editions; consequently, he can derive little or no profit from his works. By sending out early sheets, so as to give Brown a few days' advantage over Jones, he may get a small payment, but the sum may be very small. Moreover, should Messrs. Jones have noted his coming greatness, and have been the first to announce his first book, albeit quite unknown to him, they will claim to be his publishers; and although he may wish to give Brown the preference, they will feel themselves aggrieved and insist upon helping to make him famous. Should he go to America, and first publish his book there, he will find himself in a still worse position; he is like the notorious " Man without a Country "—he has positively no rights at all; he has none in America, and has none here. It was long supposed that an American author was in a similar position; but it is not so. By a fluke he has secured rights which he never dreamed of, and by means of *our* Copyright-Law, may obtain privileges denied him by his *own*. His plan is simply this : having prepared two copies of his MS., he places one in the hands of his Boston or New York publisher, with directions to publish on a certain day; the other he forwards to a London house, with directions to publish at the same time. Just before the day of publication, which is possibly at that time of the year when Saratoga is an abode more agreeable than the Fifth Avenue, he proceeds to the Canadian side of the Falls. Here he spends a few hours, and then returns, without encountering more inconvenience than saving his hotel expenses by buying a suit of clothes, on which he pays no duty on his return. Thereupon he finds that by so simple a process he has obtained Copyright in the United States, in the dominion of Canada, in Australia, India, France, Germany, and Great Britain ! We can imagine the lively twinkle of his eye as he crosses the Suspension-bridge, to think what 'cute people the Britishers are to have secured all these privileges for him.

We believe, therefore, that American authors are not very anxious about the matter. By taking a little trouble, they can secure all they wish.

English authors have not been fairly treated. They are at great disadvantage, and must be satisfied for the present to work for fame, or but for little more. Fortunately for them, the American publishers, seeing that they do what they are legally entitled to do, are quarrelling amongst themselves, and are crying out for protection.

[Here is introduced the case of an American publishing-house stated by themselves, which concludes thus :—

. . . . "A review of these facts naturally suggests the reflection that the interests of the book-trade in this country, no less than the protection of authors in their just rights, require further legislation at the hands of Congress. It is high time for the passage of a well-considered International Copyright-Law, such as will wipe away from our country the reproach of what are known as 'pirated editions.' "]

We quite agree with this. Some legislation is called for. But now comes a third party, the public, which has its rights as well as the others. We shall very likely incur some odium for admitting that the million have any rights whatever to the productions of men of letters, and may be told that emanations of the brain are as much the private property of their authors as the guineas are of the man of business. So they are, so long as they keep them to themselves ; but when they have communicated them to the world they are no longer their exclusive property. It is right that they should have a modified protection, and we think it must be admitted that English authors are amply protected in their own country. We think, however, that the American public will not be disposed to give them the same amount of protection there, nor is it well that they should have it. They are, however, entitled to some protection, and we hope the day is not far distant when English authors will reap some solid advantages wherever the English language is spoken. We are disposed to think that seven years would generally be long enough for the purpose ; although so short a time would be hard upon such men as Grote, Motley, Merivale, Webster, and others, whose lives have been spent upon their works. We take it for granted that the law, when modified, will be the same on both sides, and that Dickens and Longfellow will receive equal treatment. We are too selfish to give up our cheap editions of Longfellow, and American citizens are not what we take them to be, if they would, for a whole generation, debar themselves from popular editions of Dickens.

(From *The Bookseller*, June 1, 1869.)

COPYRIGHT IN CANADA.—Letter by the *Times'* correspondent:—" Under the English Law, English Copyrights reprinted in the United States are imported into Canada, subject to the same duty as other imported articles; but these Copyrights cannot be reprinted in Canada, the consequence being that the Canadian public is almost entirely dependent on the United States for reprints. The English author is seriously injured, inasmuch as not one-tenth part of the reprints which find their way to Canada are entered at the Custom-house or pay duty." . . . . Mr. Rose replies:—"The undersigned is ready to admit that the principle involved is theoretically at variance with the general policy of the mother-country, in so far as the object of that policy is to secure to authors an absolute monopoly in works of literature for a term of years; but it must be remembered that the necessity for this exceptional legislation arises out of a previous partial departure from this theoretical policy, which in its practical operation is shown to afford a premium to the industrial interests of a foreign country, &c. If it could be shown that the concessions asked for would result in any way to the practical disadvantage of the author, or lessen the protection which it is intended to secure to literary labour, there might be some reason for withholding them. If the rate of duty, whether import or excise, were inadequate, it would be an equally reasonable argument against the extension of the law; and in that case the rate could be augmented. But the undersigned fails to see any reason why, so long as the importation from abroad is permitted, the publication in Canada at an equal rate of duty should be withheld."

(Extract from the *Atlantic Monthly*, October, 1867.)

. . . . This work, we repeat, cost the author 24,000 dollars to produce. Messrs. Harpers sell it at 15 dollars a copy; the usual allowance to the author is 10 per cent. of the retail price, and as a rule, it ought not to be more.

(Extract from the *American Booksellers' Guide*, June 1, 1869.)

At a public meeting recently held in Montreal, respecting the Copyright-Law, it was resolved to apply to Parliament for an amendment permitting Canadian publishers to print British Copyright works upon the payment of 12½ per cent. to British authors. . . . The payment by the publisher of 5 or 10 per cent., or of a fixed sum, for a Copyright of a book, whether by an American or British author, does not necessarily increase the price of the book.

(Extracts from an Article in the *Athenæum*, July 17, 1869.)

This great question is of especial interest at the present time, in consequence of opinions and demands put forward by Canada with relation to Copyright property in the United Kingdom. It appears that for some time past a correspondence has been carried on between the Canadian Government and the Imperial authorities upon the subject of " Copyright-Law in Canada." This " Correspondence " (having been laid before the Canadian Parliament) has been printed and published. It commences with a resolution of the Canadian Senate (passed 15th of May, 1868) that the Governor-General should be prayed "to impress upon Her Majesty's Government the *justice and expediency* of extending the *privileges* of the Imperial Copyright Act, 1847, so that whenever reasonable provision and protection shall, in Her Majesty's opinion, be secured to the authors, *Colonial reprints* of British Copyright works shall be placed on the same footing as foreign reprints in Canada, by which means British authors will be more effectually protected in their rights, *and a material benefit will be conferred on the printing industry of the Dominion.*" . . . .

All the North-American colonies soon availed themselves of this Act of 1847, and Orders in Council were founded upon them ; the rights of British authors being deemed sufficiently protected by an *ad valorem* import duty of 20 per cent. upon the value of the " foreign reprints," that being about *one-tenth* of the price of the works as published in England !

There appears to have been no debate in either House upon this Act of 1847, and it seems to have escaped all public notice on the part of British authors and publishers during its progress in Parliament. From the time Her Majesty's Orders in Council enabled the colonies to avail themselves of that Act, it has operated as a stimulus and considerable premium to the " legalised robbery" of British Copyright property in the United States, and has, practically, given printers and publishers there a monopoly in " foreign reprints" of English books. The Act of 1847 is, therefore, a partial confiscation of those Copyrights which have been acquired in England under Earl Stanhope's Act of 1842, because the colonies have, for the last twenty years, been almost exclusively supplied with English books by United States reprints of those books. . . . .

In 1867 the "dominion of Canada" was created by the Imperial Act of that year, which united all Her Majesty's North American Colonies. It was then found that printing had become much cheaper in Canada than it was in the United States; and amongst the earliest Acts of the first session of the Canadian Parliament two statutes were passed —one, "An Act respecting Copyrights;" and the other, "An Act to impose a Duty upon Foreign Reprints of British Copyright Works." Under the first of these Acts, no work of "any person resident in Great Britain or Ireland" is to be entitled to the protection of that Act unless "the same *shall be printed and published in Canada*." And under the second of the above Acts it is sought to keep alive the injustice of allowing "*foreign reprints*" to be imported into Canada as a basis for that resolution of the Canadian Parliament to which we have called attention.

Such are the facts which preceded the Canadian "Correspondence." It commences with the resolution which, in effect, advocates "the *justice and expediency*" of enabling Her Majesty's Canadian subjects at their discretion (and without the permission of the owners) to confiscate the property of authors of British Copyright works upon the terms of the publisher paying such authors a royalty of $12\frac{1}{2}$ per cent. upon the price of the Canadian reprints, that being about *one-tenth* of the publication price of the work in England! It appears the "justice and expediency" of adopting this Canadian resolution has been pressed very strongly upon the authorities at the Colonial-office, and likewise at the Board of Trade, by the Hon. J. Rose, the Canadian "Minister of Finance." He frankly admits that the policy of the Act of 1847 (so far as respects the protection of British authors) has long been an utter failure; that the amount of duties received for their benefit "is a mere trifle;" and that "it is next to impracticable to enforce the law." These statements are confirmed by a letter, dated June 11, 1868, from Mr. John Lovell (a Montreal publisher) to Mr. Rose, and which appears in the Correspondence. Mr. Lovell says: "At present only a few hundred copies pay duty, and many thousands pass into the country without registration, and pay nothing at all; thus having the effect of seriously injuring the publishers of Great Britain, to the consequent advantage of those of the United States. I may add that, on looking over the Custom-house entries to-day, I have found that not a single entry of an American reprint of an English Copyright (except the Reviews and one or two magazines) has been made since the third day of April last, though it is notorious that an edition of 1,000 of a popular work, coming under that description, has been received and sold within the last few days by one bookseller in this city."

In support of the Canadian resolution, the Hon. J. Rose likewise urges the greater cheapness now of printing in Canada than in the United States. Upon this point he is also confirmed by Mr. Lovell, who says: "It is undeniable that Canadian printers would be enabled to comply with the requisite conditions (that is, of paying a royalty of 12½ per cent. to the author), and produce books, thanks to the local advantages, at a much cheaper rate than they can be produced in the States, *and so bring about a large export business.*" . . . .

This application on the part of the Canadians is answered at considerable length by the Board of Trade; the substance of that answer being "that the question raised is far too important, and involves too many considerations of imperial policy, to render it possible to comply with that application. My Lords, however, fully admit that the anomalous position of Canadian publishers with respect to their rivals in the United States of America is a matter which calls for careful inquiry; but they feel that such an inquiry cannot be satisfactorily undertaken without, at the same time, taking into consideration various other questions connected with the imperial laws of Copyright and the policy of International Copyright Treaties, and they are, therefore, of opinion that the subject should be treated as a whole, and that an endeavour should be made to place the general law of Copyright, especially that part of it which concerns the whole continent of North America, on a more satisfactory footing. The grievance of which the Canadian publishers complain has arisen out of the arrangement sanctioned by Her Majesty's Government in 1847, under which United States reprints of English works entitled to Copyright in the United Kingdom were admitted into Canada on payment of an import duty, instead of being, as in the United Kingdom, absolutely prohibited as illegal." . . . .

A circular by Mr. Purday contains the following :—

A fact transpired only a few days since of an order being sent for some of the musical works published in Bond-street, on which it was stated that they *must be " American printed copies.*" . . . It is said that the Americans have the means of disposing of 30,000 or 40,000 copies of any popular book or song they choose to reproduce. This, of course, is a fine premium for supplanting the English publisher in the sale of his own Copyright works in his own colonies.

FROM A MANUSCRIPT STATEMENT BY MR. PURDAY.

The Act of 1 and 2 Vict., c. 69, was passed into a law under the title of "An Act for securing to Authors in certain cases the benefit of International Copyright," the date of which was July 31, 1838. The 14th section is in these words: "And be it enacted, that the author of any book to be, after the passing of this Act, *first published out of Her Majesty's dominions,* or his assigns, *shall have no Copyright therein within Her Majesty's dominions,* otherwise than such (if any) as he may become entitled to under this Act." Section 9 says that no protection of Copyright shall be given to a foreign author, unless such protection shall be reciprocated to an English author by the country to which the foreign author belongs. Now, nothing can be clearer than that the Act of 5 and 6 Vict., c. 45, never contemplated giving protection to a foreign author; but, on the contrary, that it was passed solely for the benefit of English authors. . . . At last the whole matter was brought before the House of Lords, where it was decreed that a foreign author was not an author within the meaning of the Acts of Parliament, and could neither claim any Copyright himself nor assign any to an English subject, unless he was resident in the British dominions at the time he sold his work, and published it there before there was any publication abroad. This, after eleven years of litigation by various parties, among whom my brother was the most persistent defendant, he being perfectly convinced that if the subject came to be thoroughly investigated, no such claims as were set up by the monopolists could be maintained either at common law or in equity. The House of Lords, however, were not called upon to decide what was meant by the term *residence.* This, therefore, gave rise to an attempt on the part of an English bookseller to contrive a scheme which, to the not very creditable honour of English jurisprudence, as it appears to my humble understanding, succeeded. The scheme was this: An American authoress of little repute wrote a novel, one copy of the manuscript of which, it is said, was handed over, for a consideration, to this English bookseller, to publish in England; the work was got ready on this side of the Atlantic as well as on the other side, and, after agreeing as to the date of entry at Stationers' Hall, and the publication of the same in London, the lady was desired to go over the Victoria-bridge into Canada, one of the British dominions, and remain there a few hours or days, while the publication took place in London; then she was to go back again for the protection of the same work, as a Copyright, in her own country. Meanwhile, another

X

English publisher, hearing that such an artifice was about to be attempted, procured an American copy of the said work, and re-published it in a cheap form. The consequence was, that an application for an injunction was applied for by the first party, which was granted, and appealed against to the Lords Justices, who gave it as their opinion that the word "author" in the Act of Parliament was to be interpreted in its widest sense, and that there was no limitation to that word in the Act of Parliament; therefore, it was maintained that *any* author could have a Copyright in England who complied with the requisitions of the Act, and this defective scheme was confirmed by Lord Chancellor Cairns, who remarked that none of the former decisions had stated that it was other than necessary to be in the British dominions during the time of the publication of the work. This device may have facilitated the desire for an international law upon a righteous foundation, now so loudly advocated in America.

In the judgment given in the House of Lords, in the case of Boosey's assumption to the exclusive right of printing the opera of Bellini, the subject of residence in England was debated, and Lord St. Leonards used these remarkable words: "Now the American Legislature have no such difficulty. They have expressly enacted that Copyright there shall be confined to natives, or persons resident within the United States. Those are the express words of their statute." And we may remark, farther, that unless an alien author has resided at least twelve months in America, and has made a declaration in these words, "I do declare on oath that it is *bonâ fide* my intention to become a citizen of the United States," &c., he cannot obtain the privilege of Copyright in anything he may publish there. This conflict of opinion must necessarily end, therefore, in a new Act of Parliament, which has been long needed to settle this and other much-vexed questions of Copyright.

LETTER FROM THE SAME.

24, Great Marlborough-street, June 15, 1869.

Dear Sir,—I think your suggestion of the payment of a royalty upon the publication of an author's work, if made mutual in both America and Great Britain, would go far to reconcile the two nations to abandon the present unfair reprisals; more especially if it were left to the option of any publisher to reproduce such works in the form most suited to his particular trade. Some publishers choose to publish in one form, and some in another, more or less expensive, according to the taste or want of their customers. It is true, there might be some difficulty in arranging the per-centage per copy upon such a scheme; but that might be regulated according to the price and style of getting up of the work, which should always be determined upon before the work is issued.

The question of Copyright in music is one which presents features appertaining to itself exclusively. One feature which it shares along with the other fine arts is this great fact: that music is a universal language, and addresses itself equally to all nations. Its range, therefore, is far wider than literature. It needs no translation.

The taste for music is more widely diffused than that for painting and sculpture, from which it differs in a way that causes very considerable embarrassment when the question of Copyright comes to be particularly dealt with. Like paintings and statues, music may be reproduced in a permanent form; but, unlike them, the chief value of its Copyright privilege is reproduction in sounds, and, therefore, in a form unsubstantial and transient. He, therefore, who would deal satisfactorily with this branch of the wide question of Copyright has to provide for a demand, and overcome difficulties, such as do not belong to literary and artistic Copyright. But, still further, music— say that of an opera—may be separated into parts without serious diminution of its revenue-bearing value. Once more, there is the *libretto*; it belongs to the range of literature. Questions, therefore, arise, and must be provided for, with respect to the affinity of that part with the music, its reproduction in the form of translation, and its being, as it occasionally is, the work and property of an author other than the composer of the music.

There is still so much uncertainty, approaching to confusion, as to what really is the law, especially with regard to international Copyright, in this branch, that thorough revision and immediate international negotiations are absolutely necessary.

The laws of Copyright should be divested of all ambiguity and superfluous legal verbiage. In fact, they should be made so plain that "he that runs may read," and understand them. The payment of a royalty on foreign works is not a new thing here. Chappell pays 1s. a copy, besides a considerable sum for the Copyright, of the last work of Rossini—viz., the "Messe Solennelle," for the exclusive selling of the work, and for the right of performing it here. Any other information I can give you I shall be happy to afford.

I am, dear Sir, yours obediently,

To R. A. Macfie, Esq., M.P.   C. H. PURDAY.

X 2

EXTRACTS FROM CORRESPONDENCE ON COPY-RIGHT LAW IN CANADA.

LAID BEFORE THE CANADIAN PARLIAMENT BY COMMAND OF HIS EXCELLENCY THE GOVERNOR-GENERAL.

Extract from a Report of a Committee of the Honourable the Privy Council of Canada, approved by His Excellency the Governor-General in Council, on the 27th May, 1868.

" On the recommendation of the Honourable the Minister of Customs, the Committee advise an uniform *ad valorem* duty throughout this Dominion of 12½ per cent., being the rate fixed and collected in the Province of Canada, previous to the Confederation of the Provinces—and to establish such regulations and conditions as may be subsistent with any Act of the Parliament of the United Kingdom then in force as may be deemed requisite and equitable with regard to the admission of such books, and to the distribution of the proceeds of such duty to or among the party or parties *beneficially* interested in the Copyright."

(From Memorandum by the Minister of Finance.)

" Not one-tenth part of the reprints which find their way to Canada are entered at the Custom-house, or pay duty. . . . It is proposed, in order perfectly to secure the English author, that every Canadian publisher who reprints English Copyrights should take out a licence, and that effectual practical checks should be interposed, so that the duty on the number of copies actually issued from the press should be paid into the Canadian Government by Canadian publishers for the benefit of the English authors. It is believed that the English authors would benefit enormously by the proposed change. At present the amount received by Canada for duty on English Copyrights, and paid over by Canada to the Imperial Government for the benefit of English authors, is a mere trifle."

(From Mr. Lovell.)

" Montreal, June 11, 1868.

" In 1849, I believe, the Government of Canada, with the sanction of Her Majesty the Queen, gave United States publishers the right to bring reprints of English Copyright works into this country on payment of Customs duty of 15 per cent., which has since been reduced to 12½ per cent., the proceeds of the duties to be forwarded to the English authors as a compensation for the privileges secured to the American publishers.

"The people of the Dominion, and especially the printing and publishing interests, feel that they ought to possess at least equal privileges to those conceded to the foreigner. There are several establishments in the Dominion that would esteem it a great boon to be allowed to reprint English Copyrights on the same terms as are now secured to United States publishers, and would gladly pay the 12½ per cent. to the English authors on the *total number* of copies printed, sure to be very considerable. At present only a few hundred copies pay duty, but many thousands pass into the country without registration, and pay nothing at all; thus having the effect of seriously injuring the publishers of Great Britain, to the consequent advantage of those of the United States."

(Extract from Letter from Sir Louis Mallet to the Under-Secretary of State, C.O.)

"It is obvious that, looking to the geographical position of the United States and the North American Confederation, any arrangement with respect to Copyright which does not apply to both must be always imperfect and unsatisfactory, and it is therefore extremely desirable, if possible, that the Canadian question should be considered in connexion with any negotiations conducted with the United States Government.

"Another serious objection to the sanction by Her Majesty's Government of such a proposal appears to my Lords to be, that, while the public policy of the mother-country enforces an absolute monopoly in works of literature for a term of years, it is very undesirable to admit in British Colonial possessions an arrangement which, whatever advantages it may possess (and my Lords fully admit that much may be said in its favour), rests upon a wholly different principle.

"It would be difficult, if such a principle were admitted in the British Colonies, to refuse to recognise it in the case of foreign countries, and thus it might come to pass that the British public might be called upon to pay a high price for their books, in order to afford what is held to be the necessary encouragement to British authors, while the subjects of other countries and the Colonial subjects of Her Majesty would enjoy the advantages of cheap British literature provided for them at the expense of the inhabitants of the United Kingdom."

(Extract from a Paper by the Minister of Finance on the Copyright-Law in Canada.)

" The consequence of this anomalous state of the Law is that Canada receives large supplies of American reprints of English Copyright books, which are sold at a much higher rate than if printed in Canada ; while, at the same time, so generally is the payment of the $12\frac{1}{2}$ per cent. Customs duty evaded, and so trifling is the whole amount realised from that source (the total received last year for the whole Dominion of Canada being only $799·43, or 164*l*. 5s. 3d. sterling, the average of the preceding four years being only 115*l*. 1s. 3d., sterling), that so far as regards the pecuniary or other interests of English authors, for whose protection the duty was imposed and in whose behalf it is collected, the effect is practically the same as if the reprints were avowedly admitted duty free. . . . .

" It is believed that if this privilege were extended to Canadian publishers, they would avail themselves of it to a very large extent, and as the Excise duty of $12\frac{1}{2}$ per cent. could, under proper regulations, be very easily levied, a substantial revenue would accrue therefrom for the benefit of English authors; and further, that a great impetus would be given to the interests of printers, publishers, paper manufacturers, type founders, and other important kindred branches of material industry, and indirectly to the interests of literature and literary men. . . . .

" An American or any other foreign author, by publishing his work first in the United Kingdom, may obtain for himself all the benefits of the English Copyright-Law. One of those benefits, as the law now stands, is to prohibit its reprint in any portion of Her Majesty's dominions out of the United Kingdom. He can equally procure its Copyright in the United States, and the consequence is that the price of literature is enhanced to British subjects in all Her Majesty's Colonial possessions, since to them and to them only can the prohibition to re-publish apply or be made effectual.

" England does not confine the protection which she thus extends to her own authors. The foreign author is protected against all her Colonial subjects, provided he publishes first within the confines of Great Britain and Ireland. She will not recognise a publication in a Colonial possession as a compliance with the Copyright Act, but limits the place of publication to the United Kingdom.

"Such the undersigned understands to have been the solemn interpretation of the law by the House of Lords in the recent case of 'Routledge and Lowe' ('New Law Report,' Appeal Cases, vol. ii., pp. 100—121), and he would very strongly call attention to the unfair position in which the policy of that law places the Canadian publisher and the Canadian public.

"The mere circumstance of the publishing in the United Kingdom gives the author a monopoly throughout the entire area of the British dominions—that author, in the opinion of the then Lord Chancellor Cairns, need not be a native-born subject of the Crown; he need not be an alien friend sojourning in the United Kingdom; he need not be sojourning in a British Colony, but he may be a foreigner residing abroad. This protection is afforded, in the language of Lord Cairns, to induce the author to publish his work in the United Kingdom.

"If the policy of England, in relation to Copyright, is to stimulate, by means of the protection secured to literary labour, the composition of works of learning and utility, that policy is not incompatible with such a modification of law as will place the Colonial publisher on a footing of equality not only with the publisher in the United States, but even with the publisher in the United Kingdom. . . . .

"If the rate of duty, whether import or excise, were inadequate, it would be an equally reasonable argument against the extension of the law; and in that case the rate could be augmented."

TENDENCIES OF COPYRIGHT AMENDERS.

That pretensions under Copyright are becoming so formidable as to demand very serious attention on the part of statesmen and of all who desire to maintain the integrity of our national inheritance of a world-wide, heartily-united empire, and imperial freedom from odious, inquisitorial, and impracticable restraints, especially such as might hinder intellectual and moral development, will be evident to any person who takes pains to study and follow out to their necessary consequences the provisions contained in the following transcripts from a Bill lately introduced by an ex-Lord Chancellor, " for Consolidating and Amending the Law of Copyright in Works of Fine Art : "

Fine Arts Copyright Consolidation and Amendment. [32 Vict.]

Design.—An original conception represented by the author thereof in any work of fine art.

Drawing or Painting.—Every original drawing or painting, made in any manner and material, and by any process.

Photograph shall mean and include every original photograph.

Sculpture.—Every original work, either in the round, in relief, or intaglio, made in any material, and by any process.

Engraving.—Every original engraving and lithograph made upon a plate, block, or slab, of any material, by any process, whereby impressions may be taken from such plate, block, or slab, and the impressions taken from the same.

Work of Fine Art.—Every drawing, painting, photograph, work of sculpture, and engraving as herein-before interpreted.

Extending to all parts of the United Kingdom of Great Britain and Ireland, the Channel Islands, the Isle of Man, and *all the colonies* and possessions of the Crown which now are, or hereafter may be, created or acquired.

3. The author of every original work of fine art, if made, or first sold, after the commencement of this Act, such author being a British subject, or resident within any part of the British dominions at the time such work shall be made or first sold, and the assigns of such author,

shall have the Copyright of sole and exclusive right of copying, reproducing, and multiplying such work, and the design thereof, in the British dominions, by any means, and of any size, for the term of the natural life of such author, and thirty years after his death, but subject to the following conditions and restrictions; (that is to say), &c.

9. If the author of any work of fine art in which there shall be subsisting Copyright, after having become divested of such Copyright, or if any other person, not being the proprietor for the time being of the Copyright in any work of fine art, shall by any means unlawfully repeat, copy, imitate, or otherwise multiply for sale, hire, exhibition, or *distribution*, or cause or procure to be repeated, copied, imitated, or otherwise multiplied for sale, hire, exhibition, or distribution, any such work, or the design thereof, *or any part of such design*, or, knowing that any such repetition, copy, or other imitation has been unlawfully made, shall *import* or export into or out of *any part of the British dominions*, or sell, publish, let to hire, exhibit, or distribute, or offer for sale, [hire, exhibition, or ;distribution, or cause or procure to be so imported, or exported, or sold, published, let to hire, distributed, or offered for sale, hire, exhibition, or distribution, any unlawful repetition, copy, or imitation of any such work, or of the design thereof, such person for every such offence shall forfeit to the registered proprietor for the time being of the Copyright thereof a sum not exceeding twenty pounds, and not less than two pounds, for every first offence, and not less than five pounds for every subsequent offence, &c.

11. All repetitions, copies, or imitations of any work of fine art, or the design thereof, wherein there shall be subsisting Copyright under this Act, and which, contrary to the provisions of this Act, shall have been made in any foreign State, are hereby absolutely prohibited to be imported into any part of the British dominions, except by or with the consent of the registered proprietor of the Copyright thereof, or his agent authorised in writing ; and if the registered proprietor for the time being of any such Copyright or his agent shall declare, *or if any officer of Her Majesty's Customs shall suspect*, that any goods imported are prohibited repetitions, copies, or imitations of any such work of fine art, or of the design thereof, then *such goods may be detained*, unpacked, and examined by the officers of Her Majesty's Customs.

12. The *Commissioners of Customs* shall cause to be made, and *publicly exposed at the several ports* of the United Kingdom, *and in Her Majesty's possessions abroad, printed lists of all works of fine art wherein Copyright shall be subsisting*, and as to which the registered *proprietor* for the time being of such Copyright, *or his agent*, shall

have given notice in writing to the said Commissioners that such Copy-right exists, stating in such notice when such Copyright expires, and shall have made and subscribed a declaration before the collector of the Customs, or any justice of the peace, at some port or place in the United Kingdom or in Her Majesty's possessions abroad, that the contents of such notice are true. The provisions contained in the Acts now in force, or at any time to be in force, regarding Her Majesty's Customs, as to the application to the courts and judges by any person aggrieved by the entry of any book in the lists of books to be made and publicly exposed by the said Commissioners under the said Acts, and the expunging any such entry, shall apply to the entry of any work of fine art in the lists thereof to be made by virtue of this Act, in the same manner as if such provisions were herein expressly enacted, with all necessary variations in relation to such last-mentioned lists, &c.

13. *Every person who shall import* or export, or cause to be imported or exported, into or out of any part of the British dominions, or shall *exchange*, publish, sell, let to hire, *exhibit*, or *distribute*, or offer, or hawk, or carry about, or keep for sale, hire, exhibition, or distribution, any unlawful copy, repetition, or imitation of any work of fine art, in which, or in the design whereof, there shall be subsisting registered Copyright, shall be bound, on demand in writing, delivered to him or left for him at his last known dwelling-house or place of business, by or on behalf of the registered proprietor for the time being of such Copyright, to give to the person requiring the same, or his attorney or agent, within forty-eight hours after such demand, *full information in writing of the name and address of the person from whom, and of the times when, he shall have imported, purchased, or obtained* such un-lawful copy, repetition, or imitation, also the number of such copies, repetitions, or imitations which he has obtained, and also to produce to the person requiring such information all invoices, books, and other documents relating to the same; and it shall be lawful for any justice of the peace, on information on oath of such demand having been made, and of the refusal or neglect to comply therewith, to summon before him the person guilty of such refusal or neglect, and on being satisfied that such demand ought to be complied with, to order such information to be given and such production to be made within a reasonable time to be fixed by him.

14. Upon proof by the oath of *one credible person* before *any justice of the peace*, court, sheriff, or other person having jurisdiction in any proceeding under this Act that there is reasonable cause to *suspect* that

any person has in his possession, or in any house, shop, or other place for sale, hire, distribution, or public exhibition, any copy, repetition, or imitation of any work of fine art in which, *or in the design whereof*, there shall be subsisting and registered Copyright under this Act, and that such copy, repetition, or imitation has been made without the consent in writing of the registered proprietor of such Copyright, it shall be lawful for such justice, court, sheriff, or other person as aforesaid before whom any such proceeding is taken, and he or they is and are hereby required to *grant his or their warrant, to search in the daytime such house*, shop, or other place, and if any such copy, repetition, or imitation, or any work which may be reasonably suspected to be such, shall be found therein, to cause the same to be brought before him or them, or before some other justice of the peace, court, sheriff, or other person as aforesaid, &c.

15. If any person, elsewhere than at his own house, shop, or place of business, shall hawk, carry about, offer, utter, *distribute*, or sell, or keep for sale, hire, or *distribution, any* unlawful copy, repetition, or *colourable imitation* of any work of fine art in which, or in the design whereof, there shall be subsisting and registered Copyright under this Act, all such unlawful articles may be *seized without warrant, by any peace officer, or the proprietor of the Copyright, or any person authorised by him*, and forthwith taken before any justice of the peace, court, sheriff, &c.

23. Under this Act there shall be kept at the hall of the Stationers' Company by the registrar appointed by the said company for the purposes of the Act passed in the sixth year of the reign of her present Majesty, intituled "An Act to amend the Law of Copyright," three several books or sets of books, which shall be called as follows:

(1.) The register of proprietors of Copyright in original drawings and pictures:

(2.) The register of proprietors of Copyright in original photographs and engravings:

(3.) The register of proprietors of Copyright in original works of sculpture.

In the first of such registers shall be entered a memorandum of every Copyright, *or of any limited legal interest therein*, to which any person shall claim to be entitled under this Act in any original drawing or painting, and also of *any subsequent assignment* of such Copyright *or limited legal interest therein;* and such memorandum shall contain a statement of the several particulars required by the form applicable for that purpose in Part I. of the third schedule to this Act; and in addition thereto the person registering shall annex to the memorandum under which he requires the entry to be made an outline, sketch, or photograph of the drawing or painting to which such memorandum refers, &c.

*** Again adverting to the case of Ireland, let it be remembered it was only so late as 1836 that an Act was passed "to extend the protection of Copyright in prints and engravings to Ireland."

This Bill of Lord Westbury's, after having been referred to a Select Committee of the House of Lords, has been withdrawn, but only for the present Session. The reason for withdrawal is found in amendments recommended by the Committee, one of which is that it should extend only to the United Kingdom and Channel Islands. The subjoined extracts from a printed defence of the Bill, by D. Roberton Blaine, Esq., will be read with interest, as showing how influential is the quarter whence the Bill emanates, and not less on account of their allusion to Patent-right and their other interesting contents.

This Bill has been prepared by direction of the Council of the Society of Arts, Manufactures, and Commerce, in consequence of a memorial having been presented to the Council, signed by a considerable number of the most eminent artists and publishers resident in London. . . . .

There is no Copyright in the *ideas* embodied in a work of literature or of fine art. . . . .

It is quite otherwise according to our Patent-Laws. Under them the *idea* of an author is everything, so to speak, and is rigidly protected. Thus, for example, suppose A produces a new manufacture by means of a very imperfect and clumsy machine, or chemical process, which he invents and patents; and suppose afterwards that B invents a very perfect and simple machine, or chemical process, whereby he can produce the same manufacture as A, but better and cheaper than his. In such a case the Patent-Laws prohibit B from making any use of his improvement for making the manufacture of A during the continuance of his Patent, unless with his consent. This arises from its being a leading *principle* of our Patent-Laws, that where a new invention has been secured by a valid and existing Patent no one is allowed during the continuance of that Patent to produce *the same results by a mechanical or chemical equivalent.* Hence the great source of complaints and of the litigation arising under our Patent-Laws. Thus it is that a patented manufacture precludes any improvements therein except by the patentee, or with his consent, during the term of his Patent. . . . .

In Italy, at the expiration of such forty years, although any one may then make and sell copies of the work, the person doing so must, during a second term of forty years, annually pay to the proprietor of the Copyright 5 per cent. (calculated at the *published* price) upon all copies sold by the person so making and selling such copies. As to France, her Copyright-Laws are expressly extended to all her colonies. And, by the 8th Article of Her Majesty the Queen's Copyright Convention with France, dated 3rd November, 1851, *reciprocal* protection is agreed to be given in favour of Copyright works *first* published in "the territories of France," or in "the British dominions." This appears to show that both States clearly intended that such reciprocal protection should extend to their colonies. It is also stipulated by the 7th Article that "pirated works *shall be seized* and destroyed." Now the French law very justly declares the piracy of Copyright property to be a *crime* (*delit*), and provides rapid and effectual means for enabling the proprietor of the Copyright to seize both the pirate and the fraudulent copies, plates, &c., in his possession. Yet, according to the present state of the British Artistic Copyright-Laws, no such powers of seizure, as expressly agreed by Her Majesty the Queen's Convention, exist in the British dominions; nor does any protection whatever for *artistic* Copyright works extend beyond the United Kingdom; no, not even to the Isle of Man, or to the Channel Islands!

This important and novel subject is likely soon to receive useful illustration from a Parliamentary return to be moved for by the Right Hon. T. H.

Headlam. From another of that gentleman's Returns a suggestive extract is also subjoined.

It contains evidence that long ago impatience of existing restraints was in vigorous action in the British Colonies—evidence that payment of authors by royalties is a system that commands State concurrence—and evidence how over-ready the State is, or how circumstances are formed so as to compel it, to undertake work for authors and publishers by means of its Custom-house officers. On this last point I am happy also to produce an important paper kindly furnished by Michael Daly, Esq., of Her Majesty's Customs. Mr. Daly's note deserves to be pondered in prospect of the re-appearance next Session of the Board of Trade's "Trade-Marks Registration Bill." *

The extracts which I have agglomerated show that the idea of employing officers of *Excise* as well as those of Customs is seriously propounded, but this is by no means all the useful information they convey.

COLONIAL DUTIES ON COPYRIGHT WORKS.

Return of all the Colonies and British Possessions in favour of which Orders in Council have been issued under the Act 10 and 11 Vict., c. 95, suspending the Prohibition of Importation of Reprints of British Copyright Works.

NEW BRUNSWICK.—An *ad valorem* duty of 20 per cent. on the *bond fide* price of the publication, imposed on importation; such duty to be transmitted through Her Majesty's Government for the benefit of the author.

NOVA SCOTIA.—An *ad valorem* duty of 20 per cent. to be applied in like manner.

---

* Would it not be well to confine registration to *names* of firms or premises without recognising *marks*?

PRINCE EDWARD ISLAND.—An *ad valorem* duty of 20 per cent., currency of the island, imposed on similar terms.

BARBADOES.—An *ad valorem* duty of 20 per cent. to be remitted to the author.

BERMUDA.—An *ad valorem* duty of 15 per cent. on the value of such reprints, imposed on the like conditions, a deduction of 5 per cent. on the amount to be made, for the remuneration of the officers collecting the duty.

BAHAMAS.—A duty of 20 per cent. on the value of the publisher's wholesale price; nine-tenths of the amount collected to be paid to the proprietors of the Copyright on their application to the Governor.

NEWFOUNDLAND.—An *ad valorem* duty of 20 per cent. to be paid over to the author.

ST. CHRISTOPHER.—An *ad valorem* duty of 20 per cent. to be remitted in like manner.

ANTIGUA.—An *ad valorem* duty of 25 per cent. to be applied in like manner, 5 per cent. to be deducted for remuneration of the treasurer collecting the duty.

ST. LUCIA.—An *ad valorem* duty of 20 per cent. to be applied in like manner, without deduction.

CANADA.—An *ad valorem* duty not exceeding 20 per cent. imposed, to be applied in like manner.

BRITISH GUIANA.—An *ad valorem* duty of 20 per cent., after deducting 5 per cent., to be remitted to the author.

ST. VINCENT.—An *ad valorem* duty of 20 per cent. to be applied in similar manner.

MAURITIUS.—A poundage of 20 per cent. to be paid, to be deposited in the Colonial Treasury, there to be kept at the disposal of the British authors of such works.

GRENADA.—An *ad valorem* duty of 20 per cent. to be remitted for the benefit of the author.

JAMAICA.—An *ad valorem* duty of 15 per cent. An *ad valorem* duty of 20 per cent.

CAPE OF GOOD HOPE.—An *ad valorem* duty of 20 per cent. to be applied in similar manner.

NEVIS.—An *ad valorem* duty of 15 per cent. to be applied to the benefit of the author, after deducting 5 per cent. for the remuneration of the treasurer collecting the duty.

NATAL.—An *ad valorem* duty of 20 per cent. to be remitted to the registered proprietor of the Copyright.

EXAMINATIONS BY CUSTOMS' OFFICERS.

The officers of Customs are compelled to discharge various duties beyond those connected with the collection and protection of the Revenue. Among others they have to take care that foreign goods, on their importation, do not bear the mark or brand of any British maker, or such marks or brands as would be likely to give them a British character. All goods so marked and branded are, by 16 and 17 Vict., cap. 107, sec. 44, prohibited to be imported into this country. Cases are constantly occurring where such goods have to be dealt with by the Customs' authorities. In some instances the goods are confiscated, in others the brands or labels are ordered to be removed, upon which the goods are delivered to the owner, either with or without fine; and in other cases they are ordered to be returned to the port whence they were imported. But why should this duty devolve upon the Customs' officers? It is an extremely disagreeable one, involving much trouble to the department and vexation to importers. If a manufacturer or dealer in this country infringes the right of another by using his mark or brand, he has his remedy in a court of justice; but he has no right to enter a factory or warehouse, to open packages and make an indiscriminate search, with or without grounds of suspicion that his brands have been placed on the contents of the packages. Yet, practically, this is really the case with regard to the Customs' right of search for prohibited marks and brands. Why not let the goods pass without reference to brands or marks? Leave the owner of the marks to his remedy in law; and the vendor of the goods bearing such forged or false brands to the risk and penalty which he thus incurs. In this case the fraudulent dealer only will be the sufferer, while the innocent will be saved the vexation of having his goods pulled about at the Custom-house; and the Customs department will be relieved of an extremely disagreeable and troublesome duty. As to the brand, not those of any particular maker, but in their general character purporting the goods to be of British manufacture, but very little harm can result to any particular interest from the use of such marks. It will take something more substantial than such mere fictions to ruin the trade of the country; but if better goods, even if they be of foreign origin, can be obtained at the same prices as those paid for British. then so much the better for the consumer. Would it not be well, also, to relieve the Customs officers of the duty of searching for pirated works under the Copyright Act? Why not deal with the vendors here of such works, if reprinted abroad, in like manner as if reprinted here?

THE BRITISH AND FOREIGN BOOK TRADE.

The following figures, extracted from a recent Parliamentary Return, while they show a highly satisfactory ratio of increase, will probably convince the commercial reader that the International Book Trade of Christendom is yet in its infancy, and, perhaps, that the swaddling-bands and close confinement of monopoly should be exchanged for a freer and more natural system of nursing and protection :—

BOOKS PRINTED IN THE UNITED KINGDOM, EXPORTED THEREFROM.

COUNTRIES to which Exported.	QUANTITIES.			DECLARED VALUE.		
	1828.	1848.	1868.	1828.	1848.	1868.
	Cwts.	Cwts.	Cwts.	£	£	£
Foreign Countries :—						
United States	605	3,158	18,379	14,612	47,955	184670
Other Foreign Countries	1,449	2,003	10,540	33,319	30,678	181350
Total	2,054	5,161	28,919	47,931	78,633	366020
British Possessions :—						
Australia	148	1,968	18,583	3,933	27,249	148413
British North America .	364	1,131	6,919	8,178	15,156	64139
Other British Possessions	1,552	4,026	6,987	41,072	71,114	105671
Total	2,064	7,125	32,480	53,183	113519	318223
Aggregate of Foreign Countries and British Possessions.	4,118	12,286	61,408	101114	192152	684 24 3

Quantities and Value, with the Weights and Moneys rendered into English Equivalents, of Printed Books Imported into and Exported from the United Kingdom and Foreign Countries in the latest Year for which Returns have been received and the Tenth Year previous thereto :—

COUNTRIES.		Imported (for Home Consumption).		Exported (Domestic Produce).	
		Cwts.	£	Cwts.	£
United Kingdom* ...	{1858	59,71	83,598	12,286	192,152
	{1868	10,695	137,580	61,480	684,243
Russia †	{ 1857	Not	100,718	Not	Not stated.
	{ 1867	stated	73,588	stated	18,813
Sweden †	{ 1856	Not	6,938	Not	1,697
	{ 1866	stated	8,780	stated	3,569
Zollverein	{ 1856	21,098	Not	38,275	Not
	{ 1866	31,485	stated	67,376	stated
Holland	{ 1857	4,349	46,126	2,437	38,363
	{ 1867	7,228	76,659	3,555	37,714
Belgium	{1856	5,612	69,750	4,063	52,228
	{1866	Not stated	97,040	Not stated	48,760
France	{ 1857	5,438	95,224	38,542	510,352
	{ 1867	11,942	201,280	40,887	522,374
Spain †	{ 1854	Not stated		2,060	19,383
	{ 1864	1,924	8,323	674	8,929
Italy	1865	6,108	56,464	1,678	15,375
United States	{ 1857	Not	181,980	Not	57,843
	{ 1867	stated	246,539	stated	71,386

* Part Re-Exported.
† For these Countries the Total Imports and Exports are stated.

The total weight of the Book Trade of Christendom appears to be less than 200,000 cwts., which, taken at 1 lb. per volume, makes only about 20,000,000 of volumes, about a fourth part of which is sent from this country to the North American and Australian "Markets."

The *Beehive*, of 31st July, has an article on the meeting referred to in the Prefatory Note. The following is an extract, to which three notes are respectfully subjoined :—

. . . . But to abolish all protection to original inventions would' be, as Mr. Paterson justly contended, to hand over all the profits arising from such inventions to the capitalist.* This speaker would make the granting of Patents free from charge, and lay a tax on the profits of the contrivance patented. Mr. Macfie, the Member for Leith, made a decided hit when he pointed to the absence of royalties abroad, while at home they lie upon us with a crushing weight ; and, if we cannot find ease without following the example of Switzerland in abolishing Patent-Laws, and of Holland and Germany by declaring against them, there will be no help for it.

But when Mr. Macfie " denies that the inventor has any exclusive right to his invention," he makes an assertion that it is in the power of any inventor practically to disprove. Say that A has found out an invention of value, or, which is the same thing for the purpose of argument, thinks he has ; he meets with the Member for Leith, who says, " Come, my fine fellow, out with that invention of yours, for the general good ; you have no exclusive right to it." What would A be likely to say in reply ? " Haven't I ? Let me choose to keep it to myself, and who can hinder me ? " While, however, it is perfect nonsense to deny a man's right to the ideas of his own mind,† the practical question is another thing ; and it behoves us all to remember that we are members of one society, and that a society called at least Christian. Nevertheless, if A is to make his contribution to the general good, all the rest of the alphabet are bound to reciprocate his liberality.‡ . . . .

---

* For capitalist, if there were no Patents, why not say *consumer* ?

† It is *exclusive* right, not at all his personal right, to use, and right to conceal, if he has the will and power, that is denied.

‡ These concluding sound reflections are eminently suggestive.

INDEX.

ERRATA.

On page 70, two lines from bottom, read Francis instead of Joseph.

„ 92, line 13, for command read commend; and insert a comma after the word inaugurate in next line.

LONDON : W. J. JOHNSON, PRINTER, 121, FLEET STREET.

THE PATENT QUESTION
UNDER FREE TRADE:

A SOLUTION OF DIFFICULTIES

BY ABOLISHING OR SHORTENING THE INVENTORS' MONOPOLY, AND

INSTITUTING NATIONAL RECOMPENSES.

A PAPER SUBMITTED TO THE

Congress of the Association for the Promotion of Social Science,

AT EDINBURGH, OCTOBER, 1863, BY ROBERT ANDREW MACFIE,

PRESIDENT OF THE LIVERPOOL CHAMBER OF COMMERCE.

TO WHICH ARE ADDED TRANSLATIONS OF RECENT
CONTRIBUTIONS TO PATENT REFORM
BY M. CHEVALIER AND OTHER CONTINENTAL ECONOMISTS.

LONDON :
LONGMANS, GREEN, READER, AND DYER.
———
1864.
PRICE ONE SHILLING (By Post for 13 Stamps).

.

www.ingramcontent.com/pod-product-compliance
Lightning Source LLC
Chambersburg PA
CBHW021112270326
41929CB00009B/845